Laurie O'Leary was born in Bethnal Green in 1932 and went to primary school with Ronnie and Reggie Kray. On leaving school he worked with the Kray brothers in Spitalfields Market, and later as a bookmaker's clerk at Ascot, Epsom and Brighton racecourses, where he was introduced to all the top gangsters of the 1950s. In the 1960s, he managed Esmeralda's Barn, below the Twins' casino, and formed the Kray Entertainment Agency with Charlie Kray.

Laurie went on to a successful career in the nightclub industry, managing the top society club Sibyllas in 1966 and the famous Speakeasy club from 1968 to 1977. He also worked as a tour manager for, amongst others, Marvin Gaye, Martha Reeves and the Vandellas, Barry White, Peggy Lee and Steve Marriott, and was the manager and promoter of the medium Doris Stokes.

Laurie remained friends with Ronnie Kray throughout his life, visiting him regularly in both Parkhurst and Broadmoor from 1973 until his death in 1995. At the family's request, he was a front pall-bearer with Charlie Kray at Ronnie's funeral, and also a leading pall-bearer at Charlie's own funeral in April 2000.

Ronnie Kray

A Man Among Men

Laurie O'Leary

headline

First published in 2001
by HEADLINE BOOK PUBLISHING

First published in paperback in 2002
by HEADLINE BOOK PUBLISHING

6

ISBN 978 0 7472 6660 0

Typeset by
Letterpart Limited, Reigate, Surrey

Printed and bound in Great Britain by
Mackays of Chatham plc, Chatham, Kent

HEADLINE BOOK PUBLISHING
A division of Hodder Headline
338 Euston Road
London NW1 3BH

www.headline.co.uk
www.hodderheadline.com

Dedicated to
Brian Hall

My sincere thanks to:

Tony Ortzen for the stardust, Alphi, Brian and Iris,
Barbara and Scott Mitchell, Roger Forrester,
Kate Kray, Harry Howard, Diane and Claudine,
Freddie and Jan Foreman and all of the Chaps.
Wherever you are.

contents

by barbara windsor

I first met Laurie O'Leary in the early 1960s when I was singing at the Whisky-A-Go-Go in Wardour Street in the West End. He came to the club one evening with his best friend, Patrick Bedford, who asked me for a date. 'I don't go out with people outside the business,' I told him, rather loftily. Then Laurie threw his hat into the ring as well and invited me to go out with him. He got the same answer.

Laurie was one of the handsomest, most charming men I'd ever met. He had real film-star looks. So why I turned him down I don't know – I think he was so gorgeous that I was a bit overawed by him. But we have been firm friends ever since.

About a year later, I was appearing in Joan Littlewood's ground-breaking hit musical *Fings Ain't Wot They Used T'Be* at the Garrick. When I came out on stage one night and gave a cheery little wave to the audience, I saw three men waving back. There, sitting in the same row, were Laurie with Patrick Bedford, and, separately, a short distance away, Ronnie Kray's elder brother, Charlie. They'd all come to see me in the show, and obviously they all thought I was waving specially to them. As they looked round at each other and realised they'd slightly misread things, the three of them sheepishly brought down their arms. I had trouble keeping a straight face.

I'd been introduced to Charlie and his twin brothers, Ronnie and Reggie, while working in *Fings*. I had just come off stage after a performance when my pal Chuck Sewell, who was also in the show, brought them round to my dressing room to meet me. I had never heard of the Krays and hadn't a clue who my visitors were. I just remember that they were all immaculately turned out – dark suits, white shirts and sober ties – and very quiet, polite and respectful. The Twins, then in their twenties, seemed very shy and quite impressed to find themselves standing back-stage in a performer's dressing room.

I went out with Charlie for a while around that time. After the show he'd take me to the Astor, London's poshest club, though these dates could hardly be described as romantic trysts, because one or other of Charlie's mates – Limehouse Willie or Big Scotch Pat – would always come along with us. I heard people talking about his brothers, of course, but I was very young and naïve in those days and I had no idea what they did for a living.

It was Laurie O'Leary who put me in the picture. I rang him up one day and asked: 'What is it that Ronnie and Reggie actually *do*?'

'Barbara, they run the East End,' he told me.

Although Laurie was busy with his own career in the entertainment business, he remained a good friend to Ronnie Kray, as he has been to me. It was Laurie who always kept me up to date with news of Ronnie and passed messages and good wishes to and fro. For example, when Ronnie made some soft toys as a present for me while he was in Broadmoor, he sent them to me via Laurie.

A great deal has been written over the years about Ronnie Kray, but nobody is better qualified to tell the real story of his life than Laurie, whose close relationship with him lasted from their primary school days right up to Ron's death in 1995. So I am glad that Laurie's authentic version is now being published, and I am sure that Ronnie, whose great wish it was that Laurie should write this book, would have been pleased with his achievement.

Barbara Windsor
January 2001

ron does it his way

Eight weeks before Ronnie Kray died, he telephoned Stephanie King, a confidante of the Kray brothers, and asked to see me as soon as possible.

'Can you see Ronnie tomorrow, Laurie?' Stephanie requested. 'He said it's urgent and seemed excited.'

'Impossible, Steph,' I replied, thinking ahead of a meeting the next day. In fact, when I looked at my packed diary, it seemed that I wouldn't be free for at least two weeks. But maybe it was Fate that urged me to say: 'All right, Steph. Tell Ronnie I'll see him tomorrow. I'll change my meeting.'

The hour-and-a-half journey from London to Crowthorne in Berkshire where Broadmoor Hospital is situated was trouble-free, although it was raining quite heavily as I approached the outside road leading to the main gate. At this stage the drive became depressing as I climbed the long, winding, tree-lined road circling the perimeter of Broadmoor. The wind and rain lashed the thirty-foot high red brick wall surrounding the hospital. It was unusually quiet – spooky, in fact. I did not see a single person on the fifteen-minute journey through the grounds.

I finally arrived at Broadmoor, which was conveniently perched on top of a hill, obviously for security reasons. It was a place with which I was very familiar, having first visited Ronnie when he went there from Parkhurst Prison seventeen years before and regularly ever since. Back then the entrance had huge twenty-foot wide arched doors used by the vehicles carrying patients and contractors' supplies and goods. The ancient medieval-looking reception room was entered through an adjacent smaller side door. It was very claustrophobic in this jumbled, tiny room. In those days visitors signed the book with any name they chose. Nobody seemed to care who you were as long as you wrote that you were a friend or family; there was no check. When the guard with lots of keys arrived to take you to the communal waiting room, you were ushered across the small courtyard to an old Dickensian building with corridors painted in a glossy cream paint. Each corridor had a cell-like door, which was locked and unlocked by the man with the keys as you passed through. The room for visitors was like a firm's canteen, very basic, with chairs and tables scattered around the hall. When the person you were visiting arrived in the room, the waiter – an inmate – took your order. Tea, coffee, cakes, non-alcoholic beer or meat pies and sandwiches were available, so it was reasonably civilised.

The entrance now is in a newly-built, ultra-modern building with computer-controlled doors and a totally sterile atmosphere. However, in a way, it is still every bit as unpleasant as it was on my first visit back in the late seventies. Apart from modernisation, nothing had changed. The hospital was still not at all inviting. If anything, my bar-coded admission card added to the hostility. I was called to the door by a red-faced, overweight official.

'Visitors for Kray, Henley Ward!' he yelled.

Visitors are asked to empty their pockets into a tray, then pass through a screen similar to those used at airports. I went through, retrieving my keys and money, then walked with a clergyman companion across the large courtyard, accompanied by a guard, a young, talkative chap, unlike the priest, who remained silent in his thoughts.

Rightly, I guessed that the priest was meeting Peter Sutcliffe, the 'Yorkshire Ripper'. When visiting Ronnie on previous occasions, I had seen clergymen with Sutcliffe through the glass door into their visiting room next to ours. Whilst waiting for Ronnie, I often saw Sutcliffe and a vicar discussing a Bible in front of them on a table.

As we arrived the doors were unlocked and we were taken upstairs to the ward area. I turned the corner and entered the ward. There – about five feet away from me – stood Sutcliffe with a guard close by. I felt a surge of repulsion fill my body. His cold, empty eyes turned away from mine. As I looked at him with scorn, Ronnie Kray came into the area dressed as immaculately as I have ever seen him. He was well groomed, wearing a dark grey modern-cut suit, gleaming white shirt, Versace tie, gold-rimmed glasses and highly polished black leather shoes.

He had noticed my concern over seeing Sutcliffe. 'Don't let him spoil our visit, Lol,' he said, using my nickname. 'I'm in here with a few of these slags.'

A short while before, Ronnie had almost strangled a patient on his ward. Lee Kiernender, a burly young man, had a reputation for being a nuisance, hassling other people. To quote a hospital worker, Kiernender was 'trying to wind Ronnie up'. Because Ronnie wanted peace and quiet, he would just tell the man to go away. This kindness was taken as weakness. Consequently, the man caught Ron on a bad day. Ron snapped, putting his hands around Kiernender's throat, causing his face to go a shade of blue, his eyes bulging with the pressure of Ron's strength. Newspaper reports said it took four stewards to pull Ron off.

'Let's have some tea, shall we?' Ron asked. 'I've got a lot to talk about.'

'Thanks Ron, but—'

Before I could say another word, Ronnie interrupted. 'Was it black tea or coffee with milk and sugar?' he went on, seemingly pleased with his memory.

'Tea please, Ron,' I said.

'Good. I'll go and make it then.' Off Ron went to the kitchen on the ward.

When visiting Ron a number of years before, I had asked him who the young man was taking our order for refreshments in the open visiting room.

'Oh, that's Graham Young, the poisoner,' Ron had replied. He'd burst out laughing when I cancelled my pot of tea and ordered a can of drink instead. 'He doesn't make the tea, Lol,' Ron had said reassuringly. 'He's only the waiter.' I wasn't taking any chances, though.

As I waited for Ron to return from the kitchen, my thoughts strayed. Why was Ronnie still in Broadmoor? I knew he was ill with schizophrenia, but he was not a danger to the general public. Keeping him in that place did not help him. Ron had been certified insane by the authorities, then sent to Broadmoor for treatment. Apart from the initial adjusting period, he responded to medication and understood that he would not be considered for any form of release until Reggie had a date for parole. Ron never complained about the time he had done, but would always tell me how long they had been away.

'We'll have done twenty years soon, Lol,' I remember him saying when they had completed nineteen years and a bit. It was nearly two-thirds of their sentence. Normally, with remission, they would have been considered for parole, and Reggie at least would be out, but Ron knew that he could not build up his hopes. The most he could have hoped for was Reggie getting a date. That would have made him very happy.

Whenever Ronnie had a change in attitude or was violent, he would try thinking rationally about the event afterwards. He wanted to know why, and would discuss the situation with his doctors.

I remember well an incident he told me about on my previous visit. He had complained to his doctor that ward staff were opening his door in the early hours of the morning, waking him up, which annoyed him. The doctor told Ron no one would do any such thing to upset him, and that it must be his imagination. Ronnie added he was worried in case he was becoming ill, becoming paranoid again and unable to trust anybody. This really concerned him. Ron even felt that the doctor wasn't telling the truth.

So he decided to trap the ward staff he thought were responsible. Ron placed a heavy book on the inside of his room door so that when someone opened it, he would see that the book had moved. Sure enough, at about 3.30 in the morning, there was a noise and loud laughter, waking Ronnie. He jumped up, knowing he had caught the culprit.

But looking down at the door, the heavy book was still where he had originally placed it. He was satisfied and relieved because his plan had worked. That morning he asked to see the doctor and told him about the incident. The doctor explained to Ronnie that as he had been suffering from an ear infection, they had given him antibiotics. Because of this, the treatment for his paranoia had been reduced in strength, causing these hallucinations. Ron was ever so pleased that he had sussed it out for himself.

'I could have been back to square one again, Lol,' he'd said. 'When I first came here, I didn't trust anybody.'

I remembered that time very well. Ron was then very ill. He had certainly changed. If he had known that the dosage had been changed because of the antibiotics it could have saved him such distress.

Ron's mental state was now so much better, and had greatly improved in the years I regularly visited him. I was quite certain that with the prescribed medication he would be completely safe and deserved to be in a much more relaxed hospital. After all, he had been locked away for the past twenty-seven years – with seventeen of those in Broadmoor – for killing a rival gangster. Yes, I know it was a bad crime, but surely nothing when compared to today's murderers and their comparatively short sentences. Yet here he was being detained in the same wing as mass murderers Peter Sutcliffe and Ian Brady, among others.

Ronnie returned with two cups of tea in his hands. He was in a very good mood. With shining eyes and a beaming smile, he suddenly asked: 'Why didn't I think of it years ago, Lol? I want you to write a book about us. It's a good idea. What do you think?'

The questions came without a pause. Ron bubbled with enthusiasm. It would have been difficult to refuse if only to appease Ronnie, but I had to be honest.

'I can't,' I replied. 'There's been sixteen books written about your family. If you had asked me years ago, I could – and would – have written an interesting one, but now it will just be another book about "The Krays".'

There was an immediate look of disappointment and rejection on Ronnie's face. He looked totally dejected. 'You could tell the truth, Lol,' he went on, trying to persuade me. 'I thought it was a good idea, my way of getting you some money. After all, you never got that £6000 I promised you for all the work that you did for us on the film about us, and for introducing us to those publishers.'

Ronnie went on to say that he hadn't forgotten how I looked after their mother on visits. 'Don't think it went unnoticed,' he was saying.

'Ron,' I said carefully. 'I've another idea. I'll write a book about *you*! You're one of the most fascinating characters I've ever met.' I noticed a smidge of embarrassment as he nodded in agreement.

'Smashing, Lol!' he said.

Immediately, Ron began to write on a sheet of paper. 'Hold on, Ron,' I said jokingly. 'You've already written your book!'

Grinning, and with a glint in his eye, he replied, 'Oh, it's just a few things that might help you.' How could I refuse?

'Don't make me a nice person, Lol,' Ronnie added. 'Just say I was nice with nice people, but a bastard with bastards.'

Just at that moment, something occurred to me. 'I want

you to know, Ron,' I said slowly and with real feeling, 'that you've never intimidated or frightened me. I want you to know that I have always valued you as a true friend.'

Ron spoke softly but firmly, saying: 'I have never tried – or wanted – to frighten or intimidate you or your family. You are my oldest friend. And you've always been very loyal to our family.'

I thought then about my own family and the Twins. My mother, Rose, had known them since they were kids visiting our rented Victorian house in Cheshire Street, around the corner from their home in Vallance Road. When I told her of their frequent troubles and their being arrested, she would reply, 'Why don't they leave the poor little sods alone?' I had to remind her that they weren't 'poor little sods', but that is how she saw them. In her eyes it was always 'the others who must have caused it'.

Following a stroke which left her without the use of her left side and arm, my mother was housebound for some years. She never complained. In fact, if anyone showed her pity she would quickly respond, 'There are thousands worse than me, son.'

During this time, the Twins often visited with gifts to cheer her up and when she died of cancer in the early sixties, even though Ron was then on the trot from the law, he still arranged for about ten or so members of The Firm to attend the funeral to pay their respects. When I came out of the bathroom into the passageway of my parents' council flat in Bethnal Green, lined up in the hall were some of The Firm, all dressed in dark suits and black ties, a true mark of respect to my mum. Despite the sad occasion, I still managed a smile as I said, 'It's like the St

Valentine's Day Massacre!' Mum would have liked the ritual of The Firm being present as she had a great sense of humour.

Ronnie Kray was a living legend in the East End. But most of all, for me, he was a childhood friend. I understood why he wanted me to write a book about him. He wanted me to tell *my* story of Ronnie Kray. He trusted me.

Over the next few weeks, as work started on this book, I had some amazing meetings with Ron. All the time, though, he insisted that I should not try to make him and Reggie good guys. They were gangsters and paid the price, Ron conceded, although he thought that thirty years inside was much too severe. Coupled with the fact that there was no remission, it gave them absolutely no hope at all. The system was an ass; it was survival at all costs in prison. Ron said that he knew some nice people inside with the same code of respect, but there were far more he was unable to tolerate.

'If we kill or are killed in prison, it makes no difference,' said Ron. 'They are not bothered. We have ceased to be treated as humans. For instance, if a nutter tries to make a name for himself by attempting to top a Kray, it's obvious that with no hope of parole, Reggie and I would have to defend ourselves. We have no option. If we kill someone in the process, what does it matter? Our sentence will probably remain the same. It's what they expect of us. They don't understand different crimes, Lol. They treat everyone the same – bank robbers, housebreakers, mass murderers.'

My conversations with him over this period were very intimate, although Ron always feared that I would be prevented from visiting. These fears, it turned out, were justified. About two weeks before Ron's death, I visited him with his elder brother Charlie only to be told at the reception desk that I was not on the database as an approved visitor. Charlie complained – but to no avail – so I waited for him to have his visit. Not wanting to upset him, Charlie told Ron there had been a mix-up with the computers. The same thing happened again on my next visit and no explanation was given other than 'a computer error'. Yet at that time I had been visiting Ron in Broadmoor for over seventeen years.

At last, two weeks after I had been first refused entry to Broadmoor, I was again allowed to see Ron. Charlie was with me as was often the case because I had a vehicle and he didn't. It was the day before Ronnie died.

When we arrived, we made our familiar way to Ron's ward. Before heading for Ron's bed, Charlie asked a senior nurse on reception at the ward about his brother's condition. He was told there was nothing wrong with Ron's heart, but because he had been suffering from dizzy spells, a consultant was going to examine Ronnie that evening.

We found Ron in an anxious condition, lying down on his bed. He was disturbed about the monitors taped to his chest, and asked me to take them off, saying, 'You understand these things, Lol.' He thought that the monitors were taping our conversation. I explained that the discs on his chest were monitoring his heart.

'What's wrong with it?' he asked.

'Nothing's wrong with your heart,' came Charlie's quick reply.

'Then why are these fucking things stuck on me?' was Ron's equally rapid response.

Eventually, we managed to convince Ron that the monitoring of his chest was because of his heavy smoking. Reassured, he relaxed. Sitting up in bed, he looked straight at me and asked, 'Did you bring anything in?' I fumbled for an answer. 'What do you want Ron?' I said. I was going to say that we did not know if he could have anything when he turned to Charlie and asked, 'Didn't you even bring me some Lucozade?'

Charlie was taken by surprise, but I realised straightaway what Ronnie meant. Whenever they visited someone in hospital, East Enders always took something in with them. Even if the person were dying, they would still get a bottle of Lucozade. We had gone empty handed, something Ronnie would never have done – and he wanted us to know it.

As if in harmony, Charlie and I said: 'There's a shop outside in the hospital. We'll get you something in a minute.'

As we talked, Ron reminded me of my promise to write a book about him. Because he knew I was going to America, he even remembered to ask to have his regards sent to friends in the States. After about twenty-five minutes, we said we would go and get Ron some things. 'What else do you want, Ron?' asked Charlie.

'I'll have some Ribena blackcurrant juice,' Ron replied. My theory about the request for Lucozade was right. Ronnie was quietly telling us off by changing his mind and asking for Ribena.

As we left the ward, Charlie was met by a television reporter looking for an exclusive comment on Ron's condition. I went to the shop close by whilst Charlie did the interview. The shop only had small cartons of Ribena. I bought three, but was concerned about the small curly straw attached to the side. Ronnie was not so ill that he needed to drink through a straw. In fact, he looked quite strong and was speaking loudly. I did not relish the thought of offering the cartons to him. I was sure he expected a bottle and might get angry over the little drinking straws.

Ron was sitting upright in bed when we went in with the drinks. I had given them to Charlie, who took off a straw, placing it in the carton.

'A straw's better in case it gets on the clothes as it will stain,' said Charlie diplomatically. Ron agreed, adding: 'It's lovely and cold. Thanks.'

As we were about to leave, Ron praised the attendants at Broadmoor. 'They've been very good to me,' he said, waving his arms at them. I told Ron I would see him before I went to the States the following week, saying that he looked better than I had expected him to.

'I look terrible, Lol,' he said. 'My hair's a mess. I look white. My teeth feel gritty. I'll see you when you come back from America. Have a nice time. I'll feel and look a lot better then.'

It was at this very moment something happened that I was unable to comprehend. Ron leaned forward to say to me almost in a whisper: 'Look after Charlie, Lol. Promise me?' He obviously sensed something, but at the time I was puzzled.

I told Charlie what Ron had said, thinking he would give me a clue, but he just laughed, happy that Ron looked so well. 'Maybe he thinks that you are going to win the Lottery,' he said jokingly.

Later that evening, Reg rang from Maidstone Prison

asking for details of the visit and thanking me for going. He told me that a doctor at the hospital had informed him that Ron would be having a blood transfusion the next day as he was anaemic, and would keep me informed. Charlie called immediately after Reg, saying that he would be going to see Ron in the morning, reiterating that he thought he looked quite well. I told him to give Ron my best wishes.

The next morning I was half listening to the television news when I heard the announcer say, 'Gangland leader Ronnie Kray . . .' – I expected him to say that he was in hospital having tests – 'died this morning.' To say I was shocked was an understatement. I was numb and felt suddenly alone. Instantly, the telephone rang. It was Stephanie King.

'What's happened to Ronnie?' she asked. Steph obviously had not heard, but was enquiring because a reporter had telephoned her, saying, 'Have you heard about Ronnie?' but replaced the telephone before telling her anything.

'Ronnie's dead!' I blurted out. Steph screamed and put the phone down in total shock. It must have been awful for her to find out in this way, but I, too, was in shock, having seen him just hours before and was not thinking straight.

Charlie rang me at about ten o'clock. He was devastated, hardly able to speak. 'Reggie wants us to go to see him tomorrow to sort things out,' he stuttered. Charlie was obviously utterly grief-stricken. 'I'll see you tomorrow then at the prison,' he added, his voice full of emotion.

Charlie and I went to see Reggie as arranged. The prison Governor and his staff were compassionate, allowing us a visit in a private room. Reggie was obviously grieving, but seemed remarkably calm and in control, checking with

Charlie that everything Ronnie had wanted was obeyed. He wanted to know every detail of Ronnie when we had seen him for the last time the night before he died, and was pleased he was in good spirits as we left the hospital. Reg was happy that I would deliver the message to their friends in the States, wishing me a good journey in almost the same way as Ron. Uncanny, but then they were identical twins.

Reg said that he did not need any form of sedation, in spite of newspaper talk that he was heavily tranquillised, and that he would be talking with his best friends in the prison later in the day as they had been a big help to him in his hour of need. Among them was Freddie Foreman, a very close and loyal friend.

Once in New York, I had many calls from various friends of the Kray family giving their condolences. Carmine 'Wassel' De Noia phoned with respects from himself and the Pagano family. They were sincere in sorrow, sending their respects to the family. I was able to pass these on when I arrived back in London.

Ron's funeral was compared to that of Winston Churchill, something that would have amused and pleased Ronnie. The television coverage was immense. One programme carried an hourly update, showing the arrival of flowers at 6 am, with people gathering at the same time to pay their respects to a great East End character. Barriers had been put in place beforehand for the expected crowd from all over the country. As they were lifted, people began to line the route to see the spectacle of six plumed horses drawing the Victorian glass-sided carriage carrying Ron's body. The carriage was ornately decorated with masses of wreaths. *EastEnders* star Barbara Windsor, Roger Daltrey of The Who and *London's*

Burning actress Helen Keating were among show business friends to send wreaths. Friends from New York sent a Gates of Heaven with a photograph of the Manhattan skyline. Outstanding among them all were the largest wreaths from Reggie with 'The other half of me' in huge letters along with 'The Kray Twins', followed by others – 'The Colonel', boxing rings and gloves from local boxing clubs, and those from brother Charlie and family. There were hundreds of others, including some from strangers, who felt they knew the Twins and wanted to pay their respects.

The cortege left the Chapel of Rest at W. English and Sons, a local funeral parlour on Bethnal Green Road. In total, twenty-four limousines followed the vehicle supplied by the prison authorities carrying Reggie, who was handcuffed to a warder sitting beside him and accompanied by three other warders. They followed the carriage carrying Ron's body along Bethnal Green Road, which was now packed with thousands of people who were clapping and shouting 'Free Reggie now!' along the half-mile journey to St Matthew's Church, where the funeral service was being held. It was a never to be forgotten spectacle, one that showed the high esteem in which the Krays are still held in the East End.

Ron's splendid coffin of dark oak with golden handles was carried by the pallbearers – including Charlie and myself – into the church. The respect for Ron was shown by the capacity attendance: two hundred seats were taken, with other mourners standing two-deep at the back and in the aisles. The service was conducted by Father Christopher Bedford, commencing with a tape of the Frank Sinatra classic 'My Way', Ron's favourite song.

After hymns – including the haunting 'Morning Has Broken' – and some prayers, two messages were read by Sue McGibbon. The first, from Reggie and Charlie, read: 'We wish for only good to come from Ron's passing away, and what is about to follow is our tribute to Ron. It is a symbol of peace in that four of the six pallbearers will be Charlie, Freddie Foreman, Johnny Nash and Teddy Dennis. Each one represents an area of London – North, South, East and West.' All four encircled Ron's coffin in a minute's silence.

This was followed by a short, heartfelt message from Reg. 'My brother Ron is now free and at peace,' it said. 'Ron had great humour, a vicious temper, was kind and generous. He did it all his way, but above all he was a man. That's how I will always remember my twin brother Ron. God Bless. Reg Kray.'

After scripture readings, prayers and a hymn came the Final Commendation. Worded wonderfully, it went:

> Do not stand at my grave and weep
> I am not there. I do not sleep.
> I am a thousand winds that blow,
> I am the diamond glints on snow.
> I am the sunlight on ripened grain,
> I am the gentle Autumn rain.
> When you awaken in the morning's hush
> I am the swift uplifting rush
> Of quiet birds in circled flight
> I am the soft stars that shine at night.
> Do not stand at my grave and cry,
> I am not there; I did not die.

The congregation left the ceremony to the tune of Whitney Houston's wistful 'I Will Always Love You' from *The Bodyguard* film. Outside in the street, masses of people unable to get in for the service continued to show their endearment to their favourite East Ender. As Reggie, still handcuffed to a warder, emerged, the crowd spontaneously surged forward. A youth, one amongst others on the roof of a building opposite the church, yelled, 'Free Reggie now! Let him out!' This was picked up and chanted by the dense crowd who had gathered, bringing Bethnal Green Road and the surrounding streets to a standstill.

Thousands came to line the route from Bethnal Green to the cemetery in Chingford, Essex, where Ron's body was to be laid to rest beside the graves of his mother, Violet, and father, Charles, and close to the grave of Reggie's late wife, Frances. In all, an estimated forty thousand people lined the streets of the East End to witness the final journey of Britain's most notorious gangster.

At Chingford Cemetery the mourners were almost overwhelmed by the crowds waiting by the entrance to the burial ground for the arrival of the cortege. At the graveside, hundreds more had massed. Among those present were Charlie Smith, Ron's good friend and companion for many years in Broadmoor. Charlie, handcuffed and heavily escorted by warders, was accompanied by his wife Maggie.

Also present were Ron's former wife, Katie, and actors Ray Winstone and Jamie Foreman. Football was represented by Brentford manager David Webb, whilst from the fight world came Greg and Alex Steene, Roy Shaw and Lenny McLean. Frankie Fraser, a former gangster and now good friend of the Twins, was amongst the hundreds of famous – and infamous – faces in attendance. The sight and sound of low flying helicopters filming the event added to the occasion. Finally, as Reg was taken back to Maidstone Prison to continue his grieving quietly and privately, well away from the public gaze, brother Charlie, along with a number of invited mourners, went to Guvnors, an East End pub, to attend a buffet arranged by Reg.

It was the end of an era. Like him or not, nobody ever ignored Ronnie Kray. He was a marvellous friend, but a very dangerous enemy. Villains or heroes, the Krays are legendary figures who, in fighting their way out of London's poverty-struck East End to mix with famous stars and politicians, carried the hopes and aspirations of a generation of British society, and were cheered and feted by both the humble and high born alike.

And even after his death, Ron continued to make news. In December 1995, taking a look back at the year just over, the *Daily Mirror* ran a pictorial page feature on celebrities who had died in the previous twelve months. Amongst those the paper included in 'The ones we lost' were actress Ginger Rogers, former Premier Harold Wilson, novelist Sir Kingsley Amis, singer Dean Martin, John F. Kennedy's mother Rose, tennis champion Fred Perry, and comics Kenny Everett, Peter Cook, Larry Grayson, Arthur English and Marti Caine. But by far the largest picture was reserved for a dapper-looking Ron. Somehow, I think he would have approved of outflanking them all size-wise!

'if the krays were about . . .'

Countless times, recently and over the years, I have heard people talking about muggings and old people getting robbed or beaten up. The comment is always the same – 'Wouldn't have happened if the Krays were still about . . .' Such is the feeling in the East End about the Krays that locals thought they could police the area as vigilantes, such was their power. Most locals have kind words for the Twins and were not afraid of their reign as gangsters. Of course, the Krays were not a threat to the general public.

But to really understand the Krays and their enduring appeal, it is necessary to get some idea of the East End at the time we were all growing up. Even though I mixed with some of the roughest, toughest, most notorious characters, I have no criminal record, which is amazing as in the area of Bethnal Green where I was born and bred it was considered natural to engage in unlawful activities. Goods stolen from a warehouse or parked lorry – items such as cigarettes, spirits of any kind, televisions or electrical appliances – would change hands expeditiously and without any conscience or guilt whatsoever. The feeling was that the goods were insured and that the owners invariably claimed for more than the amount stolen, so it worked in their favour and was an earner for them, too. In my teens it was a way of life to buy and sell bent gear.

To be honest, it was almost irresistible to refuse a cashmere coat or leather jacket from the Harrods' sale. These were skilfully exited from the store by the many hoisters (shoplifters) who would congregate around Lyons' tea shop in Whitechapel Road opposite the London Hospital.

During the sale period after Christmas, the large stores such as Liberty, Selfridges, Harvey Nichols, Jaeger and, of course, the favourite Harrods, would be invaded by teams of hoisters from all over London, as if they had a licence to shop without any intention of paying. It was quite funny if, by accident, you went into one of the stores at this time. Along the rows of beautiful merchandise, selecting the most expensive garments, would be familiar faces belonging to the elite of that breed of shoplifter, dressed as finely as any genuine paying customer.

Words unfamiliar to the genuine customers would drift through the room – 'Nitto,' 'Sweet' and 'On your daily'. These words of encouragement and sometimes warning of store detectives watching the action were called in their own inimitable style. I should explain that 'Nitto' meant 'Don't go ahead' whilst 'Sweet' denoted the all clear. 'On your daily' meant 'Don't touch it!' because a store detective was watching. It was possible to order certain clothes in advance of the sales by giving the size, colour and order number to a hoister. He or she would delight in achieving the request, mainly because it fetched them a higher price from the buyer. This was fifty per cent of the marked price for an order, instead of one third, the usual price generally charged by the professional hoisters if they were desperate to sell.

Another of the hoisters' haunts was the Lyceum lunch-time dance hall in Covent Garden. It was brilliant at lunchtimes at 'The Ly'. Everybody seemed to be able to get there on weekdays during their break from whatever job they did. Among these were draughtsmen, solicitors' clerks and budding actors, along with the young fruit, fish and meat market workers, fresh from their early morning start. There was the added advantage of the abundance of the most beautiful young ladies working in local offices and shops also congregating at the 'Ly'. Many a heart was broken by both genders.

The boys adopted the name of 'the Chaps' to signify that whichever area you came from in London you were recognised as 'One of the Chaps'. It was considered honourable to be included. There were no leaders or committee. It was unique and you were somehow accepted or left out if not suitable. Some of today's very well-known figures in the entertainment, sporting and finance worlds – both legal and illegal – belong to this coveted group, and still meet quite frequently and revere the title 'One of the Chaps'.

I remember going down to the Lyceum and ordering a cashmere coat from Harrods off 'Tommy the Trotter'. The next day Tommy took the coat to 'The Ly' at lunchtime and Cossa, another of 'the Chaps', collected it for me. It was exactly as I had requested, but when I tried it on we both burst into fits of laughter – it was about two feet too long. Tommy must have really struggled with that one as he was smaller than me. I had it altered and until a couple of years ago, when it was donated to an Oxfam shop, it was still in perfect nick. Such is the value of Harrods!

Ronnie and Reggie never indulged in the lunchtime sessions at The Lyceum, except perhaps an occasional visit to meet Curly King or Flash Ronnie. They were busy beginning to build their reputation of fear among the older fraternity of gangsters. But Ronnie found the younger element of 'the Chaps' quite amusing. Some of them – Terry Bay, Brian Lynch, Roy McQueen, Joe Bailey and others – would often be invited to join Ron's company if he was in a pub or club.

Ron really enjoyed talking and reminiscing about those early times. I told him during a visit to Broadmoor a short time before he died of an incident many years ago at The Grave Maurice pub in Whitechapel. One night when Reg, Ron and a few of The Firm walked in, looking quite serious, a group of young chaps standing by the door were heard to say, 'Heads up – it's the Brothers Grim.' They did so in hushed tones and more out of respect than anything else. Fortunately, it was out of earshot of the Twins or their group.

Most of the young group were friends of the Twins. Funny as it was, nobody laughed. They were not stupid. In fact, it wasn't long before Ron joined their company, for he enjoyed listening to their antics. When, many years later, I told Ron about the unheard 'Brothers Grim' comment he wanted to know who had said it. When I told him I thought it was Terry Bay or Brian Hall and was not meant to be derogatory, he smiled in amusement.

'Saucy young bastards, weren't they, Lol,' he said. 'But they were very funny kids too, weren't they?'

Ron remembered that most of them were good boxers,

making reference to the ability as a young lad of Brian Hall, later to become an actor, appearing at one time with Bob Hoskins as Reg and Ron in a stage play. Subsequently, he was better known as Terry the cook in John Cleese's *Fawlty Towers*. Brian attended Ron's funeral, then sadly passed away himself not too long afterwards.

So breaking the law was a way of life for many growing up in the East End in those days. At the same time, the code of respect was very important, loyalty being paramount. The saying was, 'Never grass on your mates, whatever.' Grassing on anyone was considered really bad, but on your mates unforgivable.

For example, if you were buying something off someone, as soon as you had bought it then it was yours, whatever the circumstances. Even if it was considered to be bent, you were responsible, and if you were nicked for buying stolen goods, it would be sorted out later, probably with some help with the fine, the usual punishment.

The only exception to this rule was God help anyone who stole from a working-class home, not that there was usually anything worth stealing. More often than not, the targets were the gas or electricity meters, which held cash. This meant the tenant was responsible to the supplier, even after a robbery. If that happened, it was considered despicable by everyone. I know of a few cases when Ron sent out some of the local thieves to find those responsible for breaking into someone's home – usually an old person's – and 'doing the meters' as it was commonly called.

If found, it was usual to beat up the culprit and return the money and any stolen goods. Ron would then add some cash of his own for the mainly old folk who were burgled. He hated those low-life thieves. 'Could be your own mum,' he would say. Word soon got around and this type of burglary seemed to come to a rapid halt, hence the saying, 'All this wouldn't happen if the Krays were about today.' People really think they would have been able to stop today's violent crime. It's a nice thought, but one that I think is unrealistic because it is now a different world entirely.

The object of writing this book is not to educate would-be gangsters, to suggest that young hard nuts of today should copy the style of the Krays, for that would be foolish and futile. But in the fifties and sixties, things were totally different. It is easy to forget that the 1960s saw a revolution, not just in social and sexual attitudes and behaviour, but in music and fashion. Suddenly, the young were liberated, no longer looking like cloned versions of their parents. Youth was in; age was out.

The police and their methods have moved on, too, with forensic science being capable of the most incredible feats. These days, just a tiny speck of this or minuscule spot of that can lead directly to a conviction. Now, cases years old are reopened and solved. Today, the police use high-tech scanning equipment. Indeed, it sometimes seems that just about every corner of London's streets has close circuit television cameras. Video camera footage is now accepted in court whilst mobile phones can be tapped for evidence. All of these gadgets – and more – were then unavailable, but would make an operation like The Krays' virtually impossible today.

The Krays were men of the 1960s. As their trusted

friend, I was close enough to appreciate their growing power at that time. I am certain that Reg, Ron and Charlie would hate it if anybody tried to emulate them. It was not a very lucrative road for them or their family. At the end of the day, the 'glamour' was not very glamorous at all with the heartbreak it fetched them. The penalty of the huge sentences given to Reg, Ron and Charlie is too harsh a price to pay for such infamy.

My own knowledge of growing up with the Kray family and their mother's family, the Lees, is still very vivid. My memories are entirely different from most of the books written about the Krays.

I maintain that most stories about the Krays are rubbish. I say that because some still tell tenuous, questionable tales of ties with the Krays. In my opinion, many of the stories told today are grossly exaggerated. At times, they are laughable. If they were all true, the Twins would never have been caught, such was their power and strength.

Instead of tall stories, I will explain how I grew up with my young friends who later became the most infamous gangsters of the century. This friendship always endured, right from our childhood. I was there watching as Reg and Ron became excellent amateur and professional boxers and have visited them in various prisons. Never once was I asked or even wanted to join The Firm. Perhaps I was considered too soft. Thank God that I never had to make such a decision one way or the other.

Born in Bethnal Green in the 1930s, I can remember thinking that we seemed to be the poorest family around until I heard my mum telling her sister Lucy about a very hard-up family living nearby who needed some clothes. My auntie gave my mum some of her daughter's clothes for this family, who had a son that went to my school. Quickly, I realised that we were all in the same boat; we were all the same. Some seemed to have a better lifestyle, but they were no different or else they would not be living in our area.

This, then, is the backdrop against which I, the Krays and thousands of other families lived in the pre-war East End. Believe me, there was poverty a-plenty and no welfare state to act as a kind of cushion or counter balance. But, then, the East End was a tight-knit, caring community. Today, society has changed almost out of all recognition. The extended family has long gone, so Mum generally is not just around the corner or across the street to help out. These days, so many people literally do not know their next door neighbour. Ill-designed tower blocks had yet to appear. When they did, not only were they sometimes a blight on the horizon, but brought a blight on society, too, with their own brand of social problems.

We may have been poor; we may have dressed in hand-me-downs; we rented homes rather than being owner-occupiers. But what we did have was pride in ourselves and our families.

bombsites and baths

I have always had respect for Charlie Kray senior. I had heard stories about how nasty he had been to the Twins' mother Violet, but they did not sink in as I'd only known him to be nice and friendly towards me. As their personalities clashed, he and Ron did argue generally much more than he and Reg, but I never knew them to have any fights as has been suggested by some. Anyhow, the Twins' dapper-looking father was a small, wiry man of about five feet, seven inches and no real match for his sons physically.

On the day Charlie senior was buried, I went to see Ron in Broadmoor, staying the full two hours to comfort him. At this very sad time, Ron was extremely emotional, especially as he and Reg had decided not to attend the funeral. Their mother had died only eight months previously and the whole episode was unexpectedly marred by extensive media coverage. Their mother's funeral was the first time that the general public could see them in person, for they had been given compassionate leave.

The event was attended by thousands of curious onlookers, along with a vulture-like Press pack eager for a sensational story and photos to match. Genuine showbusiness friends of the Twins also attended, including a very distraught Diana Dors, amongst others. Ron and Reg were handcuffed to two of the tallest prison warders available. They dwarfed the Twins, making them appear unusually small, not only in stature but importance. It was an obvious ploy by the powers-that-be to try and diminish them in every possible way.

As he was an Army deserter, the Twins' father never features very much in any of the books about the Krays, for in reality he did nothing special to write about. As he was on the run from the military police, Charlie senior was not around much for us kids to see, and I never knew when he visited his family. It was only after the Second World War ended, when I was in my teens, that I began to see him. The Twins hardly spoke about their father to the Press until later on in their terms of imprisonment. It was only after his death that they gave any mileage to his life. After they were sentenced, I enjoyed Mr Kray's company. Old Charlie and I were often asked to run errands for the Twins.

Charlie had married his girlfriend Violet Lee in 1926 when she was 17 years of age. They wed in a local register office, much to the annoyance of her father, 'Cannon Ball' Lee. Their first son Charlie was born in 1927.

Later, they had another child, a girl with jet-black hair who died soon after she was born. The couple named her Violet. Reg and Ron were born within ten minutes of each other on 24 October 1933, with Reg coming first. At that time, the family lived in Stean Street, Hoxton, but in 1939 they moved to 178 Vallance Road, Bethnal Green, to be neighbours of Violet's sisters, May and Rose. Meanwhile, Violet's parents lived a few doors away at the end of the terrace. Not for nothing was the area known as 'Lee territory'.

The properties were typical two-storey Victorian dwellings with a back yard. The Krays' house had a sitting-room, commonly called 'the front room', which was kept for their best visitors and was the smartest room. A long passageway led to a small kitchen, whilst at the back of the house was a bedroom, which Charlie senior and Violet occupied. Upstairs were two bedrooms, Ron and Reg sharing the back room.

Our family – father Robert (Bob) O'Leary, mother Rosina (Rose), elder sister Kathy, myself and younger brother Alfred (Alphi) – lived in an eight-bedroom Victorian house, just round the corner from Vallance Road. The upstairs rooms of our home at 212 Cheshire Street had very large windows. We were told that the houses were originally built for the Huguenot settlers from France who needed large windows for natural light to enable them to operate their looms for silk weaving. It was noticeable that most of the homes in the area had this type of window.

Like the Krays, we had a lot of our family around us. Maisie, our elder sister, lived with my mother's mum – our gran Rose Mahoney – in nearby Menotti Street, whilst Arthur, the eldest of the family, was married at an early age to Lily Flowers, who came from Manchester Buildings, also in Menotti Street.

So the dingy back streets and houses of Bethnal Green in the 1940s were the playground of our childhood. By today's standards they were slums and not fit to be lived in. The lavatory was in the yard. A brick-built extension in the corner of the garden adjoining the house, it had a roughly constructed wooden door with a nine-inch gap at the top and six-inch gap at the bottom, probably for ventilation. It certainly wasn't for privacy, for everyone knew if you were using the loo. The strong, lingering, pungent, quite unforgettable smell of Jayes disinfectant wafts into my nostrils as I write fifty-odd years later. The lavatory may have been shabby by modern standards, but the pine seat was scrubbed daily, causing the grain to rise against the soft wood, which in turn would give users a weal on their buttocks depending on how long they had been sitting there. Not for us softer than soft toilet paper advertised today on TV with a cute puppy dog. Our lavatory paper was newspaper cut into squares and put on a meat hook. Well, it served the purpose!

Then there were the tin baths and large, white, solid-as-rock, oblong sinks where everything was washed – the crockery, clothes, even kids were sat on the draining board if one needed a bath before going to bed. To us, though, Bethnal Green – which is now quite trendy – was the very best place in the entire world. It *was* our world.

I have known Reggie and Ronnie Kray for as long as I can remember. We went to the same primary school, Wood Close in Brick Lane, Bethnal Green. Our early lives as kids were centred around the start of the Second World War in 1939, when I was six years old. Even today, my memory of those early years is vivid. The London Blitz was on. Because our houses were in the streets running parallel to a railway line, we were a target for German bombers. During raids we went either to communal shelters under the railway arches – these were considered a safe place to be – or stayed in our garden in an Anderson shelter. These were provided by the authorities. Built of corrugated iron, they housed about six people. Sometimes, though, our mother sat us underneath the kitchen table or under the stairs if the air raid warning siren screamed out that an attack was about to happen.

Most of the raids occurred at night, giving extra protection to the bombers. When the German planes loaded with bombs droned overhead, Ron, Reg and I would stand in the street outside the shelters, watching the searchlights and tracer bullets pick out the raiders in the sky. They flew so low that at times we could see the crew. Roving ack-ack guns on lorries fired at the bombers along with other guns that had been set up in local parks. When an enemy plane suffered a direct hit, everybody cheered.

Not surprisingly in view of the danger we faced, our mothers would tell us to get back into the shelters, but we ignored them, standing happily in the crowd, watching the action. I cannot ever remember being afraid, even though friends were sometimes killed. Perhaps we were too young to understand the enormity of what was happening and the grave danger in which we lived. To us, it all seemed so exciting. When the All Clear siren sounded, heralding the end of a raid, for us kids a different kind of action immediately began. We went out shrapnel hunting, looking for pieces of bombs or bullets that had exploded around us. Sometimes they were still hot. And if a fragment had German writing on it, that was considered a prize souvenir, one to be shown with pride to other kids.

When we played on bomb sites, the Twins' cousin Billy, son of Mrs Kray's sister Rose Wiltshire, would be our leader. He was about six years older than us, and naturally more mature. If we did not do the things he wanted, Billy got angry and punched us on the muscle of the arm, his bony knuckle often leaving a nasty-looking bruise. Billy was always up to some form of mischief so we liked being in his company, even if we were blamed for some of the things he did. This was often the case, yet I still have fond memories of Billy as he always protected us against the bigger boys.

During day time, as the schools had been closed, we played on the debris of newly-demolished houses, which always had a magnetism for us. I remember that on one occasion the Twins and I found a sealed cake tin among the ruins. When we opened it up, it contained some lovely home-baked rock cakes in perfect condition, so we ate them between us. It was a real luxury. But when we excitedly told my mum what we had found, she was angry and scolded us. 'They were Lil Castle's,' she exclaimed. 'She's had her house bombed, poor cow.'

Lil Castle's home backed on to ours. The windows in our house had been blasted out, too, but I still never knew us to be in the least afraid. Later, when Mum told Lil we had eaten her cakes and that we would say sorry to her, she would not hear of it. 'Let the kids enjoy themselves, Rose,' she said. 'They might be dead tomorrow.' Such a comment succinctly sums up the true spirit of the East End during the war.

At the end of the war years, we used to play outside 'Ben the barbers', at the corner of our road and Menotti Street. Ben was a Jewish character, with thick, black hair, sleeked back with Brylcreem. He had two assistants, Raymond and a younger man called Arthur, who later became famous in the area as his uncle, Charlie Cooper, won £100,000 on Littlewoods' pools. By today's standards, that sum would run into millions. The locals nicknamed him 'Champagne Charlie'. A kind man, he paid the rent for other people in his tenement block of flats in Corfield and Wilmot Streets.

As a child, it was always good to go to Ben's barber shop. He would put a board on the arms of the chair for us to sit upon so he could cut our hair. As we grew older and taller we were able to sit down without the board. That made us feel very adult, so, just as the older boys had once done to us, we teased the smaller kids who still had to sit on the board.

Ben knew most of the kids and parents in the area. A likeable man, he had a profound stutter, increased by excitement. Often, we played football – seemingly for hours – with a small tennis ball right outside his shop. The ball often got kicked into his forever open front door. Ben would come to the door with a very red, perplexed look, stuttering, 'Twinnies,' (his pet name for Reg and Ron) 'I'll go and tell your mother!' as if we had done it on purpose.

On reflection, kicking the ball into the shop was danger-ous if, as he often did, Ben was shaving someone with an open cut throat razor! But we saw no need for his threats and would tease him by saying something like, 'Give us our ball back, Ben! By the time you get the message out, it'll be dark!' Of course, the game would end there with Ben, menacing-looking razor in hand, coming into the street, pretending to chase us for being saucy. Often, he kept the ball, always giving it back to us the next day.

We all liked and respected Ben, and loved his shop, with its red-striped pole outside. Many were the times we laughed when he thought he was being discreet offering the older customers 'Something for the weekend, Sir?' We all knew that he meant Durex. And it was even funnier if someone became embarrassed, blushed bright red and pretended not to hear him. I cannot ever remember Ben trying to sell us Durex: he was probably too embarrassed to ask as he had seen us grow up from children.

As well as playing in the streets, we would also constantly be around each others' houses, which were only a five-minute walk apart. My mum, as well as working as a presser in the garment trade using a fourteen-pound iron, used to let out rooms to lodgers, as we didn't need all our bedrooms. This embarrassed me as the lodgers were very eccentric characters, but Ronnie Kray wasn't put off. One of the lodgers, known as Lavender Liz, had a dog called Rhoda. Ron loved dogs and Rhoda was very friendly with him. Ron also liked Lavender Liz's eccentricity. Liz was so-called because she put small sachets of lavender into little bags, selling them around local pubs. She had a Victorian style of dressing up, with long dresses to her ankles falling over her tall button-up boots, and a small bonnet perched on top of her head. She was very eccentric, but intelligent and well-spoken; whenever I had a conversation with her she was very kind and knowledgeable. Ron found her extremely interesting.

She died at home after her dog Rhoda had passed on a few months before. It seemed as if the dog's passing had broken her heart as we never knew Liz to have any friends. When the police came to attend to the body, they told my mother that she had thousands of pounds in her rooms. There were lots of uncashed postal orders, banknotes and letters, most unopened. It turns out that she had been falsely accused of cruelty to her beloved dog years before.

After she had been cleared by the RSPCA, the local newspapers reported her story and dozens of readers had sent money to her in support.

The police showed my mother a beautiful wedding dress wrapped in cellophane paper and covered in tissue paper. It was still in perfect condition. A newspaper story came out that she was a lady who had dropped out to live among the poor, getting a living the best way she could. This story was given more credence when a smart middle-aged man arrived at our house to tell my mother that Liz had been jilted at the altar, and that she could not – or alternatively would not – face up to the hurt of what she thought was a disgrace. He thanked my mother for looking after Liz, and was inquisitive about her lifestyle in the East End. When my mother explained that she earned her living by selling lavender in sachets, he was amused and pleased, saying that her family owned lavender fields in Norfolk, and that he was her nearest relative.

As well as hanging around each others' houses and in the streets, Cheshire Street public baths, just across the road from the Twins' house, was a daily ritual for me, Reg, Ron and quite a few of our mates. At home we only had a tin bath in the yard that we had to fill up with hot water from the copper boiler Mum used to wash our clothes. As the boiler needed wood and coal as fuel it was easier to go to the communal baths. Since most of the houses were built the same way, the baths were nearly always full at week-ends. During the week, though, we were able just to walk in without queuing. Bath night was on a Friday evening or all day Saturday for most of the locals. We often wondered how they could have just one bath a week, for we were in there every day and loved it. Weekends we jibbed in the queue and never had to wait, for the attendants knew their regulars and would always get a tip from us, giving us extra soap and fresh towels.

An old trick that was often played on newcomers to the baths was this: we would shout to the attendants, 'More hot water number six,' then wait for the person in cubicle number six to scream out: 'Turn that water off! It's too fucking hot!' The boiling water would gush out of the very wide tap on their bath. We thought this was hilarious, but never owned up to having done it, even if it was one of our mates.

One of the attendants at the baths was Charlie, a friend of Charlie Kray, the Twins' dad. It was only when I was read a book by 'Nipper' Read that I realised that after the Twins' arrest in 1968, attendant Charlie was questioned about Reggie, Ronnie and The Firm. 'Nipper' Read was, of course, the Scotland Yard detective in charge of hounding the Krays until finally arresting them. It seems the police thought that some bodies were disposed of in the furnace used to heat the water for the baths! I wouldn't know if that were true, though anything's possible, but would not have thought there would have been much left of anything by the time of asking. It was well after the murders had taken place. Fortunately, there was no evidence to prove that anything was amiss . . .

When I was fifteen years old, I started my first job at Spitalfields, at a firm called M. Boas, which supplied fruit and vegetables to hospitals and restaurants. Both Reg and Ron applied for a job there, but I was not supposed to know them as it was a condition of the Jewish bosses that they didn't employ friends. Possibly, this was because they would play about if working together and the work would not get done.

We did have some fun there, though, if only for a few months. We had to count cabbages into sacks and check the quality for hospitals as they paid good money. Hotels paid better, though, and had the pick of the crop. Restaurants were very competitive with their buying, so we had to trim the vegetables to make them look fresh, then spray water over them to make it appear that they had been freshly picked. It was quite a good job for us as we started early in the morning, about 6 am, and would finish at the latest by 2 pm, and often sooner. It was still an eight-hour day, but we liked the afternoons off.

I got the sack when Ronnie and I were caught putting a boy in a sack and tying up the top. It was a boyish prank, no more than just a bit of juvenile fun. Ronnie kept his job, but the guv'nor thought I was the ringleader, and that I had told him a lie when he asked me if I knew the Twins. Later, I found out from Ronnie that another boy, Ray Farrow, had told the guv'nor I was a friend of the Twins and he just waited until I was up to something to have a reason for sacking me.

From that job, I was able to get another one with my older brother, Arthur, in a firm called T. J. Poupart at the flower market in Spitalfields. It was a good job, and because I was adept at writing and arithmetic, I was considered too good to waste on carting boxes about and promoted to being a checker. Now that was a lucrative job for me, with all sorts of fiddles. None of us starved in that firm!

Although I had a better job, I still brooded on getting the sack from M. Boas. It upset me when Ronnie told me that Ray Farrow had got my job after I was sacked and was now the guv'nor's blue-eyed boy. It seemed about right. Farrow was a bit slippery, so I went to Hanbury Street where we used to take our tea break in Curas Café.

I saw Ray walking along with Ronnie Kray, so took my revenge on him with a good right-hander. He went to the ground, but Ronnie stopped the fight going any further. He found the incident amusing. We were fighting over a job of work, but I wondered if he had orchestrated the entire thing.

Ray was still game, though, for about half an hour later he arrived at the flower market where I was working to continue the row. He was on a bike. Throwing it to the ground when he reached the stand where I worked, he furiously went to attack me. Naturally, in defence, I put Farrow down twice more. It was funny really because he was still angry. Ray Farrow may have been a good thief, but he was not an equally good fighter.

Watching this row was a real tough-looking character, a man named Jackie Dumford, nicknamed 'Crackerjack' or 'Jacko'. He reminded me of Desperate Dan of the *Dandy* comic. Always playing tricks on people in Spitalfields Market, he was very well liked by everyone.

'Turn it in Ray,' Jacko said when he stepped in to stop the fight. 'You ain't 'it 'im yet. You're like a jack-in-the-box. Shake 'ands and be friends, boy.'

Of course, there was no winner, but it was common to settle a difference of opinion in the market with a fight. There were a lot of very strong good fighters who would not let any liberties take place. Nevertheless, it was a lovely place to work, and the characters are irreplaceable. As the songs says, 'They don't make 'em like that any more.'

Reflecting on that fight with Ray Farrow, I know now he wouldn't have shopped me. Although I had never discussed it with Ron, I think Ron had set us both up. There was nothing wrong in that. Ronnie often did a little mixing to clear the air and test the power of his friends.

they fight each other

The Krays were fighting from an early age. They both enjoyed boxing, a sport their elder brother Charlie taught them from their early teens. When even younger, the Twins and I used to climb a wall to stand and watch the fights at the Mile End Arena for free from a ledge on top of the doorway of the telephone exchange in Eric Street. We would watch boxing whenever we could, so when we heard there was a boxing booth at a fairground in Turin Street in Bethnal Green, we rushed down to see it. At the time, the Twins were barely eleven years old.

The fight was between local favourites Stevie Osborne and Slasher Warner in a bout billed as 'A fight to the finish'. This was a decider, for they had each won a previous bout against each other. However, it became obvious this would not go ahead until someone fought in a couple of supporting bouts. The crowd was getting restless when it seemed that nobody in the audience would accept the challenge of the fairground boxers.

Buster Osborne and Les Haycox were among those challenging all-comers. Believe me, they presented an awesome sight, with their scarred, battered faces and cauliflower ears. They resembled Oliver Reed's portrayal of Bill

Sykes in the film *Oliver*. They looked too nasty even for the usual odd drunken character who Alf Stewart, the fairground owner, would expect to offer to fight or at least go a round. There was the usual prize of £1 for each round that the challenger survived on their feet.

On this occasion there were no takers. The enterprising Mr Stewart, typical of the old-time fairground entrepreneur, titillated the palate of the restless audience with an offer that he would pay any of the spectators to fight each other for a couple of rounds. He added a splash of colour to his request by saying he knew the area to have an 'abundance of fighters' and he hoped that he wouldn't be disappointed.

This announcement was eagerly received by the hyped-up Kray Twins. The excitement was too much for Ronnie Kray. 'We'll fight each other mister!' he exclaimed, closely followed by his brother Reggie nodding in agreement. The shocked Mr Stewart looked apprehensively at these two young kids, but there was no decision for him to make: the crowd did it for him. 'Let's get started!' they yelled. 'Let 'em fight!' The Kray brothers, cheered by the crowd, produced a fight over three rounds worthy of a Junior Championship, and nobbins were thrown into the ring for an excellent performance.

Ron's nose was bloodied and Reg's face marked by Ron's aggression. But they had both enjoyed their debut public appearance. Returning to the dressing room, gratefully accepting praise from the professional fighters, they simply changed into their street clothes, received payment of a few shillings from the very happy Mr Stewart, then went back into the arena to stand and watch the fight they had originally come to see between their personal favourites, Slasher Warner and Stevie Osborne.

When the compere finally introduced Slasher Warner he told the crowd: 'These boys do not know the Queensberry rules of boxing as we would know them. But for those of you who have had the pleasure of seeing their previous two fights, we are in for a spectacular performance.' We all knew that the fights were arranged, but it was still thrilling to see Slasher dressed in a wrestler's leotard, looking for all the world like a boxer of yesteryear, with his hair parted in the middle. Stevie, a boxer of some repute, had support from his large family of boxers, namely Dougie, Buster, and younger brother Simon. All were good street fighters and more than capable professionals. It was an entertaining bout, as was always the case with these two. Blood was always drawn from one or the other, so it was always good value for money. It had to be to fetch the crowd back when the booth returned to the area.

Without knowing it, that night Alf Stewart's Boxing Booth started the professional boxing careers of Reggie and Ronnie Kray. On reflection, it all seems so natural, but then nobody would have known how things would turn out. They were far from gangsters at this stage in their lives. Sportsmen, yes. But gangsters definitely *not*.

The Twins soon joined the Gill brothers – Ronnie and Danny – at the Robert Browning Boxing Club in South London as amateurs. By just fourteen years of age, they had won the following titles between them: Reggie became the London Schoolboys' Champion, South East Divisional Youth Champion, London Air Training Corps Champion (ATC) and National Great Britain Schoolboys' Finalist.

Meanwhile, Ronnie was Hackney Schoolboys' Champion, ATC Champion and London Boys Clubs' Junior Champion. They competed against each other in the schoolboys' finals three times, with Ronnie winning twice to Reggie's once.

Naturally, boys of our age would congregate in small groups, mostly from the adjoining streets. Ours wasn't a gang, just a few youngsters that had similar interests, mostly sporting in our case. The fourth member of our usual group, along with Ronnie, Reggie and myself, was Pat Butler. I often wondered what his interests were. He was a skinny kid with no enthusiasm for any sport whatsoever. Pat had an eccentric, superior attitude towards us that was quite comical, and was the first one of us to carry a tool, a sabre I think it was, although he referred to it as a cutlass. I never saw him use it. Pat had it to impress, which we thought was pathetic. A couple of years later, when the Twins were about seventeen, he was sent to borstal for robbing a vicarage of some money. Pat had burgled it twice within a few months. Unfortunately for him, the second time, the priest caught him red-handed, attacking Butler with some wooden clubs used in weight-lifting.

Feeling sorry for him, the Twins were instrumental in his escape after less than a year in the borstal. Pat was not a very strong person. He wrote to the Twins, complaining about the awful place he was in and that it was too rough for him, so Reg and Ron decided to help him escape.

First, we needed a car, but as none of us drove we could not hire one. The Twins asked me to see if a friend of mine, who was much older than us, would help. This was Sean

Venables, son of Tommy Venables, an old-time, battle-scarred villain who lived in nearby Menotti Street. Would he drive us and help in the escape?

We had a meeting with Sean, a good-looking man of athletic build who was a professional boxer. He told us he would nick a car: that was no problem, but we would have to change the registration plates in case we had to have it away on our toes. This, Sean added, would 'give us more time while the cops check everything'. We believed him.

Unfortunately, when we arranged a date for the possible escape of Butler, Venables did not show up. Ronnie was very angry and blamed me, too, saying that Sean was my friend and I was responsible for him. Sean wasn't to be seen for a week or so, keeping out of the way.

In that time, the Twins arranged for someone else 'more reliable' to help in Butler's escape from borstal – and they kept me out of it. The Twins succeeded in getting Butler out, and while on the run, a friend's sister dyed Butler's blond hair jet black. This was all right until he was caught in the rain . . . and the black dye streaked down his face! He was eventually caught and given an option of going to Australia, which he grabbed. When Pat returned a couple of years later, he had adopted a profound 'Aussie' accent, deciding that we weren't his friends any more: he'd grown up. To use his words, we were 'acting like kids'. Ironically, St Matthew's, the church he initially robbed, was the very same church later used for the funeral services of Ron, Charlie's son Gary, who tragically died of cancer at the age of 44 in March 1996, and Charlie Kray. It was also the one my wife Iris and I chose for our marriage in 1961.

Ronnie never forgot Sean Venables letting him down,

though. Indirectly arranging an encounter a while later between Sean and me, Ronnie told me to be careful as Sean was going to spring me one night on my way home.

Leaving Iris, then my girlfriend, with my sister, we met one night near his home in Menotti Street. After a few exchanged punches, Sean realised he wasn't getting his own way and pulled out from his coat a vicious-looking, two-pronged, finely sharpened dockers' hook. He took aim at my face, but fortunately missed, slipping on to my jacket. This ripped it open, giving me access to a wooden mallet I had hidden there as a precaution, for I remembered Ronnie's warning that Sean would try to spring me. Sean was standing there, looking in amazement.

'You wouldn't, would you?' he asked, a bit cheekily considering he'd just tried to take out my eye with a vicious hook. He then leapt forward and I hit him on the head a few times with the mallet. As I tried to hit him again, in my eagerness I also hit my own head with the mallet!

With Venables on the ground, a crowd soon gathered. At that point, I realised I had to return to my sister's flat. Getting myself together, I placed the mallet under my arm and hastily made my return to my sister's place. On the way, in Vallance Road, I encountered PC Silvers. He, too, lived in Vallance Road, but disliked the Twins, myself and other local youths. He attempted to stop me. I hit him, and put him on his back. Suddenly, I realised the seriousness of the fight with Venables and obviously did not want to get nicked. Arriving at my sister's, I rejoined Iris.

My face was covered with Venables' blood, something I had not realised. Iris and my sister were horrified. The following day, Iris went to work at a silk factory. 'Did you hear about the murder last night?' was the question soon going around the factory. On hearing this, Iris, assuming it referred to Venables, collapsed and was taken home. However, there was no murder, just a badly mutilated head.

On reflection, it seemed Ron had been matchmaking with Sean Venables and myself. His object was to discover the physical power within his friends, something he did frequently.

I wasn't a natural boxer like Ronnie, Reg and Charlie. In my case, the competition was too strong even to think about taking up boxing, and my main interest was football. Several of the boys I played with ended up as professionals, including Stanley Carpenter (Arsenal) and Ronnie White (Charlton), and the highlight of my football career was to play in a mid-week match at Griffin Park for Brentford v West Ham. I knew then that I was either not cut out for this sport as a way of life – the professionals seemed far too dedicated – or just not good enough.

But even though I preferred football, I would go down to the Webbe Club gym, where Ron and Reg would spar as fourteen and fifteen-year-olds. The atmosphere would be electric, for the Twins always commanded an audience when they fought each other. On one occasion, the doors of the club opened wide with a loud bang, completely disrupting the sparring session. Into the gym appeared, with a couple of mates, a very loud, brash man called Crocker but known to us as Loudmouth. He started looking at the team sheet for a forthcoming club match.

In the ring Ron and Reg had by now stopped sparring because of this intervention, and everyone's attention was on the intruder. Loudmouth, looking away from the team sheet, proceeded to shout, 'Ain't this fucking club got any big boys for me to fight?'

Removing a gum shield from his mouth, Ronnie shouted back angrily, 'He'll fight you mate, won't you Lol?' Thanks, Ron, for my introduction into the world of boxing. How could I refuse?

I accepted the challenge and tried to manage a menacing look for my future opponent. Loudmouth was satisfied that he had caused an uproar and left the club immediately. He was very lucky that he wasn't able to box the brothers because of the weight difference. Ronnie looked furious at being interrupted, to put it mildly. If looks could kill . . .

The weeks of preparation for the fight between Loudmouth and myself were quite comical, with Ron, Reg, and Charlie all coaching me. I was a southpaw and all I wanted to do was hit Loudmouth with my hardest hitting hand, which was my right. I was taught by Charlie in the art of defence and stance, with the chin tucked in, feet properly positioned and how to punch correctly to produce more power. As I have said already, I was not a natural boxer. Yes, like most people from a poor upbringing you had to learn to fight to protect yourself against bullies, and I can't deny that I'd had a few street fights. But this was different. I can only compare learning to box, if one isn't a natural, to beginning to drive: it appears there is too much to remember.

Ronnie was insistent that I would beat Loudmouth. 'You can wear Charlie's shorts, high-leg boxing boots, and stockings,' he said. 'You'll look great Lol.'

'Ron, I might look great, but what about when the fight starts? Will I be able to box him?' These thoughts raced through my mind as the preparation continued. And the outcome? Here's a report of the fight in the Webbe club magazine:

'The last big fight of the evening was between two Heavyweights, who as if by mutual consent ignored the finer points of boxing rules and stood in the centre of the ring slugging away at each other as hard as they possibly could, much to the enjoyment of the crowd. Gradually, however, the Webbe favourite O'Leary gained the upper hand over the more experienced Hackney champion Crocker, who with over twenty bouts to his credit, was expected to give a better performance. It soon became obvious that O'Leary, making his debut in the ring, was too powerful for Crocker. Two knockdowns in the second round rightly caused the referee to stop the fight, saving Crocker further punishment.'

Ronnie was delighted that I had knocked out Loudmouth in good style, telling me later that I was very strong and that I could win the ABA, a coveted title. Ron's ambition for me was way over the top, but he was ever so pleased that I had bashed a bully.

The next time I was asked to box for the Webbe was at an open-air show at the Oxford City Football Stadium. Reg didn't get an opponent, but Ron did. I was informed I would not be able to box as I was a raw novice with just one fight to my credit and there was no opponent for me either. We decided to eat, but because Ron was boxing he had a light meal. The rest of us were starving, so we had the business, with all the fatty foods possible.

Returning to the ground after lunch, I was told to get ready as an opponent had now been found for me. Ron went into the ring against quite an aggressive opponent, a stocky boy who was unsuccessfully trying to pull him about so he reciprocated, adding a head butt and a few choice words. His opponent found that his aggression was inadequate against Ron. Looking to the referee for assistance, Ron's patience ran out and he just steamed in to try and knock out his man. The referee warned them again, then disqualified both.

Ron picked up a three-cornered stool that he had been sitting on between rounds, made his way towards the referee and threw it at him. Fortunately, it caught on the bottom rung of the ropes and didn't hit the person he aimed at. I was next into the ring. As I passed Ron, he said: 'You have got to knock them out to win, Lol, or if you don't you will get disqualified. Hit him up the bollocks.' Thanks Ron: this was only my second fight.

I looked at my opponent, who was short and stocky. We sparred, then I caught him with a good right punch and he went on his knees. We had a fairly average first round, but in the second I put him down again. But by this stage, I felt quite sick, with the fatty food from lunch rising into my throat. The next punch that came my way caught me in the stomach. That ended the bout. I couldn't continue and was stopped. I was as sick as a dog, physically, that is. Yes, all the money I'd paid for the lunch had been wasted. I knew then boxing definitely wasn't for me. The only consolation was that both Ronnie and I had lost, so we had something in common. I did box again for another club, but can honestly say that I never, ever enjoyed any of my bouts, even the first one.

The Twins became professional boxers in the same year

of 1950, when they were just sixteen. Their debut was at Mile End Arena, where we used to watch the boxing for free over the wall. The night of their appearance, Ron thought it funny that kids were still watching the fights free just as we did. During their professional careers, Reggie had seven fights and won them all. Ron took part in six and lost two.

At about the same time as the Twins turned professional, an incident occurred that brought to my attention how Ronnie recognised at first hand the power of reputation. Along with other friends, most Sunday mornings we congregated outside Ziggy's café in Cobb Street off Petticoat Lane. We would stand alongside a record stall with boys from other areas of London, chatting about the previous evening's action, catching up on the latest gossip. There was always something going on. Curly King, Norman Hall, Terry O'Brien, Checker Berry and Flash Ronnie are names that spring to mind. They were all good storytellers and usually had something impressive to say.

One such Sunday, we were doing the usual thing, when through the fairly tightly packed crowd appeared three heavy characters, all with Stetson hats. It was one of the most powerful gangsters in London, the infamous Jack Comer, known as Jack Spot, followed by his henchmen, Little Hymie Rosen and Moisha Blueboy, also known as Blueball, depending on how well you knew him. For all the world to see, they completely disregarded the crowd as they walked towards Ziggy's doorway. Everyone in their path moved aside, giving them plenty of space. The normally loud chatter became respectfully hushed. With their image, the three individuals dressed as American gangsters could have come straight off the set of a James Cagney movie.

When they disappeared from sight, the conversation outside Ziggy's returned to normal. I noticed that Ronnie had watched this whole charade with interest. 'I wonder what would happen if I shot him, Lol?' he asked.

'Shoot Jack Spot, Ron!' I said. 'I'd think that if you hit him we would have to start running, but if you miss, we would have to run further and faster.' Ron's reply to me was simply that I was 'too soft'.

We were kids in comparison to those gangsters. Thankfully, Ron never did carry out his light-hearted threat, but I am certain that that was when he saw the power that Spot had and began to want some of it for himself. Sadly, he acquired that power, but at a ridiculous price for him and his family.

Not long after that event at Petticoat Lane, we went to a dance hall in Hackney. We never danced much, if at all, but went there for the music, which was always good. We would meet new friends as most kids do. Occasionally, there would be a scuffle in the club, but it would soon be sorted out by Albert Davis from Bethnal Green, a very powerful man whom we liked and respected. He acted as a sort of steward, so I expect that Barrie, who owned the club, let him in for free.

One evening at the dance hall, Dennis Seigenberg, the son of East End gambling club owner Joe, was flashing a knife. Ronnie told him to put it away out of respect for Albert Davis, but Seigenberg, a very flash kid known for stealing fast cars, annoyed Ronnie with his attitude. Luckily, Seigenberg left early, for although Ronnie wouldn't have caused a problem in the club, I'm certain that he would have had a few words with him outside.

It seemed that Dennis Seigenberg had underestimated the Kray brothers. He was putting word about that he would be taking a mob up to Barrie's to 'put the Twins from Bethnal Green in their place'. Well, in 'gossip alley' on the Sunday morning before the supposed attack on the Twins was meant to occur, the rumours were flying around. It wasn't taken too seriously by Reg and Ron, as Dennis was not known for his fighting skills and they were more than capable of looking after themselves. Ron was more hurt that Dennis had not taken his warning that he was making things difficult for Albert Davis by causing problems in the club: that made Ron angry.

At an extremely packed Barrie's Club that night, with almost all the crowd from 'The Lane' there, it was obvious from overheard conversation that Dennis wasn't a very well liked person. Maybe the majority hoped that either Ron or Reg would teach him a lesson. What most people didn't know was that the Twins wouldn't cause any trouble in the club out of respect for Albert. Nevertheless, the buzz of expectancy was electric. Seigenberg arrived very late with about ten others, set on causing trouble.

There were so many people bustling down the narrow stairs into the street surrounding us as we left the club that it was impossible to know just what had happened. From all accounts, Roy Harvey, the tallest and most powerful of Seigenberg's friends, was immediately smacked in the mouth by Ron for being too lippy. It wasn't his argument anyway, but because of his size, Harvey thought he should challenge Ron. This was definitely a wrong move. Harvey floundered as he hit the ground. It seems a kick or two were aimed in his direction by some others, but not by either of the Twins. They had no need to, as the fracas was over in minutes. Seigenberg and his mates legged it. As expected, there was no opposition, and as nobody was seriously hurt, it was considered no more than a scuffle.

We walked in the direction of Bethnal Green, towards our homes, excitedly chatting about the evening's escapade, spreading across the wide pavement. It was a mob of at least thirty of us, well dressed with smart suits and collars and ties. After all, it was Sunday and we had been dancing. Suddenly, came the sight of a constable on a bicycle mounting the pavement. On coming towards the middle of the group, he shouted, 'Stop in the name of the law!' or something as stupid as that. It sounded just like a line from a hackneyed and not very good 'B' movie!

Bells of police cars were ringing in the distance, piercing the air with urgency. At times like this, it was 'leg it you're on your own'. Those bells – sirens came much later – would only mean trouble, and innocent or not, you never waited to find out or get caught by the police.

I ran across the road into a street that I knew took me alongside the Regent canal and headed through to a bridge over the Broadway. This was nearer to my house and away from any police cars, as the street by the canal was too narrow for them to chase anyone. Feeling quite safe, as I was about two miles from where we saw the copper on his bike, I came to the bridge. I was running across the road when, at the precise moment I reached the middle, a police car with headlights blazing came over the hump of the bridge directly into my path. I froze like a scared rabbit. Screeching to a halt, the police car's tyres burned on the cobbled roadway as the driver leaned out of his door. 'I've been captured,' I thought. Visions of a mean, small police cell flashed quickly through my mind. 'You stupid little bastard!' yelled the driver, probably relieved that he hadn't caught me with his vehicle. I mumbled something about being late home, whereupon he replied, 'Piss off then and be more careful, or else you will never get home' (a bit different today, isn't it?). Eventually, I arrived at my home in Cheshire Street, relieved to get into bed, wondering what had happened to the others.

Reggie and Ronnie, Tommy Organ, a fine boxer from Bethnal Green, and Pat Aucott, a friend from North London, were charged with causing Grievous Bodily Harm (GBH) on three youths, namely Dennis Seigenberg, Walter (Wally) Birch and the heavy youth named Roy Harvey.

The four who had been picked out as having caused the trouble were subjected to at least five appearances at the lower courts, then myself and Pat Butler appeared as witnesses for Reg and Ron at the Central Criminal Court, better known as the Old Bailey. Just why Seigenberg had insisted on trying to get them a jail sentence was puzzling. After all, he was no innocent party. But he had bitten off more than he could chew with the Twins and their friends. Seigenberg was probably influenced by his father Joe, who ran a gambling club and wanted to teach the Krays a lesson to keep face. After all, the Twins were only kids of sixteen years of age.

It was a daunting experience arriving at the Old Bailey to be a witness for the defence. We were taken into a room saved for witnesses only and told not to speak to anybody about the case except the defendants' solicitors. We were quite surprised when into the room came a plain-clothes man who said he was a detective and that his name was Brodie. He was red-faced and seemingly frustrated about something, explaining quite loudly and with extreme intimidation that we were 'two fucking idiots'. Brodie insinuated that we had threatened a girl called Sheila Coates. At that stage, we hadn't even heard of her and were shocked by his allegations. We told Brodie and a mate with him that we would tell the judge what he was saying, and the solicitors. They left after informing us that we would be in big trouble later on. Intimidating the witnesses did seem unusual, but it was our first time in court and we were only aged sixteen so we accepted it.

Publicity had been showered on the four accused. According to the newspapers they were the 'Chain Gang', and had used a bicycle chain to attack the other youths. This wasn't true. They had no need, and were quite capable of settling any fight with their hands. Seigenberg was known to carry tools, but the Twins knew that he was all talk. This came out in court and they were acquitted.

Dennis Seigenberg became Dennis Stafford with a name change later in life, and I believe was convicted of murder. Dennis was a nice-looking, smart man whom I liked very much when I subsequently got to know him better in latter years. It was ironic that Reg met up with him in Parkhurst, where they were both serving their sentences.

wrong arm of the law

Ron's respect for the police force diminished rapidly. In 1950, just over six months after he and Reg had been acquitted at the Old Bailey of the Seigenberg/Harvey GBH charge, Ron was punched in the back by a Constable Baynton from Bethnal Green Police Station.

Unwisely as it transpired, PC Baynton decided to move us on when we congregated outside Hookers café at the top of Mape Street in Bethnal Green Road. That night, about a dozen or so of us were standing around talking, as youths normally do, something to be expected less than a hundred yards away from the Oxford House Youth Club. Opposite, on the other side of the road, was the Mansford Mixed Youth Club, so it was only natural that boys and girls from both clubs would chat outside the café, doing no harm at all.

It was unfortunate, but of all the boys, the copper chose to punch Ron in the back. There was a dull thud as the punch landed heavily into the middle of his back, causing an incensed Ron to retaliate immediately. The rest of us ran away in all directions. I scarpered into the Oxford House club, whilst Johnny Docker, another friend of ours, sat himself on the steps of a doorway. Johnny boxed for the

Repton Boxing Club, was an England International and a very polite boy. Although we had done nothing wrong, instinct caused us to run away.

Ronnie Kray was not that quick or as eager as us to run away, so Constable Baynton, along with others from the station, arrested him. Ron was taken to the station where, it is said, quite a few of the policemen on duty taught him a lesson by beating him up in the cells. Ron arrived home badly bruised, but with his pride intact.

'The bastards could only do me in numbers,' he said angrily. 'There were about six of them hitting me, but I got a few punches in myself.'

This sort of treatment would not be tolerated today, as the hands of the police force are well and truly tied, with various safety nets put in place to stop rogue officers taking the law into their own hands and meting out rough justice – literally.

Constable Baynton went on the prowl, looking for other members of the gang who had run away. Seeing Reggie Kray, he bragged that he had just given his brother a bashing. Reg, then aged sixteen and a professional boxer, hit the copper, proving too good for him and putting him on his arse. That done, in the heat of the moment, Reg legged it. PC Baynton was furious. Twice he had been put down by a different youth. His ego was well and truly dented.

Baynton went to the Krays' house with his station Inspector. They were met by an irate Charlie Kray who, along with their mother and her sister May, complained to them about the state Ron had returned home in. Bruised and badly battered, he was sitting in the front room. The fuss created by the Kray family caused the Inspector to say that he could not allow Reg off: he had to be charged.

Then and there, they arrested Reg for hitting the copper. He was charged and taken to the police station, but the police decided against allowing their mates at the station to beat up Reg as had happened to Ron earlier. The Twins were charged with assaulting a PC. When the case went to court, magistrates at Old Street gave them both a probation order. Fortunately, this did not affect their professional boxing licences.

Because of his beating at their hands in the cell, Ron looked upon the police force as 'bully bastards'. It had a lasting impression on him. It was something he was never going to forget. And who could blame him?

From the court, we progressed to the Royal Ballroom in Tottenham, North London, situated opposite the police station there. In its day, the Royal was a grand ballroom with a large central spinning mirror ball that shone speckles of light over the audience with an effect of confetti.

It was funny to see groups lining the walls. The mainly Jewish contingent stood proudly on one side, whilst opposite them would stand the so-called strangers, those from other areas. We adopted our stance on the strangers' side, meeting and talking to various boys we had come across in Petticoat Lane. On reflection, having two sides was rather silly, but then it was a question of territory and, of course, the strong Jewish element were resentful of other areas taking over. After all, Stamford Hill, being just up the road from Tottenham, was known for its hard men, such as Tony Cohen, Harry Lee, Little Moisha, Butch Ronnie Mitchell, and brothers Tony and Benny Mulla. All of these boys were known to be very rough handfuls.

But there was a funny kind of camaraderie in the dance hall. When dancing was in progress to the music of Ray Ellington and the lovely Lita Rosa, a top singer of the day, everything was reasonably normal. When dancing stopped, there would be plenty of eyeballing between the opposite sides of the hall. They would sometimes become interested in each other, rather like predators in the jungle. If one side walked to the toilet they would often go in groups and confrontations would start.

One such evening, a group from the Jewish sector walked across the empty dance floor towards the toilets and past a mob that included Ronnie and Billy Webb, locals from Tottenham, Alfie and Charlie Curtis, Harry Skinner, Micky Stachini and Ron and Reg. Filing past these was a line of about six from the other side, the last one in the file being hard man Ronnie Mitchell from the Hill.

Suddenly, fighting started. Well, fighting of a sort, for about five of the group from Bethnal Green – including the Krays and the Webbs from Tottenham – were punching and kicking a very tough Ronnie Mitchell. After stewards came forward, the fighting stopped immediately. The mob from Bethnal Green and the local Webb brothers quickly dispersed into the night air.

When the police came and began to question Ronnie Mitchell, he replied with the obvious answer from the hard man he was. 'I really don't know who they were,' he told the coppers.

Mitchell was taken to hospital to be stitched up and still would not say who his assailants were. He wasn't afraid of a fight. No, Ronnie Mitchell had seen a bit of battle even at the young age of eighteen years. Battered and bruised, physically and mentally, his ego badly dented, he would seek revenge through his own men from the Hill.

The next day being a Sunday, Ronnie Mitchell and Benny Mulla went to the record stall in Cobb Street for the sole purpose of a comeback with these Kray brothers. As they had not heard of them previously, they asked around as to who they were. Soon Mitchell and Mulla met someone they both knew from Stamford Hill, a swarthy young Jewish character, Curly King, who began to explain who the Krays were.

'You don't want any aggravation with them,' he warned. 'They're a couple of nutters when they get started.' Curly added that they were not liberty-takers and were good fist-fighters.

Ronnie Mitchell showed Curly his wounds. 'This wasn't done with a fist,' he hissed, pointing to the damage to his ear. Forever the mediator, Curly told Ronnie to wait for a couple of minutes and he would try to find the Twins.

After a short while, Ronnie and Benny were taken into Ziggy's café, and for the first time Ronnie Mitchell met Ronnie and Reggie Kray, who proceeded to explain what had caused the fight. Someone, they said, had claimed that Ronnie Mitchell was going to sort out the person who had slapped a young Jewish kid in a cinema at Mile End, which, surprisingly, was Reggie. So when Ronnie Mitchell's face was pointed out in the Royal by one of the Webb brothers, who knew him from the Hill, they waited for him to come over their side and attacked him.

Ronnie Mitchell explained that he was not looking for any trouble; the information they had been given was totally wrong. He thought they were being anti-semitic because the kid was Jewish and was now afraid of being attacked again in the Royal. The Twins could see how this misunderstanding had occurred, asking Ronnie to shake hands and be friends. With Curly's help it became possible.

'How can they be anti-semitic?' he asked, half laughing. 'I'm one of their best friends and am Jewish, ain't I?'

Curly, a natural joker, made Ronnie Mitchell laugh, and he found it even funnier when Ronnie Kray said that he was half Jewish, too. They did shake hands and, although they went in different directions, remained friends until Ron died, even though Ronnie Mitchell told me later that because of the kicking he received at the hands of the Krays and their friends that night at the Royal, he is now quite deaf.

'Ronnie Mitchell was a very hard and game man, Laurie,' Ron told me as we reminisced many years later on one of my visits to Broadmoor. 'He came and fronted us at the lane the next day. He wasn't frightened either. A very brave man.'

Ron insisted that I should try and take Ronnie Mitchell in to see him at Broadmoor. Sadly, Ronnie Kray died before I could arrange that nostalgic meeting.

I never found any difficulty in going to the Royal. Like Curly King, I went from side to side. Nearly all my mates were Jewish, but now I understand from Ronnie Mitchell that there were quite a few who disliked Jewish people, which was the reason for their clannish behaviour at the Royal.

By this stage, the small Kray house in Vallance Road had become even more packed. In early 1949, Charlie had married Dolly Moore. After that, his mother let the newly-weds move into the upstairs room of their house.

The Twins did not like the intrusion of another family in their house, even though it was their elder brother and his wife, especially as they had lost their training room where they and their friends used to spar and chat. However, it was then that I began to see more of Charlie Kray, a handsome, blond-haired man of about eleven stones in weight with a very muscular body.

Immediately after getting married, he had become a professional boxer. Although Charlie was not championship material, he went on to win twenty out of twenty-two fights, his last one being in December 1951. This was when all three brothers were on the same bill at the Albert Hall, a sporting record. The trio had lots of people from the East End supporting them. In the programme Reggie was described as the 'sweet' one of the Krays, possibly because of his fine boxing ability. Ron was billed as the 'sour' one because, as the programme details stated, he was disdainful of the block and parry tactics, liking his verdict to come the hard way with aggression.

Unfortunately, although it was a good night for boxing, only Reg won his fight. Charlie was knocked out in the third round by an up and coming fighter, Lew Lazar, one of the famous Lazar boxing family from Aldgate. Meanwhile, Reggie beat Bob Manito of Clapham on points, whilst Ronnie lost to Bill Sliney of King's Cross, also on points. All these matches comprised six three-minute rounds.

For Charlie, boxing was largely to supplement the income from his work 'on the knocker'. In his work as a 'wardrobe dealer', Charlie would travel with his father to places outside London, sometimes as far away as Bristol, putting leaflets into letter boxes, asking if occupants of the properties had any old gold or silver to sell for cash. Occasionally, they would be offered some suits if a person had died, divorced or left home. Charlie and his father would usually say that they would take them away as rags, allowing the person who was giving them away a few shillings, or sometimes nothing at all. Of course, they had a market for everything and made very good money.

Charlie, his father and others doing similar work were called 'wardrobe dealers' not because, as someone said in a book recently, they bought wardrobes! No, it was because they would buy or steal by kindness the contents of a wardrobe if the person of the house wanted to get rid of them.

I often went with Reggie and Ronnie, doing some billing for their father and brother. If they did well in their buying, we would be given some money for our day's work. We liked doing the billing, for it was good exercise. The bill was put in the letterbox and we would go back an hour later, knocking on each door to collect our bill and see if the householder had anything to sell. If they did, we would call the 'buyer', which would be either young or old Charlie, who would try to do some business. This was called 'pestering', and the householder would usually be pleased to see them go. Hence the terminology 'pesterer' for the buyer and 'on the knocker' for the billing men. There were lots of families in the East End on the knocker, the more famous ones being the Smiths, the Tresardens and the Hudsons, Bulla and Tommy.

When Charlie stopped working with his father, he

became a partner with his old friend Charlie Ludlow, a very nice man, with jet black hair, a good personality and ideal for the job. They bought an old van and seemed happy. Charlie did not like working with his father because, although he was an excellent pesterer and made good money at it, he was a heavy drinker. We often had to meet him in the Ninety Nine pub in Liverpool Street, which was like his office. This did not suit young Charlie.

In 1951 we were due to sign on for National Service. Naturally, we did not want to go as it would break up our mates, but it was compulsory at eighteen years of age unless you were unfit.

Charlie told me about a man he'd heard about while in the Navy who was refused entry into the service because he suffered from migraines, so I went to the library, found out all the symptoms and complained to my doctor about the pains in my head. This meant that it was on record. Now I was unfit for the Army, much to the disappointment of my father, who had been a regular soldier and a sergeant. I never told him I had worked my ticket, for it would have upset him. Needless to say, I was not at all upset!

I had no qualms about not going into the forces. After my father was bombed at Dunkirk and severely burned, my mother had to travel backwards and forwards to Park Prewett Hospital in Basingstoke. It was an awkward trip, especially during wartime with all the attendant difficulties and privations, the cancellations and reduced travel, but Dad was put there because he was in the Royal Berkshire regiment. What with bombs dropping on us during the war, Dad's injuries and my mother struggling to bring us up, the

Army was definitely not for me.

But Reg and Ronnie were unable to escape service. In retrospect, if the Forces had known what they were like, I am absolutely certain that they would not have taken them in. The Army would have saved itself a lot of bother as they did not exactly turn out to be good soldiers! I am equally certain that Ronnie would not have passed the medical needed to join if he had revealed he had suffered from rheumatic fever as a young man, although he wouldn't have left Reggie anyhow. As it was, they were enlisted in the Royal Fusiliers, so their boxing careers ended.

Their two years in the Army would have been far better if the authorities had recognised the usefulness of their sporting skills. If, when they first joined the Army in 1952, either of the Twins had been considered as Physical Training Officers, it is possible their destiny, and perhaps that of the entire East End, would have been so very different. With their boxing record, they were capable of teaching all aspects of PT, but not given the opportunity, they rebelled. Either way, in my opinion the Army was responsible for their future as gangsters. The officers just could not control them.

Perhaps if the Twins had still been amateur boxers when they went into the Army, things would have been different. I am sure that they would have enjoyed training with the good quality of boxers that the Services produced. Reg and Ron were very respectful of sportsmen and showed good discipline in the gym.

I was asked by their mother to visit the Twins when they were in the guardhouse at the Tower of London after they went absent without leave or, to use a better phrase, escaped from Her Majesty's Service. She explained that if I were challenged I should just say that I was a soldier in the Royal Fusiliers. The regiment that the Twins were in was stationed at the Tower of London's barracks.

It was dusk as I walked unchallenged past the world-famous Beefeaters in their unique uniforms at the front gate and along the shadowy path to the first arch. There, a soldier of the guard stepped out from his post, leg raised high. He frightened the life out of me, so I used the password 'Royal Fusiliers'. As he lowered his leg to stamp his big Army boots on the ground, as a sentry does to make as much noise as possible, he looked at me in amazement, then continued with his duties.

I saw a building and went inside. It was a lavatory. Asking a man who was in there if he knew where the guardhouse was seemed a liberty, but how else was I going to find it? Fortunately, it was next door to where I was standing. I opened a door, finding that I was in a dormitory with about twelve beds each side of the room. I saw Ron first. His greeting was most welcoming.

'Hello Lol,' he beamed. 'What are you doing here?'

Ron was laughing away as he explained the procedure. 'We are supposed to be in the guardhouse, but if you got in, Lol, then we can get out. Stupid, ain't it?'

I gave the Twins some cigarettes that their mother had asked me to take and some sweets, too. We talked for about an hour, then Ronnie told me, 'If you don't go now, they will lock you in the Tower!' He was probably pulling my leg, but I was taking no chances so left right away, leaving by the same route that I had used to enter the barracks. It was darker by now, and I was relieved to be leaving the

Tower of London. Happily, on my way to the gate along the long, winding pathway, I was not apprehended by anyone.

I jumped a bus to a chip shop called Johnny Isaacs in Whitechapel Road. Some of my friends were outside. Getting my portion of chips, I related my tales of the night's events to a wide-eyed audience who just loved to hear tales of the Kray brothers.

I walked along Vallance Road to Mrs Kray's house as she had told me she would stay up until I arrived with news from her sons. I knocked. She answered the door, inviting me in. I began to tell her about my visit to the Tower when she cut me short. 'They are upstairs, Lol!' she half whispered. 'They've escaped again. They don't like it at the Tower. It's a waste of time.'

I could not believe it: they had got home quicker than me! The Twins were on the trot again. It was quite funny when they explained what had happened after I had left.

Ron and Reggie decided they were wasting their time there and should have come home with me, so as the door of their cell was locked for the night they devised a plan. One of them stood on a chair with a tie around his neck, whilst the other one called to the guard that his brother was trying to hang himself. As the guard unlocked the door and ran into the cell, he was promptly knocked out. Getting their belongings together and with the knowledge that I had explained to them how easy it was to get in, the Twins wanted to show it was even easier to get out. They decided to leave the Army once again.

The next time I saw them I was working in Frome, Somerset, for Kelly's Directories, a large London company. It was convenient for me to see them at the Army Prison,

Shepton Mallet, where they had been sent after a court martial at Canterbury Barracks. This had taken place after their release from Wormwood Scrubs Prison, where they served a month's sentence for assaulting a police officer in a Mile End café.

I was dressed for work, which meant I was wearing a white, stiff-collared shirt, plain tie and dark suit. I was shown into a visiting room. They walked in with amusement. 'We were expecting a visit from a solicitor,' Ron said.

I noticed that he had half a beard. By that I mean he had shaved just one side of his face. Ron explained that he had done it to confuse the authorities.

'They think I'm mad, Lol,' he told me, laughing. 'I've been tearing my singlet into strips and tying them on to the wire fence to count the days we are here. When they try and move them, I shout at them. They are still there, so I'm still in control,' he smiled.

As he winked, I detected a twinkle of devilment in his eyes . . .

ronnie comes out

While the Twins were in the Army, Charlie was still living with his wife Dolly and son Gary upstairs at Vallance Road. He was also still working on the knocker. For a short time after they left the Army, dishonourably discharged in early 1954, Reg and Ron worked with Charlie, but mixing with some of their old mates from the Army made them restless. Dickie Morgan was a thief and a wheeler-dealer so they found him exciting, and were nearly always over at his mother's house in Clinton Road, Mile End. This is where they saw the opportunity for the Regal Billiard Hall in nearby Eric Street.

They stopped all the small-time thieves and layabouts from causing problems in the Regal, becoming first managers then owners of the lease in 1954. After signing the lease, the Twins used the club regularly as a meeting place for their friends from the Army prisons where they had been most of the time when serving as soldiers. It was the beginning of 'The Firm'. It was also then that Charlie found out about Ronnie being homosexual.

When he was fourteen, Ron did not seem to have interest in homosexuals. This became apparent when we were on a camping expedition to Rye House in Hertfordshire. It had a speedway/dog-racing track, a local pub, and acres of green pastures. As we lived in Bethnal Green – which was not very green! – it was a real adventure to be deep in the country, something Ronnie referred to fondly throughout the whole of his life. It was our camping expeditions that developed Ron's love of the countryside.

We often went there for a weekend, staying one or two nights for a couple of shillings. First we stayed in tents, but had trouble with some boys from Hoxton, so we caved in their tent, pulling up their guy ropes so that their tent collapsed on them in the middle of the night. The Hoxton gang had bullied some really young kids, who came to us crying about these bullies. Ron was not then attracted to these kids, but was just being helpful.

After that, we changed from sleeping in tents to staying in a large hall for the same money. It was safer and warmer at night time. We used our own sleeping bags or blankets for a bed, sleeping on the wooden floor boards. It was good fun as we were only kids out for a bit of adventure.

It was while playing football with some other kids who went to Rye House that we noticed, in a tent in the field where we were playing, an older man, whom we called Bert, who had tried to befriend us over the past few weeks. On this occasion, Bert was watching us play, lying on his back, looking at us and masturbating. It was the first time I had seen anything like it, and can still remember that scene today. It shows that when a child is young, an act like that has a profound effect psychologically.

We all discussed the unexpected scene after our game ended. It had made an impression on us. Everyone agreed that it was terrible to masturbate in an open field while watching us. True, Bert was in a tent, but the flaps were wide open for us to see him and there were no other adults around to catch him. It was noticeable that we were all terrified by the size of his erect penis as he masturbated.

Ronnie felt the same way as the rest of us. He showed no excitement at the event or any homosexual tendencies. It was Ron who thought that we should teach Bert a lesson.

Bert used to talk to us quite a lot during the weekends we went camping. He was always there, so must have been a local man. That incident was the first time he had been indecent and we were wary of him for the rest of the day. Now, we had all changed our opinion of him.

Ronnie suggested that our blond friend, Pat Butler, should entice Bert by pretending to like him. If he reacted to the bait, we would go into his tent and pinch the camera that he used regularly to take photos of us.

The plan worked. Pat Butler was good at enticing Bert, and we nicked his camera. After we had got it, we packed up to go home, fearing he might call the police. Looking back, of course he would not have done so because of his sexual behaviour, but at such a young age we did not appreciate that.

Anyway, Butler came running across the field to us, angry that we had left him alone with Bert, and that we were packing up our gear to leave without him. This was not true, of course, as we would not have left without Pat.

'He's a dirty old bastard, that Bert,' Butler yelled. 'Got his dick out to show me. He was terrible.'

Butler was in a right old state of panic as we left, and we never went back to that place again. We all agreed on the train going home that procuring children was despicable, and never regretted taking his camera, which we sold for £3.00.

That incident apart, there were never any lewd sexual insinuations from Ronnie Kray relating to homosexuality until I began to notice his interest in boys when he was in his late teens.

The very first time I became aware of Ronnie's attraction to boys was when I had been working the markets with a dark, good-looking Jewish lad called Willy. A few years younger than me, Willy was a great speiler. His father had worked in the street markets for years, so it was a natural progression for him. Willy was a good amateur boxer, too, having a slim build and clean-cut image. His family were a typical local Jewish family and good grafters. Together, Willy and I had been working markets in Maidstone in Kent and the Oxford cattle market amongst others.

My favourite was Maidstone. We sold material from the floor, meaning we never paid the council for a pitch Licence to Trade. We were rebels and only had to work hard for a couple of hours. The material we sold was cheap but, as always, you had to help customers make up their minds. Somehow we managed to do just that, also enjoying ourselves with the tales told by our mentors, who had such peculiar names as 'Bill with the windbags' and 'Davy Binns'.

Bill had a knack of offering small brown envelopes from a tray around his neck. They looked identical. Some were empty, but others contained a lighter or watch. After purchasing one for about 10p in today's money, a customer would open it to find it nearly always empty, other than a coin to be used for a free go. Customers could choose any envelope they fancied, but somehow Bill would help them. If he pushed someone into buying one and they refused, he would tear open the envelope to produce a watch or lighter, much to the amusement of the crowd. They were called 'windbags', for punters always chose empty envelopes that were full of nothing but wind.

Meanwhile, Davy Binns was so called because of a habit of forever pushing his spectacles back onto the bridge of his rather large nose when they had slipped down to the tip ('binns' being slang for spectacles). This occurred when he was nervously operating a mock auction called 'the run out' from a stall in Petticoat Lane. Davy was a character who had a knack of separating punters from their cash in the quickest time possible and was fascinating to watch.

Willy had a friend who was a very good card player and ran a school for other card players at his mother's flat near Brick Lane, often on a Friday night. This guy's grandfather had shown him how to shave little marks onto a fresh pack of cards so they could be read from the back. So when the opposing card player was facing him with his cards close to his chest, he could read their hands by the marked cards. He always won, and hated anyone else to win even just once, although I suggested he should occasionally let them. I've had cold sweats when seeing men lose their entire week's wages to this fellow. There would have been a riot if he had been caught, as some pretty tough characters joined Willy's friend's school. These included some of the Krays' friends who were card players.

One day, we stopped after work at the Twins' house for a chat. I noticed that the way Ronnie was talking to Willy seemed unusual. Ron was very attentive, agreeing with anything he spoke about. As we left, Ronnie told him to come round to his house whenever he wanted to. Willy did not appear to notice anything unusual. At least, he said nothing later about Ronnie's attention towards him. It was after that visit that Ronnie questioned me.

'You like Willy, don't you, Lol?' he asked in a matter-of-fact way.

'Of course I do,' I responded. 'We work together and he's a good grafter. We have some great laughs while working. I like him a lot.'

There was just a slight pause, then Ronnie added, 'That Willy's handsome. He's got beautiful teeth, lovely lips and hair.'

'Leave off!' I told Ron, without a moment's hesitation. 'I ain't bent – and I don't fancy him, Ron, if that's what you're implying . . .'

Ronnie came right out with it, saying to my amazement, 'I think you do fancy him. He's lovely – and I'm in love with him.'

Ron's admission took me completely by surprise.

'What would he say if I told him, Lol?' Ron asked. He laughed loudly when I answered 'You would frighten the life out of him!' being careful not to say, 'Willy's not bent,' for it was obvious that Ronnie was now telling me that he had a gay side.

I was shocked that Ronnie had admitted being homosexual to me. On one of our journeys to the market, I mentioned to Willy about Ronnie fancying him. He was terrified.

'I'm not going round to their house without you, Laurie!' he said.

My reply was obvious – 'Then Ronnie will think we are having an affair!'

It's funny now, in this day and age, when to be gay is quite all right, but at that time in the fifties it was frowned upon. If heterosexual, you were offended when people of the same sex showed an interest in you sexually.

I could understand Willy's feelings. I mean Ronnie was not your ordinary run-of-the-mill homosexual whom you could brush aside. He could be frightening. Willy gave Ronnie a wide berth after that. He would have a conversation with Ron when he saw him in the street, but socially he remained aloof. Willy got married quite young, which ended Ronnie's interest for a long time.

It was not until Ron returned from the Army, however, that he admitted his bisexuality to Charlie. Ronnie's habit of frequently keeping company with the young lads that hung around the billiards hall had begun to annoy Charlie. Some of these boys were about sixteen or seventeen years of age, jazzily dressed in brightly coloured shirts of pastel pinks and yellows with matching jumpers. One that I remember had dyed his hair bright blond. Today, this would be quite acceptable. Now, no one would look twice, but at that time it was considered to be very feminine. These lads were a few years younger than Ronnie, who always dressed immaculately in a suit with collar and tie, and was a very mature strong man with a general attitude older than his years. Ron's friendship with these boys appeared very peculiar to Charlie, who would get annoyed when Ronnie acted childishly in the young lads' company, sniggering when he appeared. Understandably, Charlie thought that they were taking the piss out of him.

Taking Ronnie aside after one such incident, Charlie asked him, 'What's so funny about me to cause that lot to laugh when I come into the hall?'

Ronnie's reply shocked his brother. 'Don't you know that I'm bisexual, Charlie?' he asked.

Well, to say Charlie was astounded was an understatement. 'Fuck off!' was all he could say. Charlie was totally flabbergasted. 'What, you like men as well as women?' he asked with a look of complete bewilderment. 'I just can't believe it!'

After a pause and a confused sigh, Charlie went on: 'Still it's your life and I suppose you can do what you like – and will, won't you?'

Ronnie smiled, then surprised Charlie even more. 'I've been like it for years,' he added. 'Nobody can change me and I wouldn't let them anyway, so you will just have to accept me as I am, won't you? Mummy knows, too, and has done so for ages,' Ronnie revealed. 'If she accepts it then you shouldn't find it too difficult, unless you worry what people think about us. Anyway, I don't care, but I'm glad that you know.'

Charlie was still trying to take it all in. Perhaps it should not have been too difficult, but the thoughts running through his mind were not about Ronnie, but his family and friends. Charlie should not have worried for most of them had an idea that Ronnie had a gay side to his nature, anyway. I suppose it was a blow to Charlie's ego that caused him concern.

Charlie, shocked by Ronnie's attitude to being bent, mentioned it to Reg soon after, deliberately suggesting the possibility of Reg being gay, too. Reg answered Charlie with amusement, confusing him even more.

'Don't you think that boys are nice, Charlie?' he asked. 'I think I could fancy a few myself!' he added, chuckling to himself.

I would say that Reg fought the fact he could also be bisexual more than Ron, but I knew of his affection for quite a few young male teenagers with whom he kept company. Reg was a really tough, clever boxer with a dynamic punch, much better as a professional than Ron, but I had my suspicions of his bisexuality. That said, Reg kept a string of young women extremely happy in his early days. To my knowledge, Reg had a son by a girl named Anna. Ron would often goad him about this and tried to influence Reg with his own appetite for young men.

The Firm's reaction to Ron's homosexual behaviour was to be tolerant. After all, they could do nothing about it. Even if they objected, Ron would have smiled at them, saying they did not know what they were missing. Whilst Mrs Kray did not mind and showed motherly understanding, Ron's father thought it was degrading and disgusting. He never referred to it, preferring to turn a blind eye. It is important to remember that homosexuality was then illegal and for the overwhelming majority of people totally unacceptable.

Following Ron's revelation, Charlie did not go to the billiard hall as frequently as the Twins, so he would not find accepting Ron and his new type of friends too problematic.

Ronnie, on the other hand, was always at the hall and would often be behind the counter. It was quite funny to see him serving a ham sandwich, or a pork pie and a cup of tea. But there was nothing feminine about Ron. He served like a buck navvy. Nobody laughed in his company unless he cracked a joke: they were not silly. Even then, Ronnie was paranoid about people talking about him.

Ronnie liked the company of young lads, as I had noticed. I think it was because of the power the Krays were beginning to acquire that these younger boys hung around Ron, although he encouraged it. But it was noticeable they did not congregate around Reggie nearly as much.

Ron began buying some of the more adventurous teenagers rather expensive presents. Naturally, they did not refuse to accept them, but even at that stage in his life, I would not say the gifts were for sexual favours. I would stress, too, that Ronnie was definitely not interested in sex with young schoolboys and despised paedophiles.

However, he had quite a few favourites among some of the local boys, preferring those who were clean-cut, dark-haired and with a fresh complexion. Later, in the early sixties, stories circulated about Ron's 'prospects' as he called them. A rumour was put out that if Ronnie put a £20 note into your top pocket, it would follow that he wanted to sleep with you. To be honest, I do not know if the story was true or if Ronnie told someone to spread the rumour.

Ron was always playing tricks on the young boys. One lad I know told me that he had heard the rumour and Ronnie put some notes into his top pocket. Panicking, he quickly took them out again and pushed them gently back into Ronnie's hand.

'I'm not like that Ron!' the boy protested. 'It would be a waste of your money.'

As the boy hurried away as rapidly as he could, Ron burst out laughing at his obvious fear.

But Ron did have a few regular sexual partners, and strong friendships with men of a similar disposition, such as Mad Teddy Smith and Leslie Holt. Although homosexuality was still illegal, Ronnie did not hide the fact that he liked boys. The reverse happened, and he was proud of the fact, talking about Lawrence of Arabia with relish. 'He was homosexual, you know,' he would say to anyone who was interested.

During the sixties, Ronnie made a trip to Tangier in North Africa. When he got back, Ronnie showed me a letter from a young Arab. It was a real love letter.

'He loves me, Lol,' Ronnie exclaimed excitedly, proudly producing a photograph of the young man, who was about twenty years of age. 'He's beautiful. Look at his teeth. They're perfect white!'

Ron had a thing about a 'prospect's' teeth. Naturally, I told him it was because the Arab was very dark skinned.

'He wants to come to England and live with me,' Ronnie said, thrilled at the prospect of having this attractive young beau over in Britain.

Ronnie never did things by half. Fortunately, his other businesses became more interesting, so the Arab got lost in the pressure of work.

In essence, Ronnie coped with being homosexual because he was proud of it. When he was sentenced, he still had many boyfriends and always became possessive of them, doing anything he could to make them happy. I do not know if these friendships were sexual, for he never talked about sex at all to me, possibly because he knew our desires were totally different.

As far as I know, Ron discussed his homosexuality with

only a very few people. Put simply, it was a part of his nature he discovered, explored and enjoyed. He was at ease with it. It did not seem to conflict with his 'tough guy' image or cause him problems on any level. I am certain that he had lovers inside prison, for it's a fact that many straight guys enjoy temporary gay relationships whilst banged up, then return to their wives and kids and pick up family life where they left off. For them, homosexuality is only a short-term release.

As I said, to the outside world, Ron appeared tough, but everybody needs to love and be loved. Ronnie was no exception, and needed to give and take affection with another human being. He, too, had ordinary emotions, though so often publicity has dwelt on and put under the media microscope only his violent side. But it seems quite likely that he also displayed tenderness, affection and even a genuine love with some of his 'prospects'. Possibly he was almost a father figure to some of them, especially if they came from disturbed backgrounds. Perhaps there was indeed a tender, caring, romantic side to Ron's nature that only a few ever saw.

ronnie arranges revenge

The billiard hall was packed with the usual mixture of characters, a few thieves and fences, always having something to sell – televisions, electrical goods, Scotch or gin. Between them, they could get almost anything.

A few ardent snooker players were enjoying this very popular game, which was the common denominator among these characters. Lots of humour was bandied about in the Regal in Eric Street, just off Mile End Road. On one occasion, into the hall came two of the usual faces, Ronnie Sorrell and his mate. Ronnie's face was a bit the worse for wear. Forever observant and protective of his customers, Ronnie Kray went over to Sorrell, who had quite a reputation for fighting.

'Been fighting again, Ron?' asked Ronnie Kray, both inquisitive and sympathetic and not at all intimidating, for he liked the Sorrell family.

'We've just come from Vicky Park fairground,' Sorrell answered in a slurred voice, a little worse for drink, but not drunk or aggressive. 'The geezer at the boxing booth took a liberty, Ron,' Sorrell began to explain. It appeared there were no takers when they asked the audience if anyone would accept the challenge of the booth fighters.

'I agreed to do a round or two to help the booth as it was becoming boring, and they were offering a pound a round,' Sorrell continued. 'I told the geezer who was running the show that I'd had a couple of pints and not to go too strong but I'd do a couple of rounds. He said something to the guy I was going to box. When we started the bout, my opponent just sparred with me, as is usual, then seemed to change his attitude when we were coming to the end of the first round. He definitely tried to knock me out. The end of that round came and I could have swallowed it, but that's not me, Ron.'

Sorrell's mate nodded in agreement.

'Well,' Sorrell went on, 'the second round started and the geezer came straight at me, pulling no punches. He was big, strong and fit, so I was under pressure, but wouldn't swallow it. I bashed him back, but it was no match. I was pissed, too, which didn't help. Then he slipped a right hook up the Derby kelly [belly]. That floored me. They threw me out, and wouldn't pay me for the first round, either. Bastards.'

Ronnie Kray's look could be terribly frightening. As I've said many times, he hated bullies. The boxing booth's fighter and its owner had taken a liberty with Sorrell.

'What time d'they close?' asked Ronnie, wanting to go back at once. Sorrell told him it had already closed, as it was after midnight by now.

'Then tomorrow night we'll have a return,' said Ronnie Kray. 'I'll get Bobby Ramsey. He has boxed in booths, and will get his own back for us.'

By declaring himself in this vendetta, Ronnie Kray had now taken it personally. He proceeded to canvas everyone who was in the billiard hall. So it was that some thirty or forty people all promised to be at the Victoria Park boxing booth the next evening at 8 pm.

Victoria Park in Hackney was a very popular park, serving the community. It had a lido open-air swimming pool, zoo, tennis courts and football pitches, all run in a proper way by the local Hackney Council. The licensed fairground operated a couple of times a year, so in the eyes of the council everything was run to a reputable standard and there was no funny business.

Well, funny business or not, as arranged by Ron Kray, a large crowd of people gathered at the fairground for the revenge bout for Ronnie Sorrell. Bobby Ramsey's life had been a tough one, for he was a professional booth fighter and boxer. He had also worked with Billy Hill, a top gangster of the fifties. Being asked by Ron to challenge the boxer on the booth was Ramsey's forte: he was thick set, with a full, round face and thick, sturdy neck. His features showed that he had been in many scraps, for he had a flat nose, ears that were thickening and scarred tissue around the eyes.

Ramsey's shoulders and arms were very muscular, but he had a trim waist planted firmly on his very sturdy legs. Although only about five feet, eight inches, nobody in their right mind would pick a fight with Ramsey.

Ron arranged that I should accompany Bob in his car to the outskirts of the park and discreetly mingle with the audience at the booth. I met Bob at the park gates. He arrived in his large American Cadillac convertible car. The top was down as discretion wasn't in Bob's vocabulary. 'Get in, Lol,' he said, using the nickname he chose for me.

Bob was dressed in an all-white tracksuit, with a hood

attached. On the back of the tracksuit was his name 'Bob Ramsey, England', with a huge Union Jack. From his boxing days, his hands had been bandaged for protection and power.

After parking, he leapt out on to the grass verge, proceeding to punch the air in a sparring motion with grunts and groans to match. He similarly punched his huge fists from palm to palm in rotation. Bob was psyching himself up for a hopefully unaware opponent. 'Let's get going, Lol!' he exclaimed. Bob was ready for the lion's den, game as ever for the unexpected, of course. But Bob himself was the lion, wanting to teach those rascals at the booth a lesson they would not forget for a long time.

Running across the wide green expanse of parkland towards the colourful fairground, Bob's flowing robe added to the spectacle of the occasion. His arms were sparring in the air, hitting an imaginary opponent. Attention was drawn to this figure, dancing towards the booth.

Entering, I paid for the two of us, covering Bob with my body as much as I could. Ron Kray met us inside the marquee that had a ring set up in its centre. Sloping boards with slats of wood to place the heel of your shoe against were all that were offered for the spectators.

The place was packed with well-wishers from the Regal Billiard Hall, all seeking revenge for Sorrell. Ron Kray was hyped up, too, as we were talking to Bob, who stood between us. Next, from the ring, the booth owner announced the start of the evening's boxing. He began by introducing the booth fighters, about four that night. As each was introduced, there was a roar of approval from the crowd. Sorrell was looking for the man who had taken the

CERTIFIED COPY OF AN ENTRY OF BIRTH

GIVEN AT THE GENERAL REGISTER OFFICE

Application Number... Y006810

REGISTRATION DISTRICT   Shoreditch

1933 BIRTH in the Sub-district of Shoreditch North East in the County of London

When and where born	Name, if any	Sex	Name and surname of father	Name, surname and maiden surname of mother	Occupation of father	Signature, description and residence of informant	When registered	Signature of registrar	Name entered after registration
1	2	3	4	5	6	7	8	9	10*
Twenty fourth October 1933 8.10 pm 68 Stean Street	Ronald	Boy	Charles David Kray	Violet Kray formerly Lee	Wardrobe Dealer	Violet Kray Mother 68 Stean Street Shoreditch	Sixth December 1933	Scott-Swindon	

CERTIFIED to be a true copy of an entry in the certified copy of a Register of Births in the District above mentioned.

Given at the GENERAL REGISTER OFFICE, under the Seal of the said Office, the _____26th_____ day of _____July_____ 19 95

KBZ 820160

CAUTION:- It is an offence to falsify a certificate or to make or knowingly use a false certificate or a copy of a false certificate intending it to be accepted as genuine to the prejudice of any person or to possess a certificate knowing it to be false without lawful authority.

WARNING: THIS CERTIFICATE IS NOT EVIDENCE OF THE IDENTITY OF THE PERSON PRESENTING IT.

nie Kray's birth certificate

Charlie Kray senior

JERRY BLOSSOM

DAIRY

LEES CAFE

tist's impression of the view from the Krays' home on Vallance Road in the 1940s
(*Ian Bale*)

Ben the Barber's shop on the corner of Mer
Street and Cheshire Street, where we used
play as children in the 1940s. Inset: Ben th
Barber himself (right) and his assistant
(*Laurie O'Leary*)

Ron with me
holding Gary. Reg
is taking the photo
(*Laurie O'Leary*)

: to right: Cousin Rita, Ron, Gary (Charlie's son) and Reg in their back yard at
ance Road (*Laurie O'Leary*)

Charlie and Reg with their mother, Violet Kray, holding Gary (*Laurie O'Leary*)

Left to right: Dickie Morgan holding Gary, Reg, Ron and Charlie Kray (*Laurie O'Lee*

Reg with Auntie Rose (*Laurie O'Leary*)

Jack Cappell announces

INTERNATIONAL BOXING TOURNAMENTS

at

THE ROYAL ALBERT HALL

on

TUESDAY 29th JANUARY 1952

Tuesday 26th February 1952
Tuesday 18th March 1952
Tuesday 15th April 1952
Tuesday 13th May 1952

DOORS OPEN 6.45 p.m. . - COMMENCE 7.30 p.m.

Seats for each of these Tournaments may be reserved on application to Phil Coren, Jack Cappell Boxing Promotions, Ascot House, 52 Dean St., London, W.1. ('Phone Gerrard 1742-3-4). Enquiries are invited from Sports Clubs, Works, etc., for details of special arrangements for parties. Office hours, 10 to 6 p.m. Saturday 10 to 1 p.m. All applications will be dealt with in strict rotation.

PRICES OF ADMISSION:

63/- 42/- 21/-	30/- 21/-	21/- 15/- 10/6	21/-	15/- 10/6	10/- 5/-	2/6
Ringside	Stalls	Orchestra	Loggias	Tiers	Balcony	Gallery

FEB. 26th 1952 is the

SPORTSMAN'S AID SOCIETY'S BOXING NIGHT

AT THE ROYAL ALBERT HALL IN CONJUNCTION WITH MAJOR JACK CAPPELL

Welterweight Contest
Six 3 minute Rounds at 10st. 9 lbs.

Referee : RICHARD REED

LEW LAZAR	v.	CHARLIE KRAY
Aldgate		Bethnal Green

LEW LAZAR

Lew is undefeated at present and his quick, dancing feet have been responsible for his still 100 per cent. record. Managed by Jack Hyams, the 19-year-old East Ender is a growing lad whose best performances are still to come, possibly in the Middleweight division.

CHARLIE KRAY

Charlie is the oldest of the three fighting Krays. He is a good boxer with a fair right-hand punch. He is just the right type to tell us whether Lazar is going places, and tonight's performance will influence the careers of both boxers.

Lightweight Contest
Six 3 minute Rounds at 9st. 11 lbs.

Referee : CHRIS MAGGS

REG KRAY	v.	BOBBY MANITO
Bethnal Green		Clapham

REG KRAY

Reg is sweet-natured and known as the Sweet of the Sweet and Sour twins. Whoever gave them that tag must have dined at Freddie Mills's Chinese Restaurant. Possibly it meant that Reg is the better boxer of the two. A good mover with a nicely timed right-hand punch, he is booked to go far.

BOBBY MANITO

Bobby Manito is a youngster who has been coached on the right lines. During his short professional career he has had two managers. Matt Wells and Eddie Ryan, both former British champions, have each taught him something extra ; maybe sufficient for Bobby to become the first one to beat Kray.

Lightweight Contest
Six 3 minute Rounds at 9st. 11 lbs.

Referee : CHRIS MAGGS

RON KRAY	v.	BILL SLINEY
Bethnal Green		King's Cross

RON KRAY

Ron is the fighter of the two. Disdainful of the block and parry tactics, he is a lad who likes his verdict to come the hard way. He is the Sour part of the Sweet and Sour, who tonight will get the cream?

BILL SLINEY

Managed by Dave Crowley, Sliney is a former junior champion with militant tactics which he has borrowed from the former Lightweight champion. Another lad with a bright future.

The subpoena demanding my and Pat Butler's presence as witnesses at the Old Baile
for the Krays' first appearance in court at the age of 16, 1950

Me in the 1950s, at around
the time I was working as a
bookmaker's clerk in
Brighton for the Krays

...e races at Epsom. Charlie is on the far left, with Reg and Ron in the centre and ... O'Brien on the right

...ido at Victoria Park: Reg is in the centre, with Harry Abrahams to his right and ... Allford on the left (*Laurie O'Leary*)

Charlie Kray 'wardrobe dealing' outside his mother house (*Laurie O'Leary*)

Left to right: Ron, Dickie Morgan, Reg and me, mid- (*Laurie O'Leary*)

liberty with him – it was the third one announced. A thick-set, muscular young individual, he had huge biceps and acknowledged the crowd with a smile verging on a sneer, or that's how it seemed to Ron and me.

'Flash bastard,' said Ron. 'Do him Bob! He's no problem.' Ramsey agreed.

Two boxers left the ring, leaving the man who had beaten up Sorrell and a young, sinewy, muscular black guy. The booth owner went through his ritual of announcing a fair contest between all corners. A boxer would, he said, be paid a pound a round for each round he remained standing. He began to ask for 'any challengers'.

Now recognisable with his hood away from his head, Bob put up his hand, accepting the challenge. The announcer knew Bob and tried to duck out of his challenge.

'Bob Ramsey,' he said. 'You are a well-known booth fighter. Are you honestly challenging these young boys?' He was trying to infer they were innocent amateurs or inexperienced, but of course it wasn't true: they were all hard men and just did not fancy Ramsey beating them. The crowd went berserk. 'Let him fight!' they demanded. The roar was deafening – and there was nothing the owner could do if he didn't want his booth smashed up.

'All right, Bob,' he conceded. 'Glove up and let's have you!'

To tremendous applause before the bout had even begun, Bob got into the ring with a leap over the top rope. Ron and I stood in his corner at ground level, our heads just above the floor of the ring. The bout began with Bob's opponent being very apprehensive in his approach.

'Come on son, let's have a fight!' said Bob loudly. 'That's

what they're here for.' Showing his opponent a left hand, Bob threw a hard right cross that caught the guy on the top of his head. He retaliated in anger at being ridiculed by Ramsey, and he tried to throw a right counter punch.

Ramsey stepped back, pulling the guy on to a series of uppercuts and hooks, both left and right, stopping his opponent in his tracks. Fortunately for him, it was the end of the first round. He refused to undertake a second round, so the boxers were changed. Ramsey didn't care at all.

The black guy who had been watching from the side really fancied his chances with Ramsey, foolishly attacking him from the moment the bell sounded. There was no sparring, just straight aggression, with left punch followed by right in swift succession. Ramsey rode the punches comfortably, smiling as he did so, muttering something I couldn't hear. Then he counter punched his opponent, following through with a forearm smash. The black guy dropped to the canvas, totally shocked. Ramsey leapt into the air, yelling with delight, telling the first opponent to come back into the ring. 'I'll have 'em both ref!' he defiantly declared. 'Two against one.'

The first guy couldn't believe the challenge and jumped into the ring. Ramsey was so psyched up with the adrenaline running through his entire body that he pulled the black guy to his feet, throwing the other one into a corner, then caught him flush on the chin.

As he went down in our corner, Ronnie Kray gleefully punched him from outside the ring. He was as psyched up as Ramsey, with a bright red face and bulging eyes. 'You bastard!' he yelled. The black guy tried to head-butt Ramsey, but it was his game. As Bob retaliated, both opponents fled from the ring.

Triumphant, Ramsey jumped over the top rope into the crowd and we left for the calm of the Regal. It was a night to remember. Sorrell had been avenged – and all thanks to Ronnie Kray.

racket is reversed

It was one bright, sunny day and I was sitting in the front room of my parents' home in Bethnal Green with my friends Jimmy Scott and Peter Worley when it was suggested that we went to the Twins' billiards hall in Mile End for a game of snooker. Scotty was a very good player and Peter not too bad, but I was absolutely useless and agreed to go only to see the Twins.

As we approached the door of the Regal, I thought it was uncanny. Something seemed not quite right. There were no layabouts sitting on the low wall outside, whilst both the large doors to the entrance were shut. One door would always be locked back fully opened, even in wintertime if the weather was kind. When too cold, it would be left slightly ajar, so I thought it very odd, for it was a hot summer's day and the door was closed.

Scotty and Peter were not aware of anything amiss. I pushed the door open to be met by an angry-looking Ronnie Kray. Peering through the doors of the darkened entrance, his eyes were squinting as the rays of bright sunlight shone like a torch on to his face. Recognising me instantly, he greeted me with a pleasant grin rapidly changing to a scowl. 'Hello, Lol,' said Ronnie. 'We've had some trouble with the fucking Malts [Maltese]. They've been here asking for protection. We're waiting for them to come back. We'll teach those bastards!'

Ironically, it was only at a much later stage that the Twins themselves were accused of orchestrating such rackets. Now Ronnie explained that a group of swarthy-looking men had come into the hall asking for the governor of the business. When Ron said he was the boss, the leader had proceeded to say they wanted protection money from the snooker hall or they would cause him some trouble.

'Fucking cheek!' Ron said, relating the story again for the benefit of my friends. 'Stupid bastards!' he continued, hardly believing it was happening. 'I stabbed one in the hand with a bayonet I keep underneath the bar. Next I grabbed a cutlass off the wall behind the bar and I screamed at the others. Then I chased them as they ran out of the hall, smashing their car as they panicked to get away.'

Turning to my friends, Ronnie added, 'Hello, thanks for coming to help us out,' assuming that we had heard of his dilemma. Next, he beckoned us all to a wooden chest near the bar. 'Take your choice,' he ordered, pointing into the chest where there lay a collection of baseball bats, four-by-two stakes of wood, a couple of cutlasses and some pick axe handles. Scotty and Peter looked into the chest in amazement. These guys had never attacked anyone in their lives, but Ronnie's command was so penetrating that they felt they should obey him.

'Here you are chaps, I'll take those for you,' I said. Grabbing a pickaxe handle and baseball bat from the box, I winked out of sight of Ron to my mates who were terrified, although trying their best not to show it. Suddenly snooker was the last thing on our minds!

Ronnie was distracted by news that a black car with four men sitting in it had parked outside the club. There must have been at least forty people in the billiard hall, all ready for action except, of course, Jimmy and Peter, who would rather have been elsewhere. 'False alarm. It wasn't them, thank God,' I thought I heard Jim say. Peter, who owned a sleek, fast, black Ford V8 saloon, was asked by Ron to follow the car as it left its parked position opposite the hall. Meanwhile, Jimmy returned to his job at the Electricity Board.

Ron, another fellow guest and myself got into the car with Peter. I sat beside Peter in the front seat, whilst Ron and his mate were in the back. Ron was anxious to see where these Maltese gangsters were going, anticipating a full-scale war with them. Turning the tables on them at their own place would teach them a lesson. Peter was directed by Ron which car to follow. We kept two car lengths behind the dark car and trailed it through Whitechapel Road into Cambridge Heath Road. After some scary driving, we followed the vehicle into Bethnal Green Road and into Ainsley Street, watching as the car went into the local police station yard. Following a police car was nothing if not funny, but Ron was satisfied it was not the Maltese, just some nosy coppers checking who was using the billiards hall as we knew there were some unsavoury characters at the Regal.

Peter later told me that he heard Ron's mate say to him that he ought to be careful as he was pointing the gun into the back seat of the driver and it might go off. A few years later, I heard some terrible news. Jimmy Scott, my friendly electrician mate who would not hurt a fly and was one of the nicest people anyone could meet, was slashed with a razor on the face outside the Golden Bird Chinese restaurant in Mile End Road. An East End businessman friend of ours gave this news to me. He asked me to find out who did it as Jimmy was too traumatised to tell anyone and had no idea why he was a target for this attack.

I told Ronnie about the attack on Jimmy. He said he would find out who had done this cowardly act. As I have mentioned before, Ron hated bullies and in his opinion this was an act of a bully, for Jimmy was a very placid man and did not belong to any gang. Married with a beautiful wife, following the attack Jimmy did not leave his house, so totally wrecked were his nerves. The businessman friend made enquiries in the area of North London where he lived, offering a substantial amount to have the attacker punished, and to find out who it was, for Jimmy was too scared to say. It was not too long before Ronnie told me that the attacker was his brother Charlie's brother-in-law, a man named Ray Moore, and that it would cause complications for Charlie if they got involved at that time.

I had known Ray Moore since he was a young boy and could not believe he would commit such an act of violence, as he came from a good family and had had a fairly strict upbringing. It was said later that he had mistaken Jimmy for someone else. Sadly, Jimmy died of cancer a few years ago. Ray Moore was shot and killed a few years later in a domestic argument.

A friend called Joe Bailey told me how he and his mate Mickey Morris first met Ronnie Kray, when at fourteen years of age they attempted to get into the billiards hall. On entering, the pair were stopped at the door by Ron and Duke Osborne, a friend of his.

'How old are you two kids?' asked Ron.

The angelic faces of these two blond, tousled-haired, wide-eyed kids looked up at Ron as they answered unanimously, 'Seventeen.' It was an obvious fib – and Ronnie knew it.

'You lying little sods,' he said. 'We'll smack your arses and take you home to your mothers if you come back again. Now go home. It's dangerous to hang around here.'

Ron smiled as he and Duke returned into the billiard hall. These kids were streetwise and much older in attitude than their age. They knew that a few of their mates frequented the place and wanted to teach Ronnie and Duke a lesson for refusing them entry. They collected some bricks and heavy stones from nearby and began to throw them on to the flat roof of the hall and at the wire-caged windows, creating a terrible din inside the Regal.

Then Joe and Mickey hid inside an abandoned car left on some ruins beside the Regal. Suddenly, the hall doors flew open. Led by Ronnie, a posse of men ran into the roadway, brandishing pickaxe handles, looking everywhere, thinking that a rival gang was attacking the hall. Finding no such thing, a bemused Ron and his mates re-entered the Regal once again.

The two culprits were very amused at the result of their deed. When it seemed safe, they emerged from the old car, but devilment was still in them. They lit a piece of rag and put it into the petrol tank. An explosion occurred, the blast throwing them both to the ground.

For a second time, panic prevailed in the billiard hall. Thinking that they were being bombed or shot at, again led by Ronnie, the posse ran out into the street to be met by a smouldering car and two blackened scallywags sitting on the ground yards away from the vehicle. Covered in soot, they looked like characters from a Dickens novel.

'You stupid young bastards,' Ronnie roared. 'You could have been killed!' However, Ronnie felt deep concern for the boys' safety, taking the dazed kids into the club and getting them cleaned up. He sent out for some T-shirts to replace their torn shirts. Their trousers were passable, if a little dusty.

These tough kids showed no reaction to their irresponsible deed. They had no visible injuries. Now relaxed, they thought that the entire potentially dangerous escapade was very funny.

'Can we join the billiard hall now, mate?' asked a chirpy Mickey Morris. If they had not suffered in the blast, I am sure Ron would have given him a clip on the ear.

'Come back when you're older,' he said with a slight chuckle. 'Right now you're getting sent home in a cab.' Ron was genuinely caring in his attitude towards Joe and Mickey. They were just kids to him then and their destiny was undecided.

Much later in their lives, both Mickey Morris and Joey Bailey, who had made an impression on Ronnie's life as a couple of urchins, were favoured by him to run messages for him. Joey didn't lose his fearless cheekiness. Ronnie was very vain. Being a bit slippery, Joe often told him that he had seen a shirt that would look nice on him at Albert's shirt shop in Aldgate, almost next door to the famous

Jewish salt beef restaurant Blooms.

By now, the former urchin had grown into a smart and trendy teenager, so Ron gladly accepted Joe's judgement. Ronnie would ask Joe to go and get him a couple of the shirts, telling him to get one for himself. Joe, of course, expected that. Often being told to keep the change, too, his street wisdom was paying off.

While Joe was happy to be in Ron's company, running errands, Mickey Morris preferred mates of his own age and did not like being lectured by Ron about keeping straight and going to work. Mickey became a bank robber along with some mates, ending in them going to prison. He died a few years ago from a heart attack at a young age. Meanwhile, today Joe is an actor/London black taxi driver. You never know, you might have travelled with him!

lust for power

It was now the mid-1950s and word about 'the mad Twins from Bethnal Green' was spreading among the villains of East London. Their old mate from their Army days, Dickie Morgan, had introduced Reggie and Ronnie to a very well-known local family in Mile End, the Levys. The fact that there were so many in that family gave them a sort of power in the neighbourhood. They were a really nice family, likeable rogues collectively, and did not see the Twins as enemies but befriended them. This meant the Twins were able to establish themselves at the Regal in Mile End, even though it was off their manor.

The Krays' reputation as tough nuts was furthered when they accepted a peculiar type of challenge from some hard characters from Poplar and Bow. They had let it be known that they were getting pissed off with the Krays' threats of power in these areas, moving in to Mile End with the Regal, getting a reputation, and already having a following in Bethnal Green.

Several men who extended the challenge were somewhat older than the Twins' twenty-one years, and threw down the gauntlet at The Coach and Horses pub in Mile End Road, within walking distance of the billiard hall.

Ronnie Kray walked into the saloon bar with an old friend of his, Pat Butler, the same man who, as a boy, stood beside me as witness for the Twins when they appeared on a charge of GBH at the Old Bailey in 1950.

Charlie had left a message at home for Reg that Ronnie would be in The Coach and Horses and for Reg to meet him there as soon as he came in. Instantly, Reg went by taxi to Mile End Road. It was after 10 pm and he hoped that he had time to get to the pub before it closed. Reg jumped out of the cab, not knowing just what he was going to find. As he entered the saloon bar, Ron and Pat were standing at the bar, close to the door where Reg had entered.

Ron greeted him with, 'You took your time! Those bastards have been looking for a row. I only had Pat with me, so I've had to bite my tongue till you came.'

Reggie eyed the mob of older men along the other end of the bar. 'Flash bastards,' he murmured. 'Do we know them?' he asked, turning to Ron.

'I don't give a fuck if we do,' was the reply. 'I think that's the mob who have been putting it about that we are getting too big for our boots.' Ron then turned to Butler, saying, 'Pat, you don't want to get involved in this. It's for Reggie and me. You slide outside and stay out of it. We are better on our own in this argument.' Ron also knew that Butler was not a fighter. Butler went into the Mile End Road, taking up a position on the opposite side of the road to the pub. The Twins pretended to ignore the men in the public bar and quickly rushed out of the pub a few minutes behind Butler as if they had swallowed it.

The men chased after them, but the Twins were too quick for them. Those who pursued Reggie and Ronnie thought they had run away and searched for them along the road. Unfortunately for them, the Twins had doubled back rapidly into the door of the public bar and charged at the men's friends, who were unprepared and slaughtered at the bar.

Hearing the commotion, the others raced back into the bar to help their friends, who were lying about the pub floor. The Twins could box, the Twins could fight, and at that time were more than capable of beating their enemies. Among the others running into the bar was a man from Bow, Billy Donovan, who nearly lost an eye in the battle.

With Billy Donovan in hospital, the rest of the action defused. The Krays' strength and fitness helped them overcome the odds. They made certain that Billy Donovan, the most powerful of those fighting them in The Coach and Horses, was looked after, sending Charlie to find out if he had lost an eye. This battle was the beginning of the Krays' lust for power. It was the talk of the East End for weeks.

Their acclaim reached all parts of London, which meant visits to the billiard hall from some of their old mates from the Army days. The Nash family from North London, the Morgans, Dickey and Chunky, Paddy Austin from Hoxton, Curly King, Bobby Ramsey and the Levy brothers became very friendly to the Twins, who were running the manor that they had all considered theirs before the Krays took over the Regal.

Reggie and Ronnie had achieved gangster power in their early twenties – and this was no mean feat. The reason, as the men in The Coach and Horses had found out, was simple: the Twins were good on the cobbles, were better than average as boxers, and kept themselves fit.

They were now also using tools and guns. Ronnie was

following in the footsteps of his American idols, the Mafia, and his main hero, Al Capone. He realised the value of power and fear. Ronnie already had a reputation for violent outbursts of temper, which made the underworld wary of him. As a young man, he was being compared to Mad Frankie Fraser, who, unfortunately, began to work with Ronnie's new rivals, adding power to the Richardson gang from South London. It was strange that the Richardsons were becoming enemies as Charlie Richardson was in Shepton Mallett Military Prison with the Twins.

Businessmen were offering deals, most of them unlawful. This attracted Ronnie's gangster brain: he made no secret of the fact he was going to be a top of the range gangster. He realised the need for joining with other leading families from other areas. In this field, Ronnie was very loyal. He made an idol, too, of Billy Hill, but strangely enough it was his fifties' gangland rival Jack Spot who offered them their first taste of working at the races at Epsom, Brighton, and Ascot.

It was organised by booth boxer and gangster Bobby Ramsey with Jack Spot's backing. Spot arranged for a man from North London to fund them and their pitch at the races, known in the business as a 'joint'. Spot also arranged a pitch for them, so although they knew nothing about racing, Reggie and Ronnie went to work there in 1955. We had some fun learning about the racing gangs. Ronnie appointed me as his clerk. It was a bit daunting for me that, on request from Ronnie Kray, I was to be a bookmaker's clerk at Epsom!

The Twins learned, too, that Spot was planning to use them with their up-and-coming reputation in the East

End. I can remember one day a year or so later in Brighton. There were four of us working the races together – the Twins, myself and my friend Sean Venables. Spot asked the Twins to stay the night at a bed and breakfast place. When Reg and Ron said they didn't have a change of shirts or underclothes, Spot asked their sizes and arranged for Reg to meet him in a restaurant along the front near the beach. From the car we saw Reggie talking to Spot. Ronnie, who was armed, thought Spot was arguing with his brother. Knowing that Ronnie favoured the alliance with another idol, Billy Hill, I thought that he would not hesitate to shoot Spot if he gave him cause.

As the three of us sat waiting in the car for Reggie to return, Ron became agitated. 'Let's do the bastard Spot if he thinks he's going to use us,' he said.

At that point, Reg returned to the car, saying, 'He's offered us some poxy cheap shirts, so I told him that if he wants us to stay, we will be back in an hour for silk shirts like the one he was wearing.' Ron was proud of Reg and said that we should sit on the beach while we were waiting.

As we sat on the deck chairs, I stayed with Ron while Reggie went for a dip with Sean. About a hundred yards away up the beach, a rowdy mob were burning deck chairs. Ronnie became paranoid. 'Quick, tell Reg and Sean we are going to be attacked!' he yelled. 'Get out and get dressed quickly.'

They both ran from the sea, not bothering to dry themselves, and put on their clothes while dripping wet. As they were doing this, Ron produced a rather large revolver. 'Don't worry, take your time you'se two. I'll shoot the bastards if they come too near,' he assured them – and he meant it.

'Let's fuck off now,' Reg said. 'I'm fucking wringing and am not going to let Spot see me like this. He'll think we're fucking tramps.'

The mob on the beach, although very rowdy, were not aware of us at all, and were just drunken revellers acting stupid. We never waited for Spot, but went home, returning the next day as if nothing had happened, although Ronnie's respect for Spot was diminishing rapidly.

# of gangsters and guns

Ron Kray had a fascination for old-time fighters, villains, and thieves. Through him, I was introduced to an ex-heavyweight fighter of Greek descent, although he liked people to think that he was Italian. We were in old Bill Kline's gym in Fitzroy Square, near Warren Street, off Tottenham Court Road in Central London.

'This is Tony Mulla, Lol,' said Ron, obviously in awe of him because of his reputation as a heavyweight and his involvement with gangsters.

The tall man being introduced shook my hand with a soft grip, not trying to impress with his powerfully large hands. Tony Mulla was a handsome man, one who obviously had his share of ladies. He certainly looked Italian, with olive skin and jet black hair. Tony was powerfully built, stood over six feet tall and had a good personality to match.

He had stopped boxing professionally a short time previously. Ronnie promised to meet him to obtain some knowledge of the club scene that Mulla professed to know and wanted to advise the Twins about.

Word about the Twins had now spread among the criminal fraternity in Central London, especially Soho. Tony offered advice and wanted to point them in the right direction. Additionally, wisely, he also thought they would be better as friends than enemies.

Tony drove us to the Bar Italia, a café in Frith Street, Soho. Ronnie was not stupid and knew Mulla was showing off his close friendship with the Kray brothers. In a café that was used by a majority of the villainous faces in the West End, word would spread like wildfire that the Twins were with Mulla. After all, Mulla lived in Hackney and was proud to be an East Ender.

Listening to his tales of growing unrest in the West End between Jack Spot and Billy Hill, Ronnie was silently amused by Mulla's inside knowledge. These former partners were now enemies, both apparently claiming to be King of the Underworld.

'He's a bit of a lunatic, like me,' Ron said of Tony Mulla, who smiled faintly in acknowledgement. 'You are, ain't you, Tone?' Ronnie added with a grin, being pleased of his friendship with this big, powerful man, who towered over him. Although taller and extremely well-built, Mulla was giving Ronnie quite a bit of respect, aware of his reputation as a schizophrenic, subject to bouts of mania, switching from nice to nasty in seconds. Ronnie's jokey comments showed that he enjoyed the company of this man.

'He's very tough, Lol, ain't you Tone?' Mulla smiled, but seemed embarrassed by Ron's admiration. 'It took six men to cut him to pieces. They attacked him in his flat, Lol, but he still earned their respect by not grassing on them.'

Ronnie asked Mulla to tell me the story of this vicious attack a few years before. 'Another time, Ron,' said Mulla. 'It wouldn't look good if anybody heard us talking about it in here. Open up old wars, so to speak.'

Ronnie understood immediately, agreeing, 'Of course, it wouldn't look good, Tony.'

Ron then became restless, as if bored with the conversation he was pursuing, but not wanting to upset his friendship with Mulla. 'Shall we go, Lol?' he asked. Feeling a bit uncomfortable in this café, I agreed. Believe me when I say that there were some pretty nasty and ugly characters going to and fro in those days.

When we left, we walked through Old Compton Street into Tottenham Court Road, and got a Number 8 bus from New Oxford Street towards Bethnal Green and home. Conveniently, there was a bus stop at the top of Vallance Road. On the journey home, Ronnie explained that Mulla was a good boxer, who had survived to the finals of a heavyweight competition promoted by Jack Solomons, the top promoter of the day.

Ronnie said that Mulla's biggest problem was that he did not have the dedication needed to be a great fighter. He preferred easy money from wheeling and dealing, and loved having affairs with women. But Ron still admired him, telling me that Mulla was used as a go-between between two rival gangs, the White family and the Carter family, taking messages from one side to the other. These included messages that were, in fact, insults.

All went well until the day one of the gangs chose to teach him a lesson. Breaking into his house and getting him to send his wife and child out for something, they proceeded to slice his back and legs with razors.

'Don't cut my face!' Mulla shouted at them during this attack. Ron told me that this was a very brave gesture on his part – and his attackers did leave his face unmarked.

I could not quite think why it was so brave. How could this huge man allow these men to cut him at will just for taking messages for them? I thought that was very strange, but then realised that if he had tried to fight back anything could have happened. 'They could have killed him, Ron?' I asked.

'Yes, but they never. You see, Lol, they just taught him a lesson. I suppose there's more to it than I've heard, but I still think he's a tough bastard to survive that.'

I met Tony Mulla many times after that first meeting with Ron Kray. I enjoyed his company. Although he liked to portray the image of a top villain, I noticed that in certain people's company he was not so flash. In these circumstances he became quite subdued rather than his usual flamboyant self. One person whom Mulla seemed wary of was Ronnie.

On one occasion, Ronnie asked me to pick up something from Mulla at his flat over a shop in Hackney.

I rang his doorbell. After I announced who I was, Tony's voice came across the intercom. 'Push the door and come up, Laurie.'

Climbing the stairs, I met Tony at the top. He was wearing a black silk dressing gown. Very impressive he looked, too, especially in view of his size.

'Go into the front room for a few minutes,' Tony said. 'I'm in the middle of shaving.'

Instantly, thoughts of the mob that had attacked him a few years before popped into my mind. Glancing around, I saw that the flat was tastefully furnished, really rich in style. 'Nice place, Tony,' I called to him through the door. 'Not bad for Hackney, is it? Is this where they attacked you?' I asked him, feeling uncomfortable about it.

Tony appeared at the lounge door wearing only a pair of white Y-front pants. He turned round to show me the scars on his back, buttocks, and calves. There were long, thin tracks on his back. By this time, the fine cuts had healed and were disguised by his olive skin. I tried to imagine how horrific that attack must have been, although I do not think it is ever possible to put yourself in someone else's position, for no two people are the same.

When he came into the room again, Tony was dressed in immaculate style, totally casual with black trousers, open-necked silk shirt and a gold buckled belt. Tony told me never to sit on the fence. 'Take sides,' he advised. 'At least you will know that you will have somebody to back you up in an argument. I was a fool and very flash. I thought that nobody could touch me and I would be a friend to both sides. It was alright until one side got fed up and took their vengeance out on me. How stupid of me! At least they left my face alone, but the scars that no one can see, Laurie, will never heal.'

Mulla meant the deep scars of the mind: they would always be there. At the risk of stating the obvious, physical scars heal. But those you cannot see with the naked eye, ones deeply embedded in someone's mind, heart and soul, can remain open psychological wounds for years.

What I had to pick up were some boxing books that Ronnie had loaned to Mulla. Tony gave them to me and advised me to be careful, saying, 'It's a dog-eat-dog war, boy.'

Calling me 'boy' was not being disrespectful. It was Tony's form of friendship. But if he had called either of the

Twins 'boy', they would have exploded with anger as they hated the expression.

At this time, Ronnie's confidence with firearms was getting noticeably stronger. I remember an occasion when the Twins had a meeting at their home. I had popped round as I usually did and Ronnie ushered me into their small front room. There must have been about sixteen or so others in there already – two of the Nash family, the Keys from Edmonton, Big Tommy Brown from Tottenham and quite a few others, including Tony Mulla.

I have no idea what the meeting was about, but Ronnie produced a small silver Beretta pistol, saying that it had jammed. He gave it to Mulla, who put it to his eye. At this point, I was standing next to Mulla.

'It's got one stuck in the breech, I think,' he said. 'Look down the barrel, Laurie. Can you see anything?'

I did not like looking down the barrel of any gun at any time, but when he was holding the butt, then pushing it towards my face for me to look down, I got an immediate impression of my head being blown off. Pushing the barrel away, tentatively I declined. 'Leave off, Tony,' I said. 'It might go off!'

Ronnie Kray looked at me, laughed and said, 'Laurie's frightened you'll blow his head off!'

Tony Mulla put the nose of the gun to the floor and tugged on the butt. He must have pulled on the trigger, for there was an almighty 'Bang!' as the gun exploded. The bullet went through the carpet and floorboards, just inches from the feet of both Mulla and myself. I can remember little or no concern from the others in the room: it was just as if this was a normal occurrence, although somebody told Mulla to be careful.

Suddenly, the door of the room flew open. It was the Twins' father, Charlie Kray senior. 'You can fuck off, all of you!' he shouted. 'I'm surprised at you, Laurie. Ain't you got better things to do?' he asked, looking right at me, ignoring the others.

Ron Kray exploded at old Charlie. 'You silly old bastard,' he fumed. 'It was an accident. D'you think he done it on purpose?'

If there had been a meeting, it was soon stopped by the gunshot and old Charlie's intrusion. When Charlie left the room, Ronnie just laughed out loud, saying, 'You could have blown Laurie's head off, Tony! I thought you knew something about guns.'

I felt lucky, but as the ringing was very loud in my ears, decided to leave the rest of the men and made my farewells.

Soon afterwards, I found out that Ron felt that Tony Mulla was becoming more wary of him and his brother Reg. This became apparent when I was at the Twins' house and Ronnie called Mulla for something he was supposed to have arranged for him.

Ronnie shouted abuse at him down the telephone, telling him to meet us outside the London Hospital in Whitechapel. Whatever it was Tony Mulla was meant to have done had really upset Ronnie.

As Mulla approached from across the road to our spot away from the main entrance to the hospital, Ronnie did not greet him with a handshake, but a volley of abuse – 'You took a fucking liberty. That's the last time I'm going to tell you, Mulla.'

Ron used his surname. This showed disrespect, but Tony

Mulla, this giant of a man, kept quiet, not even trying to explain to Ronnie. I was embarrassed for him, for the scars of the terrible razor attack must have taken their toll. As I walked a few feet away from the one-sided argument, I could hear that Ronnie was furious.

'Fuck you, Mulla!' he said as we left to walk down to his house. Many people go red in the face – puce even – and rant and rave when angry. Ron never did, though his face would contort if he were really riled. But the look in his eyes was enough: that said it all. Ron did not need to shout or even to raise his voice by one decibel. His eyes had tremendous impact. He would peer with them half closed, almost as though looking through a gap in a door.

Ronnie did not elaborate on the argument during our walk along Vallance Road. It must have been about a mile from their house to Whitechapel Road, but that journey seemed to take forever due to the sullen mood Ron was in. Arriving at the Twins' house, I was happy to enjoy a quiet and welcome cup of tea with Mrs Kray.

'Who's upset him, Lol?' she asked. 'He's got a face like thunder. Has he had a row?'

'I think it was a disagreement with somebody,' I explained softly. 'I was with him, but kept out of the argument. It was too one-sided and I felt sorry for the man.' I kept my voice down. I did not want Ronnie to give me a bollocking. He was in a vile mood . . . and that was when he was at his most dangerous.

'I'm going to May's! See you later, Lol,' said Ron cheerfully.

Mrs Kray laughed with me when Ronnie had gone next door to his Aunt May. 'She can handle him when he's like this, Lol,' Mrs Kray explained. Even so, I decided not to wait for Ronnie, so leaving for my own home, I asked her to tell Ron that I would be around tomorrow.

After the row, Ronnie fell out with Tony Mulla. Although he spoke to him from time to time, he never talked about him much.

It was a few years before I, too, was to see Tony Mulla again. By this time, he was the owner of quite a few clip joints in the West End, in partnership with his old friend, Alf Melvin. I was with one of my oldest friends, John Cosgrove. We had popped into the club the Twins owned in Gerrard Street, to see who was about in the West End and to use the men's urinal.

I bumped into Tony Mulla, who was very drunk. But I had always liked him, and it was the first time I had seen him so inebriated. He was barely coherent. 'Hello, Tone!' I said, using the urinal next to him.

'Hello, Laurie. How are you?' he mumbled with some difficulty.

His mind must have been on a suicide course, for his next sentence was not too clever. 'You tell those brothers my only guv'nor is my baby.'

Mulla's earlier advice to me came in handy. 'No, Tony. You tell them yourself. I'm no message carrier: you told me that years ago. Look what happened to you, mate!'

I was not fazed by Mulla's request. After all, perhaps he was still embarrassed that I had heard Ronnie give him a bollocking. 'Tony, you're pissed mate,' I added. 'Why don't you get a cab home?'

These were the last words we exchanged, for I never saw Tony again.

Going to Vallance Road the next morning, I was greeted by Ronnie. 'Hello, Lol,' he beamed. 'So you had a row with Mulla last night in the El Morocco.'

I was happy to put him right that I had not had a row with Tony Mulla, but we were just talking and he was extremely drunk.

'Well,' Ron riposted, 'someone told me that you were arguing with him and he just walked away from you.'

This was totally untrue, but one of Ron's spies, to curry favour with him, had carried a message to Ronnie that he knew he wanted to hear. Whatever I said to Ronnie would not convince him that we hadn't argued at all. He wanted to believe that we had.

The unfortunate end to this tale of Tony Mulla is that he was shot and killed by his partner Alf Melvin because Mulla owed him some money and slagged him off in front of some of the girls at one of their clubs. Big Alf Melvin, a very likeable person, had both his pride and ego hurt. He killed Mulla and put the gun into his own mouth, resulting in two senseless deaths. Mulla fell down the narrow stairway, landing on the pavement outside their club, which was called The Bus Stop, at 24 Frith Street, Soho. The next day, newspapers christened it 'The bus stop murder'.

the watney street mob

The progression of the Krays in the world of violence and power was noticeable by their advancing success in the night club world. In 1954, soon after they were discharged from the Army, they had acquired the Regal Billiards Hall. Two years later, they were encouraged by Bob Ramsey to join him and Billy Jones, a wheeler-dealer from Wapping, in the Stragglers Club near Cambridge Circus.

Situated on the ground floor of a house, the club was members only. Though in the West End, it was far from plush, but licensed to serve drinks later than pubs. However, the terms of the licence were often overlooked with drinks being served after hours, resulting in an occasional police raid. The police, though, often purposely overlooked the illegal drinking on the basis that at least they knew where to find various villains.

The club attracted a large number of East Enders, who were encouraged by Jones to drink there. Jones had sway with the allocation of dock labour, men then being employed for a specific day. A gang of men from the Watney Street area of Wapping often visited the Stragglers. They included George Cornell and various other dockers. Problems arose with their behaviour, which included general drunkenness and loud swearing. To try and control this, Ramsey had suggested bringing in Ron and Reg, a job they accepted with relish as it marked their first toe-hold in the West End, an opportunity they had craved.

With the Krays on board the Stragglers started to make money, but trouble was just around the corner. An argument occurred between a Watney Street docker, Jacky Martin, and Billy Jones about the supply of dock labour. Martin severely beat up Jones. Subsequently, Bob Ramsey – Jones' partner in the Stragglers Club and a stronger force – retaliated and in return thrashed Jacky Martin. Next, Bobby Ramsey was coshed by Martin and the Watney Street dockers in The Artichoke, a pub in the East End. Billy Jones, Ramsey and Ron went looking for Jacky Martin at The Britannia pub in Wapping, but he was on the missing list, so they turned on his brother Terry instead. Ramsey attacked him with a knife and hurt him badly. Then Ron, Bobby and Billy went out looking for any other of the enemy that they could find. Ronnie had a gun on him and Ramsey a bloodstained knife. Their clothes were bloodstained, too. When a police car stopped them they could not believe their bad luck. All three were charged and found guilty. On 5 November 1956 Ramsey was sentenced to seven years whilst Billy Jones and Ronnie got three years each.

Bobby Ramsey and Ronnie Kray fell out soon after the trial when Ronnie had a confrontation with Ramsey in Wandsworth Prison. He had been told by a friend that Ramsey was talking badly about him.

As they passed each other on a landing near their cells,

although they were each accompanied by a screw, Ronnie threw a punch at Ramsey, knocking him to the ground. Although Ramsey is a big, tough man, Ron was full of pent-up vengeance from their trial. He displayed an inner strength that Ramsey was unable to comprehend.

Ramsey was puzzled by Ronnie's action, but when asked if he wanted to bring a charge against him, he declined with a smirk.

'Help the law because of a difference of opinion between two friends,' said Ramsey. 'Not me mate!'

When I visited Ronnie in Wandsworth Prison it was noticeable that he was becoming very paranoid. Nevertheless, he settled down at Wandsworth alright. Ron met and became friendly with Frank Mitchell, 'The Axe Man', saying he would make sure he was alright when he came out of prison. 'The Axe Man' was so-called because he had escaped from serving a short term in prison and broken into an old couple's house and held them hostage with an axe he had found. He was recaptured and sentenced to life without any release date.

But things took a turn for the worse when Ron was transferred to Camp Hill prison on the Isle of Wight. This move changed his general attitude and he became really paranoid. Going to see him when he was in Camp Hill was not pleasant as Ron asked lots of questions. Suspicious of both Charlie and Reggie and their business dealings, he felt left out of things. On top of that, someone told him that Bob Ramsey had now called him 'a grass'. That was the last straw and completely changed him.

Ron flipped in the games room, smashing things up and lashing out at all and sundry, telling them that they were 'all a load of fucking idiots'. Put in a padded cell, Ronnie was transferred to the psychiatric ward in Winchester Prison, Hampshire, where he appeared to be recovering from a serious bout of melancholia.

Unfortunately, this coincided with the death of his favourite aunt, Rose, who died of leukaemia. When he was told the sad news, Ronnie just broke down and cried, sobbing hysterically, once again becoming violent with all those around him. Because of his behaviour at Camp Hill prison – the sole reason for his transfer to Winchester – and the violent reaction to his aunt's death, Ronnie was put into a straitjacket and certified insane in December 1957.

In February of the next year, he was transferred to Long Grove Mental Institution, Epsom, Surrey, where after some months of treatment came a remarkable improvement as far as his doctors were concerned. Despite this, his request to be returned to prison was refused temporarily. This caused him to be concerned that he would be in a mental institution for much longer than his sentence, making him disturbed once again.

The strain on Reggie was beginning to tell, too, but he had a plan for Ronnie. At that time, I had absolutely no idea what it was as Reg confided only in people involved in the scheme. As it turned out, it was as simple as it was audacious.

The day before the plan was put into practice, my friend Curly King and I went to visit Ron. Happily, we found him in a really good frame of mind. Curly made Ron laugh with his tales of the West End and the clubs he visited. Looking around the table where we sat drinking endless cups of tea until our time to leave, Ron was just like his old self. 'See you soon!' was his parting message. As it turned out, it would be sooner than we thought, or at least it was in my case. Curly knew of the brilliant plan to help Ronnie escape from Long Grove.

The very next day after my visit, Reg, his close friend George Osborne, Curly King and a few others went to visit Ron. Unknown to me, a message had been passed to Ronnie by Curly the previous day. While I was getting some tea, he was told which clothes to wear and to be ready for the escape. Ron was obviously hyped-up, but was told to keep his medication to a minimum so that he would be alert when the daring plan was put into operation.

On a Sunday in June, 1958, two visitors' cars to Long Grove Hospital arrived along with many others from all over the East End of London to see patients, who were mainly from the boroughs of Bethnal Green, Hackney, West Ham and Poplar. It was not at all unusual for cars with men sitting in them to be in the car park. The hospital was for mentally ill patients with only a very small percentage of them being criminally insane, so security was not as strict as in prison.

Georgie Osborne and Reggie went in as the two visitors allowed to see Ron. They were sitting at the table talking to him when, literally behind the back of the unsuspecting duty nurse, Ron changed into the cashmere overcoat Reg had been wearing and quickly swapped seats with him.

Ron, now wearing Reggie's overcoat, walked past the duty nurse. This left Reg in an identical blue suit to the one Ron had been wearing, sitting there with Georgie Osborne, laughing and joking, with Ron now on his way back to London and temporary freedom.

Reg and George Osborne were questioned by the local police, but they had nothing concrete to hold them on, so both were released some time later. Meanwhile, once free, Ronnie went to his home in Vallance Road. Presumably, the police must have thought this was the last place he would head for and failed to carry out an extensive search.

Reg did not make any contact with Ronnie until over a week later. Not surprisingly, the press and media coverage over Ron's escape was causing considerable interest, so Reg had to bide his time before seeing Ron again, knowing that he would be tailed if he tried to contact him immediately. The plan was to keep Ron free for a few months. Under the rules at that time, if a prisoner who was certified insane escaped and remained at liberty for longer than six weeks, he would have to be recertified when recaptured. With the certification lapsed, Ronnie would be able to give himself up and return to prison to complete the small remainder of his sentence. All Ronnie had to do was to stay hidden and keep out of trouble.

This was easier said than done. Ronnie was hidden in a caravan that belonged to a friend in Suffolk who owed the Twins a favour. The first weeks were fine, but Ron's minder began to find it tough keeping him occupied. Ron was restless, and soon wanted the company of a young man. Reg arranged this for him, but Ron was growing impatient. He wanted to leave the caravan for London, which Reg thought far too risky.

Ron, however, had his own way. He went to London, even attending a party of very close friends. Ron so enjoyed this that he wanted to repeat it. During his stay at the farm in Suffolk, Ron underwent many changes mentally. Under an assumed name, he was taken to see a doctor. The GP re-certified him, and pronounced him sane and of sound mind. Unfortunately, Ron started acting suspiciously once again, becoming paranoid. Even getting him back to London did not help. By this point, he was really becoming dangerous, so dangerous that the family agreed for him to stay at Vallance Road despite the constant fear of recapture.

In his impossibly anguished state of mind, Ron thought the whole family were spies and not really his mother, brothers and aunts. He had experienced a complete nervous breakdown. In desperation, they agreed to inform Scotland Yard that they had found Ronald Kray and were turning him in to them. The whole episode had something of a farce-like quality about it, for the police were amazed and thought it was a hoax. When they finally arrived, Ron seemed relieved to go with them. The family wept as he left them, but knew his problems were out of their hands. Ron really needed professional treatment. But the ploy had worked. Ron returned to Long Grove, from where, following treatment, he went back to Wandsworth, a prison he knew.

After leaving prison in 1959, Ron returned once again to the security of his childhood home in Vallance Road and the comforting presence of his family and friends, but his behaviour was still peculiar. Ronnie's doctor advised him to go for a course of treatment as an in-patient at the local hospital for nervous diseases, St Clement's in Bow, just around the corner from their Regal Billiards Hall. Ron was there for a short time, but his return to normality was not to be. Whatever Reg and Charlie did was not good enough for Ron. He was still extremely suspicious of them.

Ronnie's moods could swing from nice to nasty in a very unpredictable way. When having a discussion, at times he found it difficult to say the right words. Whom he was with affected how he dealt with this. If it were one of us, being friends, he would laugh out loud to cover up when he couldn't say what he meant. However, when Ron was trying to get across a point in a serious discussion with business associates, his face would become red with frustration. Ronnie's eyes bulged and altered and he would place the palm of his left hand across the bridge of his nose. Next, he would gently rub his left eye, the index finger spread to the right eye. With his head bowed, Ronnie would be searching for the right words. If he could not find what he thought were the correct ones to have a real impact in the conversation, he would explode in anger. Often, this was not with the people with whom he was having a conversation, but with himself for his inability. Only he could criticise himself. When Ronnie was in that kind of mood, he would either guarantee to seal a deal with fright or, not quite understanding him and to avoid an argument, business associates would agree a deal or just politely leave, never to be seen again.

All those really close to Ronnie Kray were, at one time or another, subject to a volley of abuse. Some reading this might say, 'But I never was.' I can assure you that anyone in this category was not really close to Ron. There are a few exceptions to this rule, and they know who they are, but I was not one of them. Ron often raged at me, if not face-to-face then certainly in letters.

Ron's behaviour was inconsistent. Soon after getting out of prison in 1959, Ron bought a caravan and sited it in

Lovatts Yard in Brady Street, Bethnal Green, about two miles from his parents' house. He encouraged Tommy Brown, an ex-heavyweight fighter from Tottenham, to live there with him, deciding that he would be a traveller. Ron was always going on about his family being Romanies.

The yard was a large, open lorry park. Try and imagine how funny it looked to see Ronnie, with his gangster image, driving in and out of Lovatts Yard, doing business in sharp-cut suits, then changing into his gypsy mode, with rolled up shirt sleeves, waistcoat and striped webbing braces on his trousers. Tied to them would be a scarf that had been loosely hung around his neck, and his trousers would be rolled up to the top of his boots. Ron became 'Ronnie the Totter'. He loved this change in his life, which lasted for a couple of weeks until he became bored.

Shortly afterwards, he bought a beautiful flat in Cedra Court, Hackney, from Ronnie Mitchell's mother. Ronnie Mitchell, of course, had had the fight with the Krays at the Royal Ballroom many years before. It proves just how small the world is really, for Ronnie Mitchell is the father of my good friend Scott, who is married to my other great friend Barbara Windsor.

In Ron's absence, Reggie had been busy extending the empire. An illegal gambling set-up had been established in Wellington Way, right next door to Bow Police Station. In 1958, Reg and Charlie had opened their own small club, the 'Double R', in a large house in Bow. The décor was nothing special. Like most of the clubs in the 1950s, it had red flock striped wallpaper and wall lights, and a small dance floor and stage. The entertainment was provided by a resident trio comprising drums, bass and piano, with appearances from top pub acts. Occasionally, stars such as American singer Billy Daniels and Blind Lenny Peters appeared there, too.

Humble as it may have been by West End standards, the club drew celebrities galore, such as Judy Garland and a host of others. Once out of prison, Ron enjoyed meeting and greeting in the Double R. Although the Twins were rapidly acquiring a reputation for brutality towards other gangsters, they were drawn towards the glitter and glamour of celebrities, both national and international. Ron and Reg both coveted and cosseted the stars, attending their various West End shows. For their part, the celebrities enjoyed the aura of gangsters at the Double R, so were more than happy to visit it in then murky Bow.

The club was a success, and soon the Twins had opened another East End Club, the Kentucky in Stepney, a plusher version of the Double R. The big-time arrived, though, when, with the help of Les Payne, the Twins' so-called partner, Ron and Reg took control of Esmeralda's Barn, a casino and restaurant in Wilton Place, just off Knightsbridge. It was their venture into the echelons of the rich and famous, away from their now tame life in London's East End. They kept the Kentucky Club in Mile End Road, but Esmeralda's was the classy environment they preferred. With a lord as co-director, they felt they were at last on their way to really rich pickings.

one look said it

September 17 1961 was the day that my girlfriend Iris Jones and I were married at St Matthew's Church, Bethnal Green. We had known each other since we were young teenagers, being introduced by my cousin Jean Hall, daughter of my mother's sister Lucy. I have since weathered the storm quite a bit, but Iris still looks fantastic, just as she did on our wedding day.

After the church ceremony, we travelled to the Grand Palais in Commercial Road. Formerly a Jewish theatre, the entrance hall was typical, having a tiny box office and stairs leading to a grand elaborate hall. This boasted bronze-tinted mirrored walls, huge sparkling chandeliers hung high from the ceiling, plush red seats and tables set for the guests to arrive.

Lobster, smoked salmon and two large, fresh poached salmon sat raised in the centrepiece of a most stunning presentation of gourmet food. The fish and seafood were gifts from our friends from Billingsgate fish market, Georgie and Billy Adair, Davey Thurlow and Lennie Appleton. Meanwhile, the catering was by a great mate with culinary degrees, a Geordie called John Walton. A chef extraordi-naire, he made reference to the fact that it was probably the first time he had cooked a ham for a yiddisher affair! Another good friend was head barman Patsy Bedford, with most of the booze supplied by our best man Peter Worley. With such a fine spread, the family was in raptures. It was great to see my mother and father and Iris' father, Sonny, having such a good time. They had deserved it.

The evening was attended by other friends and guests of both families. Among my guests were Ron Kray and Reg with his fiancée Frances Shea, a young, very pretty girl he had met through her brother Frank Shea, an old friend from Hoxton. Also there were Checker Berry, Freddie and Maureen Foreman, Charlie and Dolly Kray, Margie and Ray Winstone, Ray Farrow, and Joe and Sheila Willshire. That's not to forget Billy and Rita Adair, George and Janice Adair, Jack and Sheila Fennings, Jimmy Smith, Tommy McCarthy, Frankie Tovey, Tommy 'Ginger' Marks and his wife Annie, and Freddie Clempson. There were also a few friends from Canning Town among the couple of hundred who attended the evening celebrations.

The entertainment was supplied by the Checkmates and the Ike Hatch Trio – from the Starlight Club off Oxford Street – with a drunken drummer named Billy George. The Twins had arranged for Ricky Stevens, a singer from Hoxton, to appear and sing for us. He was top of the hit parade that very week with 'I Cried For You'.

We had a very nice evening, without mishap, although an auntie of mine told me that she decided to get drunk because she thought that if a balloon burst that night, it could have been mistaken for gunfire and she might have been in the middle of a gunfight! It was a joke, of course, but our mixture of guests included those who in later years made criminal history of the highest degree. Fortunately, it did not begin that night. Iris and I never had any children and are still happily living together in the East End, with the memory of that happy, special day still very fresh in our minds.

Two years later Ray Winstone, a close friend of mine and father of the *Minder* actor also called Ray Winstone, went for a drink at the Kentucky Club owned by Ron, Reg and Charlie in the Stepney part of Mile End Road.

The club had been featured in a recent film, *Sparrows Can't Sing*, a story about the East End, starring true East Enders James Booth, Barbara Windsor and George Sewell. Written by Stephen Lewis and directed by Joan Littlewood, the film was based on a musical from Stratford's Theatre Royal, a workshop for budding actors.

The Kentucky Club was a nice place to relax and have a chat. It was quite busy, but Ray and I were able to find a quiet corner and were discussing a boxing match we had seen when Ronnie came over to greet us.

'Nice to see you both,' he said. 'Having a night out?' Ron enquired, offering us a drink.

'I'm glad you came in, Laurie,' he continued, 'as I want to talk to you about running a club for us in Knightsbridge.' Ron explained that they wanted a club in the room below their casino at Esmeralda's Barn.

I listened intently, but politely refused, saying I did not want to work in the West End. Ronnie asked me to think it over, adding, 'It's a really nice place, Laurie. You would be perfect for it!'

After a short while, Ray and I left. On our way to the car,

he commented, 'You're mad refusing that opportunity!' I respected Ray's judgement, but repeated that I did not want to work in the West End.

'It's in Knightsbridge, a really lovely area,' said Ray. He convinced me to return to the Kentucky Club.

As we entered, Ronnie was standing in the reception area. 'Is that offer still on?' I asked. A broad grin came over Ron's face. 'I knew you would be interested, Laurie,' he said. 'With your knowledge of the music business, it's a marvellous opportunity. You'll love it!' With that, Ron gave me an address where I would see him the next day.

He insisted that the proposed dancing club would have no alcohol or drugs. 'Just let nice people use it,' Ronnie firmly instructed. 'And strict membership.'

When the club finally opened, we decided that the policy should be soul and blues music, so I had to find a disc jockey with the necessary knowledge. I interviewed a young blond guy, James Hamilton. About six feet, four inches tall, he had an incredible knowledge of the soul scene. James also had a wonderful collection of discs, backed with close contacts with the specialist blues and soul SUE label, featuring artists like Ernie K. Doe. Blues singer Betty Wright was also on that label, which was just the right combination for our clientele. James also claimed to have found the hit 'Go Now' for the Moody Blues, and had just returned from an engagement in the United States as a disc jockey. All in all, he seemed perfect for the job so became the resident DJ at the opening of the club.

Later, we introduced live music, with groups like The Bo Street Runners. One of its members was Mick Fleetwood, who subsequently formed the famous Fleetwood Mac group. Another very popular group, established by some of the Old Harrovian Club members, was A Band of Angels. They had a tremendous following of debs and their male counterparts. Ron was extremely pleased with the clientele we attracted, and frequently told me so. Out of A Band of Angels came Mike D'abo, who later replaced Paul Jones as lead vocalist with Manfred Mann. Another band member, David Wilkinson, later became the manager of the late Peter Cook, and currently manages funnyman John Cleese. Meanwhile, Angels' vocalist John Gaydon, along with his best friend David Enthoven, formed E & G Management, looking after the affairs of King Crimson, Bryan Ferry and Emmerson, Lake and Palmer.

I remember one young man, Sparrow Harrison, who had a speech impediment and stuttered quite badly, except when he was singing. This amazed Ron, who told Sparrow he was very brave to front a group with his handicap. Ron was pleased that he and his group – Sparrow and the Gossamers – played at the club. They had a very strong Chuck Berry influence. One of its members was a QC's son, and his father later became a judge at the Old Bailey. When Ron saw this in the *Daily Mail* he was greatly amused.

However, he was not quite so happy another time when a different group – Casey Jones and the Engineers – rehearsed in the empty club one afternoon before appearing there the following week. I should add that one of its members was the then unknown Eric Clapton. In latter years, during their imprisonment, Eric wrote a letter to both Reg and Ron. I delivered it to Ron in Broadmoor. Eric had written to them because

Ron composed a poem for Eric and his then wife Patti Boyd.

As they were rehearsing, one of the minders came down from the casino upstairs. 'Ronnie said to tell the band to be quieter,' he said. 'They're having a meeting upstairs.'

About ten minutes later, the same man came back. This time the message was, 'The Colonel's getting angry! The music is too loud, Lol. They can't hear themselves speak.'

Ron's nickname of 'The Colonel' was given to him by that colourful character Curly King. Incidentally, he also called Vallance Road 'Fort Vallance'. This amused the Twins – and the names stuck. Ronnie relished being called 'The Colonel'. It flattered his vanity.

I asked the group to turn down their amplifiers a bit. They motioned as if to do so, but within five minutes the door opened. In walked Ron, immaculately dressed. His eyes were fixed on the group. Without saying a word, he slowly walked the thirty-five feet to the small stage area where the group was playing. The nearer he got to them, the quieter they became. When Ron was about five feet away, they were almost silent. He just stared at them with his penetrating eyes.

Ron's presence was electric. Without saying a single word to the group, he turned to me and said, 'You see, Laurie, the boys can play quieter if you ask them to.' With that, he walked back to the meeting upstairs in the casino.

'Who the hell was that?' someone asked.

'Ronnie Kray, one of the owners,' I explained. Suddenly, the boys had lost their appetite for rehearsing. Casey Jones, Eric and the others decided to pack it in and rehearse at a later date.

You see, Ron had charisma. It was not as if he would have harmed any of the group. He liked their music, but it was interfering with his business upstairs. One look from him was sufficient. His eyes and expression said it all. There was no need for words.

a fearsome force

It was business as usual at Esmeralda's Barn. Situated on the first floor, the reception area of the Barn Twist Club was comfortably cushioned between the ultra-smart Esmeralda's Barn Casino Club on the top floor and the Cellar, a late night haunt of high-class lesbians. This was placed on the ground floor. The building was very important to the Krays since the family became directors of all these three establishments.

The members of the Cellar club usually arrived after they piled out of the Gateways club in Bayswater looking for an extra hour's drinking and dancing. They were able to benefit from the Cellar club's midnight licence, such were the antiquated licensing laws in the sixties.

Ronnie just loved the importance of keeping the Casino Club to a high standard. The Twins were happy to abide by the code of conduct set by the club, namely evening dress and bow tie. Ron and Reggie still looked fearsome, but were handsome in their finery.

One night, three rather dishevelled looking men attempted to get into the club. As they were not members, I had no reason to warrant their entry and disliked their attitude. I stopped them, trying to explain that it was not their type of club and that we did not serve alcohol. I could see they were becoming aggressive and asked a friend, George Last, an ex-heavyweight fighter and dock worker who was helping at the club at Ronnie's request, to mind the door.

I went out into the main road in Knightsbridge and asked a passing policeman if he would just show his uniform to deter these guys. I really thought they were idiots. The reason I made this request was that I honestly thought I was doing them a favour. If Ronnie or Reggie walked into the club and saw these prats acting like gangsters they would not be as patient as me.

I know for certain that the Twins would have reacted badly. These blokes were idiots and deserved a wallop. If Ronnie or Reggie had witnessed this disrespectful behaviour it would have created a possible massacre and I did not want to be any part of a likely nicking, so used the logic of prevention being better than cure.

But it was to no avail. As I walked up the wide wooden stairs to the door of the Barn, I heard raised voices. Opening the door, I saw George on the receiving end of some heavy verbal abuse. At six feet, two inches tall, George was more than capable of handling himself when fit, but he was under the handicap of having to wear a leather support around his waist due to an injury at the docks.

As the cop and I entered the small reception area, the idiots looked first at me, then at the policeman.

'What d'ya think you're gonna do?' the larger of the three men said in a very loud, menacing voice.

The cop was amazed at their violent attitude, and just looked at me in bewilderment. At that point, I once again tried to reason with the men. 'Come on lads,' I said. 'It's time to go.'

'Fuck off, you cunts,' was the belligerent reply.

I was getting angry trying to appease them, so made a request to the officer. 'Can I assist you to get them off the premises, officer?' I asked.

His reply was lacking confidence. 'They are a bit large, aren't they?' said the copper.

Taking that as a 'Yes', I exploded with rage, hitting the nearest one with a left hook that must have carried all my pent-up anger. The guy just collapsed. I turned to George who, fortunately, had grabbed the largest of the men. The third guy was about to attack George, so I chinned him. He dropped to the floor and held on to the banisters, much to my surprise. Another punch rendered him helpless.

By this time, George was tussling with the really heavy bully. They tumbled down the stairs to the bottom, still holding on to each other's shoulders. 'Mind your head!' I called to George. I threw a punch at the man's head, cutting him above his right eye. Blood poured into it. Although he did not budge very much, he mumbled, 'They've done me!'

Looking over George's shoulder, the large man said to me, 'You're fucking dead tomorrow.' By this time, the policeman had drawn his truncheon and was shouting loudly. 'Come on!' he ordered. 'That's enough!'

I thought the moment was appropriate for me to take the piss. 'Take their names officer,' I suggested with a smirk. He proceeded to take their names and addresses. I was interested to see who they were and, looking over his shoulder, I noticed that they all came from the Isle of Dogs in the East End.

'Don't you want to charge them?' the officer asked.

'No,' I replied. 'I think they've learned their lesson.' I had not even creased my tie or suit in the skirmish, so thought it unnecessary to have the trouble of charging them, too.

At this point, Ronnie Kray walked into the entrance to Esmeralda's from the street. 'I saw all this officer,' he volunteered. 'They are hooligans, and don't know how to conduct themselves in this area. It's too nice for them. This man is a gentleman,' he said, pointing at me.

'It's all right, it is all under control,' I said, thinking that it would not be good for us to get involved with these idiots any further.

At that point, the policeman made the men leave the premises. He then went on his way, but not before I had the presence of mind to take his number. Fortunately, I found that to my advantage later on . . .

The rest of the night went along as usual. That would have been the conclusion to this story, but at around 8 pm one night, about fifteen days after the incident, I was drinking a cup of coffee in the club entrance when two men aged between forty to fifty years and reeking of alcohol came up the stairs. They were quite shabbily dressed and although not aggressive at first, requested entrance to the club. When I explained it was a members' club and that it was empty as it was too early, they turned nasty.

'Who's gonna stop us then, boy?' demanded one of the men.

Well, sometimes people take my kindness as a weakness and I exploded. These men hit a nerve. I threw the coffee cup and saucer to the ground saying, 'You people make me sick!'

The coffee splashed over their feet. Looking shocked, they said in chorus whilst pulling out some form of ID card, 'CID. You're nicked!'

I was not unduly worried. What would be the charge? Splashing them with coffee? Not very criminal, is it? At that point, Big Pat Connolly, a Scotsman and a member of The Firm, came down the stairs from the casino.

'Pat, tell them they can't nick me for throwing coffee at them.' I said.

'Hello, Pat,' said one of the bullies. He had a few words with them.

'You've got to go, Laurie,' said Pat eventually. 'It's a serious charge!'

With that, the bully detectives told me I had to accompany them to the station. As I sat in the back seat of the police car, I noticed that they both stank of alcohol.

They drove me to Gerald Row Police Station in Belgravia, a very clean old building with flowers around the entrance. Once inside, I could not take in the desk sergeant's words. I am sure he said, 'Attempted murder and GBH', but knew I had nothing to worry about as I'd done nothing serious and I would not get nicked for fighting.

Ron sent a friend to see me at the station. To stop her worrying, I asked him to tell my wife that I would be working at the casino all night. Sitting in the cell, I wondered what all this was about. I was numb. 'They must have got it mixed up,' I thought. 'When was this supposed to have happened?'

After a night in the cell trying to work out what was happening, and refusing the early morning tea and toast from a kind cop, I was taken in a Black Maria to Great

Marlborough Street Police Court with more prisoners collected on the way. The court is next to the stage door of the London Palladium.

I had no idea of the procedure, as it was my first time in court as a defendant. I had been a witness for the Twins at the Old Bailey in their teens, but that was different. When I was called, the judge read the charge that I had caused Grievous Bodily Harm to three men. The simple fact that nothing about a murder was mentioned gave me a feeling of relief.

I was represented by a solicitor arranged by the Twins. He got bail for me, and as I came out of court I was met by a friendly driver telling me that Ronnie wanted to see me at his mother's house in Vallance Road. It was there that he explained what had happened.

After the event with those blokes at the Barn, two of The Firm, Limehouse Willy and Billy Exley, were coming out of the Cellar club and caught the tail end of the fight, or so they said. Being worse the wear for drink, they thought they'd teach the mugs a lesson and, carrying a very large knife, they followed the men about five hundred yards away from Wilton Place and the club. Coming up behind them, they decided to spring them.

As they attacked the men, their victims turned on them, taking the knife off Billy Exley and punching him so hard that he went down on the ground. Willy was coming unstuck, too, so they both ran. Billy was tripped up and they booted him in the face. Willy pulled him up, but two plain clothes policemen who were observing another incident ran over and pulled the guys off Exley. In the confusion, Limehouse and Exley sprinted away. Not wanting to get involved with the police, they licked their wounds.

Ron and Reg were very loyal and paid for the defence of George and myself. We appeared in court about five times – and on the last occasion things looked bad for us. The blokes who tried to gain entry to the club had conveniently mixed up the two fights and, to get themselves off, said it was me and George who had beaten them up and lied to the judge in court.

I realised that the policeman was our most reliable witness and asked for him to be called. When he got into the dock, it seemed he had lost his book containing their names and did not remember much of the incident at all. Not surprisingly, I was angry to think we were being fitted up and explained the full story from my point of view to the judge.

He challenged the PC, who said he had lost his original notebook or it had been stolen from his locker! There was too much doubt in our favour and the judge found us both 'Not guilty'. George and I were relieved that we were not having to go to the High Court.

I asked my solicitor to apply for costs. When he requested this, the judge replied, 'Ask the Kray twins for costs. I am certain they will oblige.'

I was right: the CID did not care who they nicked as long as it was a body. The Twins paid for everything, though, and were loyal throughout. That's the stuff of true friendship, isn't it?

a twist of fate

A very good friend and business associate of mine was taking a young lady friend out for the evening. Although married, he felt the environs of Knightsbridge would be a safe enough distance from his palatial family home in Kent to enjoy a tête-à-tête with his friend.

Knowing that I ran a night club in the area, he invited me to join him and his companion after they had watched an evening of professional boxing at Earls Court arena. I had told him that the Barn Twist club that I managed was unlicensed, purposely protecting the Twins' more lucrative investment, the licensed Esmeralda's Barn casino club on the top floor of the building.

'Can we be your guests in the casino, Laurie?' asked my friend. 'I like a gamble and I'm sure my friend would love it, too.'

I declined the offer, for my friend had mentioned that his girlfriend was secretary to a leading crime reporter, Tom Tullett, who was not exactly enamoured of the brothers' operation in London, having written unkindly about them previously.

I arranged to have some time off and meet them after the fights had finished, telling them that we could have a drink and a chat at 'Le Monde', a quiet little drinking club at World's End, Chelsea, run by Georgie Osborne's wife Jeanette, a vivacious beauty. The club was generally very busy during the daytime, so I assumed that it would be empty by the time we arrived after 10 pm. I collected my friend and his petite young lady, who I thought would have seemed out of place at a boxing match, portraying an air of dignity as she climbed into the back seat of my Humber Super snipe saloon car.

Arriving at the club, I was astonished to be met by the presence of at least thirty or more men standing in a small, closely-packed group away from the bar. Quickly glancing around, I recognised Ronnie Kray and some more of the faces with him. My guests were signed in as Mr and Mrs Richards and I signed in as Mr Levy, a business name I sometimes used.

Placing my guests as far from the bar and the powerful-looking group of men as I possibly could, we sat down at a table set along a wide passageway. We were at the other end of the room from the counter and about thirty feet from the main dancefloor. I hoped that we had hidden our lovely lady guest from the eyes of any boozy Romeo with devious intent, but I had a premonition that trouble was not far away.

There were two swarthy blokes in the corner of the bar. When I went up for a round of drinks, I established that they were not with the other crowd in the club. The two roughly dressed men were boozy and noisy, one much more so than the other. I knew that their behaviour would grate on Ronnie, who hated loud, flash people, so just hoped that he knew them and they would respect him.

I ordered drinks for my friends, who were oblivious of the possible danger I had anticipated. Of course, I was also with a crime reporter's secretary and would be very unpopular if there was any trouble. Collecting our drinks, I noticed as I looked into a mirror at the back of the bar that the taller and louder of the men was trying to get some form of eye contact with me. I stared straight ahead, pretending not to notice him, but watched in the mirror.

I have been around too long to get into that one. The ingredients are always the same – eye contact, the smile, the insult, the battle. I didn't want a row then, as it would have been disastrous for my guests, who were such nice people and I did not want their evening spoilt by a drunk. It may have been that this man wanted to impress my pal's girlfriend with his toughness, but I didn't intend to find out, so I quietly returned to the table.

Put yourself in my position. If the man had started a quarrel with me, thinking I was alone with my two friends, he would have been shocked to find that all the others in the club were pals of mine, too. I had mentioned quietly to Ronnie Kray while at the bar that I had popped away from Esmeralda's for a quiet drink with these lovely people for a little while. After all, Ronnie was my boss, though he understood that I would never take liberties. I told him my reason for not taking them into the casino at Esmeralda's and he agreed.

Ron said that he would tell the others so we would be left to ourselves in the quiet end of the club. I also knew that if the man in the corner had dug me out, I couldn't have swallowed a challenge in front of my pals, so the consequence would have been disastrous for him with the mood

Ronnie appeared to be in. I could tell something was upsetting him, but unless he told you what it was, you never asked. However, he seemed very restless.

After a few minutes, I was aware of the man who had been trying to catch my eye heading into the toilet. The next thing I knew, Ronnie was whispering in my ear, 'Get him out of the carzey, Lol.' Ronnie placed a hand gently on my right shoulder as I sat facing my friends with my back to the men's toilet. 'The bastard called me fat. Fucking cheek.'

I turned round, trying to shield Ronnie from my friends for obvious reasons. Ron had a knife in his hand. I stood up, ignoring his instruction to get the man out of the toilet. Placing a bar towel around the knife, I walked Ronnie back to his friends.

Someone managed to get Ronnie away from the club. Another older man said to me that Ron was going to the 'Cambridge Rooms', a restaurant the Twins had recently taken over in Kingston, Surrey.

Returning to my seat at my guests' table, I was planning to pacify them, hoping also that they had not seen too much. They were full of questions: 'Do you know these people?' 'Who were they?' 'What was that all about?'

As we spoke, a commotion was taking place in the toilet behind us. My friend's eyes widened as he looked over my shoulder. Not looking round, I purposely smacked him with my open hand on his cheek. My action worked, as both my friends were shocked at me.

I had deliberately distracted them from seeing a man smothered with a large towel being carried out from the toilet. Rapidly, I explained he had injured himself falling in a drunken stupor onto a hand basin, smashing it from the wall. I added that he had cut his head so badly that an ambulance had been called, and that it didn't look nice with those two gawping at him, even though his face was covered in towelling.

I am certain that they did not believe me, but it was all I could offer as an excuse, and did not want them to be witnesses to any act of my friends whatsoever. They were having an illicit affair anyway, so Mr and Mrs Richards were to all intents and purposes unavailable.

We left the club, making for my two-tone car that had been left with its parking lights on in the road directly outside. A small crowd was standing around two men, who looked as if they were either crouched or sitting on the kerbstone a few feet away from my car. As we pulled away, I heard someone say, 'There they go.'

At that point, I'd no idea what had happened in the Le Monde club. Ronnie had obviously 'done' someone, but I was just glad to get my friends out of the way. They had enjoyed a good drink, but I wasn't drinking, having to go back to my job at Esmeralda's, so drove my guests to a taxi rank. Would you believe that they thanked me for a lovely, if different, night and said that we should do it again some time!

I wasn't in the club for more than half an hour when Reggie, who hadn't been at Le Monde, rang Esmeralda's wanting to talk to me. 'The fellow is in a bad way, Lol,' he said. 'Ronnie cut him for calling him a "fat bastard" and telling him that he was a good fighter once, but is too fat now.'

The story was unravelling. Ronnie went into the toilet with the man, who was expecting a straightener with fists with him, not to be cut with a knife as badly as he was.

Ronnie was incensed by the man's remarks in front of his mates, and flipped. Reggie told me the police knew I was at the club and that the Twins would be with me if I got a pull. Naturally, we would protect Ronnie.

The man who had originally looked for a row with me had, unfortunately for him, caught Ronnie on a bad night. Luckily, he survived and was visited in hospital by some members of The Firm, who found him to be a very likeable chap, really. It was the same old case – the booze was in and the wit was out.

Although Ronnie was delighted with high-class guests to Esmeralda's Barn and the Barn Twist club, he could not abide lesbians, and was directly responsible for closing the Cellar club. At that point, the Cellar was fetching in about £500 a week to his coffers. Apart from the fact that it was then a tidy sum, the Cellar was never any trouble to either of the other clubs in the building.

'Close it, Laurie!' Ron demanded. 'It's filthy what women do,' emphasising the 'filthy' and making his loathing very obvious.

'But our mums are women, Ron,' I replied.

'They're different,' came his quick response, not wishing to be outdone. 'They are real ladies, ain't they, Lol?' he said, with the accent on the ladies, which he pronounced deliberately slowly.

'That's a bit hypocritical of you, ain't it, Ron? And the club's getting you £500 a week.' I defended the Cellar as the girls running it were nice people.

'Don't matter! Close it soon,' was his reply.

One day, it finally was closed as Ron had requested,

much to the annoyance of Reg and Charlie. Of course, Ron had the final say in the matter.

Soon, the building started to lose money, but Ron was happy for it to remain a West End haunt for The Firm. Joey Bailey, the cheeky kid who had blown up a car outside the Regal and ended up running errands for Ronnie, told me of an incident one night at Esmeralda's. Ronnie gave Joe a bag to keep in a safe place. It was very heavy, so Joe hid the bag underneath a table, safely out of harm's way, he thought. The next day, Ron asked Joe where the bag was.

Ronnie was furious when Joe told him that he had put it under a table in my office without telling me. 'Go and get it right away!' he ordered. 'We're going to the East End.'

Having retrieved the bag, Joe and another man called Ossie were driven by Ronnie to Commercial Road. The journey was horrendous, as Ron was a terrible driver, keeping to a twenty-mile-an-hour limit and hitting pavement kerbs on the way.

Arriving at a club called Farmers, Ron proceeded to take three guns from the bag, giving one to each of them. 'Come on,' he instructed. 'I've got to see someone in here.'

It was obvious that Ron expected to be obeyed. Putting the gun in his pocket, Joe was still puzzled by Ron's behaviour. Entering the club, Ronnie saw the person he was looking for.

'Go outside and start the car up,' he said, turning to Joe. 'And keep the engine running until we come out.'

Joe did as requested, wondering how on earth he had got himself into this position. He never knew what happened in the club, but Ron and Ossie came out after a couple of minutes, hurriedly jumping into the car. Ron told Joe to drive them to Esmeralda's.

On the way back, Ron commented on Joe's driving skills. 'You're a good driver Joe,' he said. 'Ain't he a good driver, Ossie?'

Ron turned slightly to Ossie, who was sitting in the back of the car. A non-driver, Ossie grunted in agreement, just happy that he wasn't experiencing Ron's awful driving.

As they neared the club, Ron asked Joe how long he had been driving.

'About eighteen months,' he replied confidently, with a half grin.

'Well, like I said, you're very good,' added a very impressed Ron.

They entered Wilton Place, and as Joe parked the car outside the Barn, Ron asked him, 'How long have you had a licence?'

'Oh! I haven't got one,' said Joe with a smile.

Ron was furious. 'You silly bastard!' he spat out. 'You could have got us into a lot of trouble. We were uninsured, too, and you could have got nicked.'

Ron went into a sulk with Joe, not speaking to him for a few days. He had completely ignored the real trouble they would all have been in if, due to Ron's dreadful driving, they had been stopped with guns in the car. And it would all have been his fault . . .

Eventually, though, Ron lost interest in Esmeralda's and became more concerned with the new restaurant, the Cambridge Rooms. The Barn was finally closed due to a massive tax demand from the Inland Revenue. He never paid, of course!

a lord and a laddish act

In July 1964, the *Sunday Mirror* carried a headline that read PEER AND A GANGSTER: YARD PROBE. The feature stated that meetings had been taking place between a leading London gangster and a famous peer.

Derek Jameson, then picture editor of the *Sunday Mirror*, was ecstatic. What a scoop! When a few photographs were delivered to the paper showing the Conservative Lord Boothby and Ronnie Kray together, the editor was delighted. This was a real exclusive. As this all occurred just before a general election, this would shake the Conservatives considerably.

But the next week's newspaper was headlined THE PICTURE WE MUST NOT PRINT. The paper stated it had a photograph to prove the identity of the peer and gangster. But when Boothby found out that the story was about him and Ronnie Kray, he was suicidal, according to a close friend. The year before, soon after the Profumo scandal, in which John Profumo resigned as a Member of Parliament because of his association with a high-class call girl, Christine Keeler, Boothby had been made a Life Peer by Harold Macmillan. Ironically, the Premier's wife Dorothy had been Boothby's lover for over twenty-five years.

The new Lord Boothby was saved by the production of more photographs that also showed two other men. One was Boothby's lover Les Holt, the other Mad Teddy Smith, the dark-haired lover of Labour MP Tom Driberg. Now an attack on Lord Boothby would backfire with disastrous effect for Labour leader Harold Wilson.

Dramatically, offers of assistance arrived for Boothby from two of the Labour Party's top legal men, Arnold Goodman, Harold Wilson's solicitor and confidante, and Gerald Gardiner, QC. The resulting action went as follows.

Scotland Yard issued a statement saying they were not investigating the case. The *Sunday Mirror* offered an apology to Boothby with an out-of-court settlement of £40,000. Ronnie Kray received an apology from a junior member of the *Mirror*, but no money was ever mentioned. It was a complete and utter cover-up.

The only good derived for the brothers Kray was explained by Derek Jameson. If anything were given to Fleet Street about them, the answer was: 'Forget it. They are dangerous. They cost us forty grand. Leave 'em alone!' This action gave the Twins carte blanche with their underworld activities as far as the Press were concerned, but not Scotland Yard and 'Nipper' Read, the policeman determined to nail the Krays.

A pattern was forming: they were becoming personal targets of Read. While delving into the activities of The Firm, Read was contacted by Hew Cargill McCowan, a high-class homosexual. McCowan had re-opened 'The Hideaway', a club formerly run by Albert Dimes and Frankie Fraser, conquerors of the former King of Soho, Jack Spot.

When the club opened, it was suggested by a member of The Firm that a pension should be paid to stop any trouble occurring. When this was refused, the club had a visit from a drunken Mad Teddy Smith, who proceeded to wreck the joint, throwing things about and generally breaking things up. This was ridiculous, so the new owner, Hew McCowan, called the police.

The case was passed to Nipper Read, who thought that it was the breakthrough needed to nail the Kray gang. Witnesses, including McCowan, were willing to appear along with the manager of the club, Sidney Thomas Vaughan.

Lord Boothby was persuaded to seek an intervention on behalf of the Krays in the House of Lords, causing uproar when the case did get to court. As before, the Krays filled the newspapers, along with Mad Teddy Smith. But the evidence against them was not sufficient to encourage the jury to find them guilty. Witnesses had been got at, causing McCowan and Read's case to collapse. Much to their annoyance, ironically, the Krays bought the lease of The Hideaway, becoming the new owners. They renamed it 'El Morocco'.

I was invited to the opening night, along with my brother-in-law Ron Turner. It was interesting to see the different types of guests as they arrived. Many were sporting personalities from the worlds of boxing and football. This was to be expected as the Twins were good sportsmen and loved mixing with stars.

As the club became more crowded, I found a place alongside the bar counter. Tucked out of the way, a comforting breeze brushed our faces when a door from the kitchen into the yard at the back of the club was opened. Alongside us was Spurs international footballer Dave McKay, nursing a broken leg that was still in plaster. It was rumoured that Nipper Read was invited by the Twins. He would have been game to be present with such a motley crew.

After a short time, journalist and author Daniel Farson appeared. Farson was an obnoxious-looking, drunken friend of Hew McCowan – now the former owner of the club and loser in court to the Twins. Farson talked rather loudly, in an irritatingly camp way, for all and sundry to hear about his unfortunate friend Hew. It was quite funny when Ronnie Kray came over to me, completely ignoring Farson.

'Do me a favour, Lol,' said Ronnie. 'Would you sling him out discreetly? He's trying to cause trouble for us on behalf of his friend, but with all these people here and the Press it would not do us any good if we did something ourselves, would it?'

Ronnie Turner and I waited for Ronnie Kray to get away from the bar area then moved each side of Farson, who was portly and intoxicated so could have caused a scene. Taking an arm each, before he could say a thing, we bundled him through the kitchen door into the back yard, then lifted him into an empty dustbin, plonking the seat of his arse in first. Farson's weight wedged him tightly up to his armpits, so that only his arms and legs were visible. Although he was shouting, the noise of the entertainment in the club and the kitchen drowned out his voice entirely. A word to the kitchen staff to let him cool down worked wonders, too. Before we left, we told Ronnie Kray what we had done.

Thanking us, he told us that he thought it was 'Marvellous!' How quietly we had done it, too.

The opening of the club attracted much publicity, and the photos in the papers the next day had all the usual suspects – Ronnie, Reggie and Mad Teddy Smith. I didn't know Mad Teddy Smith all that well. However, I had known Les Holt for many years. Then in his early twenties, Les was only about five feet, seven inches in height, but with a good muscular physique gained from the boxing ring at his local Lion Boys Club. He was a good boxer.

I well remember the first time I met Les, for it was also the first dance hall I can recall the Twins and I going to. Held at Shoreditch Town Hall, it was exciting for us in our early teens to mix with boys and girls from another area.

Shoreditch Town Hall was a large, old, imposing building situated opposite the magistrates' court and police station in Old Street. The older boys would play a dice game for money, but as this was illegal, they used the vast area of the cloakroom or toilets to gather round in a circle, throwing dice. It was comical to see the gamblers scarper away when policemen from the nick opposite raided the hall looking for the gamblers, who jumped through the toilet windows into a yard outside, panic-stricken lest they got caught.

It was amusing for us to watch as we were not gamblers and did not get involved. On reflection, both things were stupid – for the police to raid the toilets to catch these gamblers and for the boys to escape. The fine was usually trivial, but it made you a criminal, and for some of the elder boys that was not good, especially if it were reported in the local newspaper. These raids occurred nearly every week, so made going to the Town Hall a bit more exciting than just dancing, at which we were not very good anyway.

Mingling with the crowd after a raid, I met a boy called Ronnie Holt, who was looking for a friend who'd had the misfortune to be genuinely going to the toilet when a raid had happened. He was concerned as it was the boy's first time at the dance and Ronnie was responsible for him. When we located the lad, he was delighted with the experience, telling us proudly how he had managed to outwit the coppers by pretending he was only using the loo and that they had believed him! This was the truth, but the excitement made him feel like a villain. He told this story to all his mates with relish. From that day on, I struck up a friendship with Ronnie Holt, who lived with his parents in New North Road, Islington. They all crammed into a small terraced house on the bridge of a canal. All told, there were nine children in the Holt family.

During my friendship with Ronnie, I became familiar with most of this likeable family. They were typical of the time, poor but happy, like us. I enjoyed my visits to the Holt household, which was where I met younger brother Leslie, who already had a reputation as a scoundrel, having been sent to an approved school for delinquents. Life is often so strange, for who would have predicted that in the years to follow Les Holt would become a key figure in the peer and gangster scandal of 1964?

Much of what actually went on at that time – and the circumstances of Les Holt's mysterious death in 1979 – I only found out much later. When the Kray Twins were arrested in 1968, I had a visit at home from Les, who was not his usual flamboyant self. He was more seriously intent on discussing Ronnie Kray with me, anxious that Ron knew things about him and would implicate him in their trial.

Les suggested that I tell the Twins he had placed with a solicitor all the details of any dealings he had had with Ronnie Kray and others, although he never specifically explained in great detail just how he could have been implicated in their arrest. I was left wondering about his strange request. Les was able to confide in me enough to say that the information he had to disclose about Ronnie and others would certainly rock the political world. I hastened to tell him that in my opinion the Krays were in enough trouble themselves without having to worry about him or his friends. I added that I would not mention him to Ron or anyone else, as doing so might cause the police to take an interest in him and could bring everyone concerned unnecessary grief.

Exactly as I had forecast, no mention of Les was ever brought up in the case against the Twins, and they certainly were not going to volunteer any information that might implicate themselves, for they were fighting for survival.

I often thought about Les and his meeting with me in 1968. Although I saw him many times after the Twins' imprisonment, we never discussed anything of a criminal nature, and he never hinted about the meeting we had when the Krays were first charged. To all intents and purposes, Les appeared to be settled in his antique business until his strange death in 1979 from an overdose of Valium during an operation to remove warts on the bottom of his feet. Then, quite recently, I received a telephone call from Frank Kyrello, a friend of mine in Leeds.

Frank asked me if I would appear in a documentary entitled 'The Peer and the Gangster', giving me a number to call. Purely out of interest only, I called the producer of the programme, who asked if I would attend their offices in Soho to discuss the project. Obviously, I agreed. Although I knew I had nothing to tell them about Ron Kray and Lord Boothby, it would be interesting for me to know just what they were up to. I said I would expect payment if I had any information for them, knowing darn well that I had not, but I made it seem more authentic by suggesting a fee.

Arriving at the offices, which were situated above a small terraced house in Beak Street, I announced myself on the intercom and climbed the rickety stairs, arriving at the entrance to a room about twelve feet by ten feet in diameter. There were a couple of desks, which made it appear very overcrowded. Leading from this room was another small office. On a wall were cinema advertising posters. One showed a film about the American General Patten, whilst a wall opposite had another of Winston Churchill.

I could see why they wanted to talk about Lord Boothby; it was going to be about politics. I knew then that the information they required would be over my head, as I was not into politics and would have nothing to interest them.

'Mr O'Leary?' The quiet, friendly voice from a young lady receptionist greeted me. She then introduced me to the producer, who appeared from another room. He was a very pleasant man. After I was given some coffee, he began to explain just what the documentary was about. They were investigating the relationship between Ronald Kray and Lord Boothby. The producer asked if I would mind him asking me some questions, beginning with did I know about any affair between Ron and Boothby? I told him I knew that Ron was interested in young, athletic teenagers with beautiful teeth, but that, somehow, I felt Boothby did not fall into that category. Next, he produced a photograph showing Mad Teddy Smith, Lord Boothby, Ron Kray and Leslie Holt. Did I have any information on Teddy Smith? Did I know if he were still alive? Did I know where he was?

When I gave a negative response, the producer seemed disappointed that I did not know much about Teddy Smith at all, except that he had disappeared before the arrest of the Kray firm in 1968. His information that I had some unpublished photographs that maybe they could use was futile, too, for I would not let anyone use photos that I had of the Twins or friends unless it was to benefit them in some way. I let the producer know that since the 1950s I had acquired many photographs of Kray associates, but none of Teddy Smith. I wondered what information he was looking for on Teddy Smith. His attention on him made it all very sinister. Did they know something that I wanted to know?

'Who's that?' I asked, pointing to the photograph that included Les Holt with the others. He explained that he was the son that Boothby had always wanted: there was no more than that at all.

It seemed he had nothing further to tell me and obviously I was not interesting enough for them. It was explained to me that the programme was a low-budget documentary and I left, making a note of the date expected for the transmission. I neither wanted nor received any payment for my interview.

But my interest in Les Holt was renewed, and I decided I would try once again to contact my old friend, his brother Ronnie Holt. Apart from anything else, I wanted to feel happy that I would not upset the family by anything I would write about Les here. For example, did they know about his activities and his homosexual relationship with Lord Boothby? I did not want to be the one to break that news to them.

I was unsuccessful in finding Ronnie Holt. I tried by telephoning several R. Holts in the area of London he had lived, even leaving messages on answerphones, but to no avail. But by a stroke of excellent good luck, I was attending the once-a-month meeting of the London Ex-Boxers' Association in Kings Cross with my good friends Terry Bay and Terry Spinks, a former Olympic Gold Champion boxer, when I bumped into young Billy Meek, a good friend of Les Holt for many years.

We talked about Les and his involvement with Christine Keeler and Boothby. It transpired that I knew almost as much as he did. It emerged that Billy, too, had been asked to appear on television to talk about Les on 'The Peer and the Gangster'.

Billy caused me some amusement by telling me that they had suggested filming him in silhouette. He remarked that with his flat nose and obvious nasal tone he would have been recognised by a blind man.

On Monday 23 June, 1997, I settled down with intent to watch the programme, which formed part of the TV channel's *Secret History* series.

Ronnie Kray and Lord Boothby were the main characters in the programme. Later, I found out the entire feature had been written with the full co-operation of John Pearson, author of *Profession of Violence: the Rise and Fall of the Kray Twins*. Mr Pearson had vital information given to him by Violet Kray whilst he was writing his book. This included a case full of press cuttings and letters from Boothby, including photographs.

The programme related how Lord Boothby, a man of upper-class breeding, met and fancied Les Holt enough to fall in love with him. Les was a poor boy from a deprived area of London. Meeting Boothby was something he could only have dreamt about. Of course, it helped that they were both bisexuals. Boothby was attracted by the smartly dressed youth with nice features, a chiselled jaw, a shock of brown hair that fell loosely over his brow sufficiently to highlight his devilish eyes, and a smile that produced a set of gleaming white teeth. In 1963, Boothby wrote to Holt's parents, giving them cause to be grateful to him for looking after their son. After all, this figure of respectability had taken Les under his wing, introducing him to the arts, the world of opera and West End shows. Now divorced, Boothby talked of Les as the son he never had. Of course, what they did not know was that he had said the very same thing about a young black dancer he had met in the 1950s . . .

Writing in the *Independent on Sunday* in June 1997, John Pearson pointed out that what Boothby did not know was that Les Holt was having an affair with Ronnie Kray, too. It all started to make sense to me now, with the bits of information I had collected, added to the conversations I'd had with Les, the anxiety shown by him when the Twins were arrested, and his suggestion that I tell Ronnie about his dossier lodged with his solicitor. But what had Les and the Krays known, and about whom? Was this the key reason why the Krays had been kept in prison so long? And what about Les Holt's mysterious death?

blackmail beckons

'They killed him, Lol. They thought he knew too much.' So said Ronnie Kray when I visited him in Broadmoor and we were discussing Leslie Holt.

'I feel sorry for his family, sad really,' he continued. 'They are only working class like ourselves, Lol.'

Leslie Holt's job was as a window cleaner, working for a large company in the City. Like most lads of his age in the area, he indulged in petty thieving. It was nothing too big, just little bits to help with his meagre wages. In his job, the occasional portable radio or camera was sufficient until he was rewarded with a better paid position cleaning windows in high-class houses in the plush Knightsbridge and Kensington areas.

This disappointed him in many ways, for although his wages were a little better, the pilfering came to a standstill. Through the windows of these grand, often five-storey, houses he was unable to see the rich pickings of the smaller, more modest homes in suburbia. All these splendid properties in the classy areas contained were lots of paintings of old people, an abundance of gigantic furniture, desks with ornate lamps, but nothing for him to take discreetly and sell, so his weekly earnings were reduced despite a salary increase.

Speaking with some friends of his dilemma, it was suggested that he should steal a small painting or vase, but as Les wouldn't understand their value, how would he know what price to get when he sold them? Les, who was quite a bright young man, spent a little money on antique books, but these confused him even more as all this old furniture looked the same. Then, another friend told him about the early morning, open-air, Friday antique market in Bermondsey, south-east London. Just down the road from Tower Bridge, it still runs today and attracts tourists from throughout the world, all eager for that special bargain. Furthermore, I believe it's the only market in the country where, due to some old charter, it is quite legal to offer nicked goods for sale.

This was more like it! Les just loved the type of people in the antique business. Now, Les' attitude changed and he became Bohemian, with his hair a little longer, clothes a touch more casual. Once Les gained sufficient knowledge from his new friends, he soon made his sideline more profitable than his previous one in suburbia. His new friends in antiques loved Les' amiable personality, for he was very likeable. Naturally, Les sought out the rogues who would buy his ill-gotten gains. In his own way, he was quite a laid back character, not at all brash. Although married, he had an eye for the ladies, attracting those of a higher social standing, probably cleverly calculated by Les.

The young debs of the time found the rough and smooth shades of his lifestyle in line with their lust for adventure, so he was nearly always in the company of a beautiful young lady, keeping his bisexuality close to his chest. The value Les gained from his new high-flying associates urged him to look for more lucrative pastures. He became interested in the locked drawers of desks and cabinets, for maybe they held keys to a safe. His background of thieving made the most difficult, supposedly thief-proof lock child's play to his deft fingers.

What he was to find surprised even Les. Some of the owners of these valuable properties were very influential people, government officials and politicians among them. In their locked drawers and safes, he found many books and photographs of an illicit nature, whetting his appetite and creating an interest that he found irresistible. Perhaps the owners of these photographs – often of a pornographic nature – would pay to get them back, stolen or not, with no questions asked?

From information given to me later, it seems that Les began a very lucrative business in blackmail. Some of his more mature lady friends were high-class prostitutes who Les felt would be useful in his new business. Somewhere along the line, he also attracted a homosexual element of politicians and professional businessmen, among them Lord Boothby.

He became involved with celebrities of all kinds and one day he did much to liven up Jubilee Street, Stepney. In the early sixties I owned a fruit shop there that I had bought in 1958 off Alex, a man whom I knew from Spitalfields. He was a wheeler and dealer and always had something to sell cheap – bent or otherwise – so no questions were asked.

Alex could get almost anything, so I thought a fruit shop would be a good idea. I understood fruit and veg from the market time, so knew lots of firms to buy from and the salesmen who would possibly arrange good deals. I gave

Alex £100 for the lease, the rent being £4.00 a week.

Jubilee Street is in Stepney's predominantly Jewish area. It was a wonderful community, with a good selection of shops – Jack the baker's, Morrie Clapper, the delicatessen, and John Bright the newsagent and tobacconist. There would be queues at Gold Brothers' chicken shop, at the fried fish shop that used batter made with matzo meal and at the wet fish shop. Then there was Manny the barber, Gordon and his Ladies' Shoe Shop, the salt beef shop just around the corner and Ginny Kornblum, the sweet shop. Nancy, a retired call girl, was always ready to tell tales of when she was a girl and how she robbed punters of their money if they wanted more than her company. The favourite was to 'spin 'em over', to use her expression.

'Them Yanks, they deserved it, Laurie,' she would say. 'They had loads of money and was so flash.'

It was a street so colourful that it exploded with character. I loved it there. Nancy, the old brass, would be in every day, often nicking something from the elaborate show of fruit and veg. Another lady would bring back some of her fruit saying that it had gone bad. Of course, I changed it, until her sister warned me not to do so.

'She keeps it on a shelf above a radiator, Laurie,' she said. 'It's sure to go off, darling.' After that, there were no more exchanges for her.

Of course, I was not making a profit from the fruit and veg, but had kept up the good work of the previous tenant, Alex. I became a fence, in the beginning purely because people came in asking if Alex could get a television or other goods, why couldn't I? Alex would pop round frequently to supply his regulars with bent gear.

One day, great interest was aroused when Les arrived at my shop driving a top-of-the-range Jaguar E Type convertible, a present from Lord Boothby for his favourite 'son', Les told me excitedly. His very glamorous companion was Miss Christine Keeler.

The high-class call girl, prominent in the recent Profumo scandal trial, slid from the low passenger seat. The sight of Christine's long, slender legs was enough to stop the traffic of ladies crossing the road outside the shop as they took their children to the local Redmans Road Primary School. There was a buzz of excitement. The street hadn't seen anything as thrilling since I tried to sell pork sausages in the shop and Jewish locals threatened to boycott it!

Leaving Christine with my assistant Barry Shotter, Les insisted that I enjoy a ride in his new toy. I lay rather than sat in the plush leather passenger seat, which was still warm from Christine's shapely backside, with my legs at right angles to my trunk. Les accelerated away, pushing my head into the back headrest rather roughly.

'Hold on, Les!' I said. I felt that I should let him know we were in a cobblestoned Victorian road, not Brands Hatch racetrack. I arrived back at the shop after a most unpleasant ride; for me it had been too fast, in a residential street with children crossing the road.

By now Barry Shotter had managed to get a large group of people to form a queue outside the shop as excited locals entered in twos, talking to Christine and requesting autographs. I overheard conversations outside the shop, with people collectively saying what a lovely girl she was, and that, 'They must have used her,' meaning, of course, the government of the day. 'She's beautiful,' people added, and I had to agree.

Les was very proud of his association with Christine, suggesting that he had almost 'made it' in his fantasy world of fame. It was noticeable that he was flattered by the attention he had caused by their visit to see me. I liked Les and was pleased he came to see me with his famous friend. As it was, the customers talked about it for many weeks, forever asking when Christine was coming back.

Another time when Les surprised me was during my period of managing Esmeralda's Barn. During a comparatively quiet night, he suggested I leave someone else in charge of the club for half an hour as he wanted to show me something. We went to a mews house close by in Knightsbridge. It was only a short distance from the club.

Les put his fingers to his lips, motioning for us to be quiet. As we entered through the front door of the house, in the dim light I could see the room was elaborately furnished in period style. Gently pushing open a door to another room, we entered a small bedroom with fitted wardrobes and sliding mirrored doors.

Easing open a door, Les pointed to the back wall of the dark, empty wardrobe. I wondered just what he was doing and why the silence?

'It's a two-way mirror,' he whispered.

As I peered into the darkness, I then realised that I could see through the back panel of the wardrobe into the next room. The scene I witnessed was that of a masked, naked man whipping a young, nude girl spread across a mechanical horse, the type used by gymnasts. She was fastened at her hands and feet. The whole thing was perverse. I had seen nothing like it before or since.

'What does he get out of this?' I whispered to Les.

Again, he motioned me to be quiet. With fingers placed on his lips, his eyes gave a glance to the street door.

I waited until we left the house for Les to explain that the man was a leading politician who paid £100 to the girl for each lash of the whip. Les also explained that the house was once owned by Stephen Ward, the psychiatrist who committed suicide after being implicated in the Profumo scandal.

I did not need the brains of a prime minister to realise that Les was involved in a very suspicious business. Christine Keeler at the shop with him; now Stephen Ward's house; stories of blackmail; all gave me reason to believe Les was perhaps a leading figure in procuring women or men for these high-profile characters.

I saw Les spasmodically and could not help but notice he was always in the company of a beautiful lady, often with good-looking young boys, too. He never shunned me, but always had time to visit me at home in the East End or at Esmeralda's. Similarly, he always had time for a conversation, was forever pleasant and very likeable.

Les never boasted about money, but just seemed content to climb socially, enjoying his circle of friends. He would frequently visit Esmeralda's to see Ronnie Kray and we would chat for a while.

In a sense, Les Holt led a curious life. But his death was even more curious, for Harley Street doctor Gordon Kells was charged with his unlawful killing by administering a massive overdose of anaesthetic prior to operating on him.

Kells' defence was that due to a minor brush with

another vehicle on the way to his surgery, his concentration was clouded and he accidentally gave two separate doses of anaesthetic. Holt was rushed to hospital, where he later died due to complications.

At the resulting Old Bailey trial, Kells was found 'not guilty' by a jury, leaving the court a free man. Holt's family and friends were disgusted by the verdict. His sister Pat and niece Tricia Hepel were among those who shouted 'Murderer' and 'Lying murderer' at Kells as he left court.

Les' family were incensed that no evidence was provided to show the jury that Les Holt and Kells were involved in criminal activities. They were prepared to testify that they knew from Les himself that Kells was supplying information for him to burgle the homes of some of his influential clients. It was thought that, because of this, Holt was blackmailing Kells. Therefore, there was a very good reason for Kells to want Holt out of the way.

Holt's sister Pat had been intrigued by Kells' continual telephone calls to her asking if Les was around. When told that he wasn't, Kells had appeared to be in a state of panic. A couple of days of these enquiries about Les and his whereabouts ended when Kells called to be told by Pat that Les was in fact at home. With more than a sense of urgency in his voice, Kells told Pat that Les should not go to his home as it was surrounded by police, and that he would get in touch later. Bearing in mind that he was a professional man, Pat thought Kells' behaviour strange and irrational. She told Les about the call and noticed that he seemed quite unperturbed.

A short time later, Les Holt was troubled by warts on his toes. Kells performed the operation, resulting in his death.

Kells had a peculiar relationship with Les Holt, according to Kells' secretary Ricki Greasley, who was also a friend of Holt's. Apparently, they frequently teased each other when they met about wearing suspenders and garters. Ricki felt that Kells fancied Holt, and knew that they were doing some business together concerning Kells' clients.

Holt would often overpower Kells with his tremendous personality and persuasion. Consequently, his manipulative power may have been too troublesome and scary for Dr Kells. Perhaps, as Ronnie Kray suggested to me, someone else ordered Holt's demise. We shall never really know now as Kells took the secret to his grave when he died of a heart attack in 1997.

mayfair madness

Although knocked back after the failure of the Hew McCowan trial, Nipper Read had also been investigating the long firms instigated by the so-called brain of the Kray organisation, Leslie Payne, from south London.

Long firms were long-term frauds, which worked by illicitly deceiving suppliers. When payment was due, the firms closed down. I bought quite a few things from their 'long firms', all on invoice, so they were not stolen goods as far as the police were concerned. In fact, I had even sold a few bits and pieces to a security guard in our street. He insisted that he had an invoice to produce at work in the government building he was guarding. Carpets and electrical goods were always popular and easy to sell.

I did not know what a long firm was at the time, and just thought they were buying job lots cheap. All this was happening about the time Leslie Payne was around the Twins. I never liked him. Payne looked down his nose at you as if he was something special. He was a crooked snob, which is funny now, I suppose, but then he was an obnoxious bastard. I remember an incident one day at the Kentucky Club in Whitechapel where we would meet to discuss the week's business, my interest at that time being the Barn

Club underneath the Casino at Esmeralda's. Out of the blue, Les Payne accused me of buying records for my own use out of the club's finances. About three pounds a week was the amount of the accusation. Even then, it was a small sum. We were sitting with our figures for the club, both wearing collars and ties, so using his tie, I grabbed him around the neck at the top, pulling him down to the level of the table.

Big Pat Connolly, the door man at the Kentucky, ran over, but before he could interfere, Ronnie Kray appeared at the back of me. Pulling the hair near my ear, he whispered, 'Let him go, Laurie. We're getting a few quid with him.' I was really angry, but knew I had to let go. I think Ronnie found it amusing that I had lost my temper and that the smarmy Les Payne had been subjected to this humiliation. He never tried it on with me again. I would have been mad to nick off the Twins, wouldn't I? But if I had let Payne get away with the accusation, I would have been in much more trouble than a tugging of my hair. Afterwards, Ronnie and I often laughed about the incident.

But Les Payne was still around two years later, and making a lot of money for the Twins through the long firms. By this time, I was managing the society club Sibylla's for an elite group of directors that included Beatle George Harrison, Sir William Piggott-Brown, the top amateur jockey, and the evergreen disc jockey Alan (Fluff) Freeman.

This club attracted a high profile clientele, which was cleverly orchestrated by one of its directors Terry Howard, who worked in advertising. Sibylla's was a small restaurant/ discotheque situated in Mayfair's Vine Street, a narrow, winding cobbled road suitable only for the width of one vehicle. Situated between Piccadilly and Regent Street, I guess it was probably built in the days of the horses and carriages.

Entering from Regent Street, Vine Street already had three established night clubs. Al Burnet's Stork Rooms was the most famous. Directly next door was the less famous but well-run Hirondelle. Both were used by the Twins. At the time, a few doors along, was Bill Bentley's Oyster Bar, which was frequented by many a celebrity. Being next door to this prestigious seafood restaurant was one of the reasons why Sibylla's directors thought that their site was perfectly positioned.

On the other side from Bentley's was a rather infamous clip joint called Pipistrello's, which was usually visited by out-of-town businessmen looking for women of the night to entertain them. Invariably, they were taken there by black cab touts, who made a favourable living from this type of establishment. Once fares had gone in and paid the entrance fee, if customers chose to order their drinks and sit with a hostess, the taxi driver would receive the entrance fee for bringing the custom to the club. For that reason, there was often a queue of taxis lined outside Pipistrello's.

This type of club charged very high prices for their drinks and entertainment, so it wasn't unusual to see the odd person or two being thrown into the street after they had been parted from their cash with promises of a sexual encounter with one or more of the hostesses. Hence the expression 'clip joint'. The punters had been well and truly clipped of their cash!

Just why the directors of Sibylla's had chosen this site

for their exclusive club was actually beyond belief: they were obviously not streetwise. The other clubs were frequently used by London's gangsters. That kind of passing trade would have been difficult to eliminate.

As well as being manager, I was also expected to supply live musical entertainment whenever needed. I was able to find the groups through a company that we had already established, namely The Charles Kray Agency.

Getting the club prepared for the opening night in June 1966 was quite exciting, with many meetings and gatherings of those involved with the décor. Always heading these meetings was a lovely dark-haired, chisel-featured man called Kevin McDonald. In his thirties, he had wild ideas for the club. Consequently, his name fronted the club, trading as Kevin McDonald Associates.

Sibylla's was capable of 138 covers, so was quite small and intimate. Kevin engaged a well-known interior designer of the time, David 'Monster' Milanaric. In demand with the biggest stars of the day, he had just completely re-designed at high cost Mick Jagger's Cheyne Walk house in Chelsea, so it was quite a coup to get 'Monster' to design Sibylla's.

He did an excellent job, choosing an unusually cold shade of blue to be the overall colour. The tables and banquettes were covered in leather and the walls in blue felt, decked in mirrored panels. This clever combination gave an effect of spaciousness that somehow worked in making the club appear much larger.

The launch of the club was a tremendous success, with an avalanche of requests for membership, which was both very selective and expensive. The next couple of weeks saw the appearance of some very famous artistes, including

Chuck Berry, Joe Cocker, and Bill Hayley and the Comets. Agents were queuing to get their groups into this rapidly famous and fashionable club.

Sadly, after about three weeks, news drifted through that Kevin McDonald had died. I was told to keep quiet about the tragedy, and that the news could finish off Sibylla's. Nobody ever explained to me just what had happened to Kevin, of whom I had grown very fond. It appeared that he leapt off a roof in, I think, Chelsea or Fulham while under the influence of something or other. What a terrible waste of life.

As manager, I worked alongside one of the most professional restaurant managers, Paul Hadju, who took great pride in being able to recognise celebrity faces as they arrived. Paul is a very likeable man, but a class snob!

If – as often happened – James (now Lord) Hanson arrived with a party, Paul would give him an over-the-top greeting, saying, 'Hello Mr Hanson! Usual table, sir?' With a beaming smile and gleaming teeth, he just loved the association of such powerful people, albeit in his case a working one.

Once, Paul made a goof. I came into the club past a queue on the stairs and noticed George Harrison and his wife Patti. I asked Paul why George was in the queue, saying, 'Get him in quickly!' He was shocked.

'Where?' he asked. 'Show me. I don't believe you.'

Sure enough, George and Patti *were* patiently waiting for admittance to George's own club. At that period, George was in Maharishi mode, his beard and moustache being longer than usual. Paul hadn't noticed him.

'Mr Harrison,' he said. 'What are you doing in fancy

dress? I didn't recognise you.' Oops! An embarrassed Paul showed the Harrisons to the best table in the club – and why not after all that!

George, John Lennon and Paul McCartney used the club frequently, along with their childhood friends Terry Doran and Mel Evans. I do not remember Ringo Starr visiting the club much, but had many conversations with John and Paul, and was particularly fond of Cynthia, John's first wife and a lovely person. John's psychedelic Rolls Royce was often parked outside the club when they were in for the night. I could go on forever about incidents at Sibylla's, with household names from all walks of life adding colour, both good and bad!

'Laurie, can you do us a favour?' It was Ronnie Kray on the phone at Sibylla's. 'If I can, Ron!' I replied readily, wondering just what the favour might be. However, neither Ron nor Reg had ever put me on the spot in the past and I knew they would not do so now.

Ronnie explained they were having a meeting with some foreigners at the Society Club in Jermyn Street. The visitors only spoke French, and the man who was supposed to be the interpreter for them was useless. 'Can you come over here and talk to them for us before it gets too embarrassing?' Ronnie added. 'We've got to have someone we can trust.'

Ten minutes later, I arrived at the club reception to be met by an anxious-looking Ron. He was very pleased to see me, leading me to a table in the centre of this high-class restaurant. Reg greeted me with affection, and they introduced me to their guests, two very tough-looking European characters. It appeared they were discussing something they called 'the product'. I thought it was diamonds or firearms, but never felt comfortable enough to ask. It certainly was not drugs. I was able to establish this in a later conversation.

Ron began the meeting with a rather profound remark. 'Tell them we're not fucking frightened of them or their friends in Brussels!'

I began with a very diplomatic translation, merely saying, 'The Twins have no fear.'

The reply from the person nearest to me was, 'Le même chose,' which means likewise. He was not at all intimidated by Ron's body language. Diplomatically, I translated those three words into quite a few words – 'They said that they haven't come here to prove any power, and appreciate the reason for the meeting in London is to see if there is any possibility of future business.'

Thankfully, Ron accepted that explanation. With a frown, Reg urged me to tell them to get to the point of the meeting. The feeling across the table was electrifying ... and my position as the interpreter was uncomfortable. One slip of the tongue, one mistaken translation, and I was certain a battle would begin – with me right in the middle of it. Here we had two very powerful sides not giving an inch. While seemingly friendly, they were acutely aware of each other's threat.

Answering Reggie's question as to the meeting, the speaker began, 'They have a grass working for them ...' Telling of a meeting in Brussels with some of their men and a representative of the Krays, suddenly there was a police raid on the house they were in. It was surrounded and all their friends were arrested, but the Kray man got away through a window. Telling the Twins of this event and of the grass caused Ronnie to ask, 'Who's a fucking grass?' He was getting quite heated. I asked the foreigners to name the grass. 'Joe Kaufman, the American,' came the reply.

Ronnie heard them say that. As if they expected it, Reg got up from the table, went into an adjourning bar and appeared with a man in his forties. He was good-looking, but with a sickly, false smile, firmly fixed like a puppet. And who was it? None other than Joe Kaufman in person, the man who only seconds before had been accused of being a grass.

My position at this meeting was only to translate, but it was becoming obvious to me that I was in the middle of something very serious. I could see the concern on the faces of both sides. Ron explained to Kaufman that I was a childhood friend and that they fully trusted me as their interpreter. Reg then began without introducing Kaufman, so I knew he wasn't too pleased with him.

'Laurie, tell him what they have just said,' he said, leaving Kaufman standing as he returned to his place at the table. I proceeded to tell the American the story as explained. Kaufman interrupted me rudely and confidently, saying: 'No, it wasn't like that. It's not true – and I'm not a grass! I saw a means of escape through a window. That's all.'

As he came to the end of his denial, Kaufman was forced to raise his voice as a fiddler, in a surreal piece of bad timing, had approached the table playing gypsy music. At this moment, I found it hard to concentrate. What I did not know was that Ron always tipped the man to play his favourite tunes when he was in the club. But now he was briskly tipping him to play elsewhere. Was he confused or what?

Kaufman's loud, brash attitude was annoying me. I did not like this flash man. 'Shut up and listen to the full story!' I blurted out. I could not hide my emotion. This was a serious allegation from the foreigners, and he was possibly causing a dangerous confrontation that I would rather not be involved in.

Central to it all was the fact that I just knew Joe Kaufman was lying. After I shouted loudly at him to shut up, his face was a picture of astonishment. Trying to wriggle his way out of the situation by telling further lies did not help. In fact, it made things worse for him. Here he was being tried for his sins and the judges were proving very hostile. For him, the game, as it were, was well and truly up.

The foreigners were absolutely right. Kaufman *was* a grass, and at that time was working for the police against the Krays. He gave evidence against the Krays at Reg and Ron's trial.

They dismissed Kaufman from the room. The matter of 'the grass' seemed to be settled. The Europeans were content with the result, happy that the Twins had been able to control the matter satisfactorily.

With both sides now thanking me for my assistance, I began to relax, though I still felt hot from the intensity of the meeting, the heat of the room, and the thought of what might have been. The two foreigners embraced me as I prepared to leave, and I could feel the bulge of guns as we hugged closely. This proved my fear that the confrontation between Ron, Reg and the continentals could have been nasty.

I was thanked by the Twins for my involvement and, leaving the club, I welcomed the chill of the evening, breathing the heavenly polluted air with relish and a great deal of relief. The short distance across Piccadilly into Vine Street was covered in minutes. The outside neon sign of Sibylla's was welcoming. It was hard to reconcile the situation I had just left at the Society Club with the environment at Sibylla's. None of our clientele would have understood, or even believed me, if I'd tried to explain, so I had nobody to tell about where I had just been.

Arriving at the door, I bumped into Brian Jones of the Rolling Stones giving his car keys to Pedro, our Portuguese car valet. As we walked down the steps into the club, Brian asked if his girlfriend, Anita Pallenberg, had been in that night. When we were at the bottom of the stairs, the blue glass doors of the club room were opened by John Lennon, who was leaving with his buddy Mel Evans, a lovely giant of a man. As they passed, Brian muttered something. John seemed not to hear him, as he did not respond.

After a short while, Brian Jones came into the reception area to tell me that he 'wanted to punch a bloke, named Bill the Pill, who is in the club'. It appeared that he had spiked his girlfriend's drink when they were recently in St Tropez. Brian was a little the worse for booze or some other substance, so to placate him, I explained that it might be possible when the club was closing later on, but not at that moment: the club was busy with nice people and it would not look good for him. I added that I didn't like pill-pushers anyhow and he could hit him later, hoping that Bill would have left by that time.

Unfortunately, Brian took me at my word. At around

four in the morning, when we were about to close, Brian chinned 'Bill the Pill', knocking him down on the dance floor. Brian was stockily built, but as Bill was slight and frail it was no big deal. Brian then took leave of his senses, proceeding to arrive in the reception area throwing challenges to all and sundry, shouting, 'Anybody else want some?' and looking straight at me with an evil eye. But after the venture at the Society Club, this was child's play. A word in Brian's ear was sufficient to enable him to calm down and leave without any more concern. He'd had his revenge.

I was happy for the night to end, returning to the comfort and safety of my council flat at Horwood House in Bethnal Green.

a single shot

The Richardson gang was headed by Charlie and his brother Eddie. Among other members were 'Mad' Frankie Fraser and George Cornell. By the mid-sixties, the gang was acquiring power from underworld gossip concerning the torturing punishment they doled out to their enemies. A fear factor was created amongst those dealing in porn, gambling, night clubs and other circles closely associated with villains.

On the other hand, the same operators of those night clubs and porn shops in the West End of London were receiving other gossip about the Kray twins from Bethnal Green, who were becoming very strong and would challenge the Richardsons' power if necessary. The inevitable war was brewing.

Ronnie Kray was incensed when he heard that George Cornell, an East Ender by birth, was spreading gossip designed to put down the Kray Firm. A story circulated that Ronnie had tried to befriend a man to get closer to his younger brother, whom he fancied. This was instigated by George Cornell to belittle Ronnie. At the same time, Cornell is supposed to have called Ronnie 'a fat poof'. Whether Cornell said those words or not I wouldn't know, nor would

I expect many of the others who have told the story in their accounts of the Krays to know, either. In any event, legend has it that Cornell did, but the many books about the Krays all give different times and places. Nevertheless, it has been recorded and is mentioned time and again by the media when referring to the murder of George Cornell in The Blind Beggar pub in Whitechapel Road. I know that whenever he said it – if he indeed did – it would not have been in earshot of Ronnie Kray, for I also know for certain that Ron would have acted immediately rather than wait for the right time. Ronnie's schizophrenic mood would have demanded instant retribution.

In the early hours of the morning of 8 March, 1966, at a club called 'Mr Smith's' in Rushey Green, Catford, southeast London, a group of men had been enjoying a drink among other business. Whether they had been operating a protection racket at the club is not really certain, but they may have been.

According to one story, Eddie Richardson and Frankie Fraser decided to pay a visit to the club. Again, accounts differ. One story had it that they had been invited by the owners of the club to discuss the possibility of them minding it and putting their amusement machines in the bar.

In the early hours, it appears that Eddie Richardson told the owner to close the bar. This infuriated the regular clientele, who were still enjoying a drink. They were not going to be intimidated by the members of the Richardson gang and wouldn't back down. Abuse was bandied about by both sides until the action began, with Peter Hennesey from the regulars and Eddie Richardson for the intruders fighting each other. This led to a very rowdy scrap. In fact, anything went. Chairs were broken and used as weapons, a fracas comparable to the Wild West.

Then the general fighting was disturbed by a single gunshot. One account says the weapon was fired by Dickie Hart, acknowledged as a friend of Ronnie and Reggie Kray. Other guns were then produced and fired, causing a great deal of injury on both sides.

Hart ran from the club, followed by Fraser. The pair were found by the police in the hedges of a local garden. Hart was badly injured, having been shot in the face, whilst Fraser was suffering a broken leg from gunshot wounds. Eddie Richardson and other members of his gang had also been badly injured. Indeed, it appears that the Richardson gang had come off rather badly.

Their opposition, apart from Dickie Hart who died of his wounds, were able to get out of the way, although injured. Frankie Fraser was charged with Dickie Hart's murder, but later acquitted. This affray did not help the reputation of the Richardson gang.

Early on the morning of 9 March, the day after the incident, I went as usual to the house of my friends the Kray twins. I would often walk the short distance from my parents' house in Cheshire Street and had done so since a kid. Sometimes, the Twins were in. At other times, the door would be opened by their mother.

It was about 10 am when I arrived. On this occasion, the door was opened by an agitated Ronnie Kray. 'Come in, Lol.' He welcomed me with a cautious greeting. 'There may be people outside here watching the house.'

Anxious to get his words out and bubbling with

enthusiasm, Ronnie added, 'There was a gunfight last night in a Catford club.'

After closing the street door behind me, we stood in the passage as he went on, saying, 'It's a shame, but one of our good friends, Dickie Hart, was killed.'

Ronnie's eyes were on stalks as he continued. 'Richardson and Fraser's been shot, too, but I don't know if they are dead. They tried to take a liberty with some friends of ours, but came unstuck.'

Ronnie's expression was a mixture of excitement and vengeful rage. We were still standing in the passage in the same spot as he continued to tell me all the details as he knew them, adding, incensed, at the end, 'That bastard Cornell wasn't there, Lol.'

I could tell he was hell-bent on some form of action against his enemy, not then knowing that it would be so rapid. Mrs Kray offered me a cup of tea, telling Ronnie not to keep me waiting in the passage.

'He makes me laugh, Lol, keeping you there,' she said, amused by his behaviour.

I must say I found it peculiar, too, but thought it best not to mention the fact, bearing in mind the hyped-up mood Ron was in. 'It's all right, Mrs Kray,' I replied, and agreed with her that 'I'd love a cuppa tea.'

Here we were discussing murder and mayhem. In the circumstances, it seemed incongruous being offered something as everyday, as thoroughly normal, as a cup of tea, but we went into the kitchen area, followed by Ron, his shirt-sleeves rolled up. His two-inch-wide, embroidered elasticated braces, with brown, kid leather button fasteners, were fixed to his trousers, in the American gangster style familiar to him.

'Come and have a drink tonight, Lol, to celebrate,' he added. 'We'll be in The Widows in Tapp Street.'

As I seldom drank with The Firm, I knew I would not be going there, but nodded, saying, 'I've got to meet someone early, Ron. Maybe later?'

Ron smiled mockingly, commenting, 'You've always got to meet someone when I invite you out. Don't you like my company?'

I was pleased he was able to smile with me, then agreed with Ron, if only to humour him and stop him talking about the previous night's fight at Mr Smith's.

I could not believe the news when I heard it on the radio the next morning. 'A man has been shot dead in a murder at The Blind Beggar public house . . .' said the unemotional, purely factual tones of a BBC announcer. He mentioned that two men were being hunted for the murder of George Cornell: they had escaped in a car immediately after the shooting.

It seemed that George Cornell was sitting at the bar counter of The Blind Beggar, comfortably perched on a stool, talking with his friend Alby Woods and another man. They were chatting across the bar to the barmaid, who had just started her evening session. The door from the street opened. Naturally, they looked towards who had come in. It was two men, who walked unhurriedly over to George.

As if to acknowledge Ronnie Kray, the man in the lead, George, putting his hand in his pocket, said, 'Look who's here! Get them a drink.' At that moment, Ronnie pointed a Mauser pistol at Cornell's head and fired. The blast knocked him off his seat. Ian Barrie, the other man with Ronnie Kray, fired into the ceiling.

Pandemonium broke out. The men with Cornell ducked into the toilets, whilst another customer locked himself in the ladies' loo. The gunshot noise was deafening. Despite this, one old boy, still sitting at a table with his pint, was unmoved.

As calmly as they had entered, Ronnie Kray and Ian Barrie walked out of the pub into Whitechapel Road and climbed into a car that was waiting opposite The Beggar. It was being driven by Scotsman John Dickson, another member of The Firm, who took them back to The Widows pub in Tapp Street, Bethnal Green. Meanwhile, back in The Beggar, an unnatural silence had descended.

The barmaid, poor cow, was mortified. She had run screaming into the cellar, returning to sit at the top of the stairs, waiting for something to happen, expecting to be shot at. The confusion in her mind caused the silence to be deafening. The only sound was a record of the Walker Brothers singing 'The Sun Ain't Gonna Shine Anymore'. It played repeatedly, having jammed on the jukebox. Ironically for George Cornell, this was now actually true.

The voice of the pub's guv'nor, Patsy Quill, was very welcoming to the barmaid. She could hear him talking on the telephone to the police and ambulance services. Replacing the phone, he saw her cowering on the steps of the cellar. Talking to Patsy recently, he gave me his version of that night of horror:

I heard what I thought was either the backfiring of a car or gunshots. Suddenly realising it was in the pub bar downstairs, I checked that my children were locked up safely, thinking it could have been a robbery, then went down the stairs into the pub. I saw what had happened and phoned for the police and an ambulance. I saw the barmaid sitting on the stairs in a state of shock. I asked her what had happened.

Through tears, she told me that Ronnie Kray had shot George Cornell. She was about to say something else, when I raised my voice saying, 'I thought I've told you that you don't know anything or anybody when anything happens in the pub.' Thinking of comebacks, police, witnesses, I didn't want more problems caused for us. All these thoughts rushed through my mind. Then, realising that the barmaid was traumatised, I lowered my voice and asked her just what had happened. Now she was totally confused, even with me.

'I don't know anything,' she blurted out. 'I don't know who it was. You've just told me that I don't know anything and I've forgotten who it was. I've forgotten everything.'

The barmaid was so frightened that I just agreed with her, telling her it would be all right. I went into the bar. It appeared empty except for George, who was lying on the floor where he had been sitting. The stool was upturned just beside his head, which was covered in blood. His shirt was drenched in blood, too. The smell was foul – a mixture of blood, gore and gunpowder.

As I bent down, I noticed he was still breathing. The barmaid gave me some tea towels, which I put under George, holding his head in my arms.

Thoughts travelling rapidly through my head were of the consequences of the night. I had heard that morning of the previous night's murder at Mr Smith's in Catford, and that the Richardsons were involved. Now this. Although an East Ender, George Cornell was very much a member of the Richardson gang, so there would be some sort of repercussion, probably gang warfare.

Trying to make George Cornell comfortable until the ambulancemen came, and with those thoughts going around my head, I felt a presence nearby jolting me into reality. Glancing to where I had heard a slight noise, I saw, without looking upwards, a pair of rather well-worn men's black boots. The trousers were suspended about four inches above the top of the boots.

Slowly looking up, I saw that the man had a belt tied tightly round his waist. His short jacket was opened wide to reveal a pair of braces, with a scarf tied to them. A newspaper hung loosely out of his jacket pocket.

Still holding George, I was now straining my neck to meet the face of the owner of these weird clothes. His face peered down at me. He still had on his flat costermonger's cap. Then, with an expression that was as sombre as one would have expected at the time, he spoke.

'Fuck me,' he said. 'I guess he won't be drinking any more booze, will he?'

It was the old boy we knew just as Old Pop. He had been in the pub throughout all the shooting and everything. Pop seemed as cool as a cucumber, but I later realised he was in shock; he had just popped in for his regular pint and had witnessed a shooting that was later to become a murder.

The ambulancemen arrived to take George first to a local hospital, then on to another hospital in Maida Vale, where he died later that night.

Ronnie Kray arrived back at The Widows pub excited and pleased by the action of the night. The celebration of the previous night's battle at Mr Smith's paled in comparison. Ronnie let it be known, first to Reggie, that he had shot Cornell in the head and did not expect him to live. Word soon spread among the guests in the pub that Ronnie had shot Cornell. The atmosphere changed dramatically. People on the fringe of The Firm's activities did not want to be involved in gang warfare. It had been all right having a drink with them, but their bottle suddenly capsized when Trouble with a capital 'T' loomed a little too close for comfort. After all, The Blind Beggar was only a few minutes away from The Widows, which emptied quite rapidly, leaving only members of The Firm to congregate and arrange to meet at a pub in Walthamstow.

Someone was told to go and see if Mrs Kray was all right in the Twins' home. There was no member of The Firm at Vallance Road when Olive Cornell arrived, screaming at Mrs Kray about her son and that he had killed her husband. It was Mrs Kray's sister May, who lived next door to her, who argued with Olive before shutting the door in her face. This caused Olive Cornell to throw a brick through a window of the Kray family home. Neighbours called the police, who whipped Mrs Cornell away. She was charged with abusive behaviour, and later had to pay a small fine.

This same lady had earlier arrived at The Beggar. She had been telephoned by Alby Wood, George Cornell's friend, who had been with him at the bar. It was before police began questioning people who had been at the scene. When she arrived, naturally she caused an uproar, screaming at all and sundry and telling whoever was there to own up to having seen the person who had shot her husband.

Afterwards, many people felt that her behaviour was unbecoming, for wasn't her husband a member of a rival group? Surely the events of the previous evening at Mr Smith's were warning enough for George Cornell to at least stay away from his rivals' territory?

The next day, the hunt began. The investigation into the murder at The Blind Beggar was underway, with witnesses being sought by Scotland Yard. They had little or no luck: everybody knew that Ronnie Kray had shot and killed George Cornell, but without proof from witnesses there would be no charges. Good work for Ron was executed by loyal friends, who were asked to 'have a chat' with those present on the night of the murder.

The Twins were off the plot for a while. Although questioned about Cornell, Ronnie was confident nobody would dare to be witness against him, least of all the barmaid, who was unwilling to identify anybody associated with the murder. Ronnie felt he had emulated his mentor Al Capone with his deed and was untouchable. His justification that, 'I've done one of their mob because they did one of ours,' was slightly twisted, as the row in Mr Smith's was nothing to do with the Krays at all.

In fact, it had been purely a Richardson affair. Rightly or wrongly, with elder brother Charlie Richardson in South Africa, Eddie Richardson and Frankie Fraser had decided to sort out any problems at the club, with or without the permission of the owner, or indeed the resident group of locals, who had resented being told when they could or could not drink. They may have been associates of Reg and Ron, but Dickie Hart, who was murdered in the battle, was not, as has been reported, a cousin of the Krays. This confusion may have been because Ronnie Hart was a distant cousin of the Kray family and gave evidence against The Firm at their trial.

When I saw Ronnie Kray the morning after the row at Mr Smith's, he stated that Dickie Hart was a good friend of theirs. I did not know him personally, but knew that at that moment Ronnie felt genuinely sorry for Dickie and his family. I am certain he also felt an urge to use that as an excuse to kill George Cornell. When told he was on the manor the night after the murder at Catford, Ron took it as an insult to them and Dickie Hart that he had the audacity to show his face in a local pub. Although Cornell was a regular drinker at The Beggar, unfortunately his timing was wrong for him that night.

Ronnie also told me later that he never liked The Beggar and would not have killed Cornell if he had been in Ron's own local, The Grave Maurice, also in Whitechapel Road, as he liked the guv'nor there. I am sure he wasn't thinking straight when he said that, as the guv'nors of The Blind Beggar pub were really likeable and quite friendly with the Twins, although I am certain, too, that the Quills wished George Cornell had been in The Grave Maurice that night.

Patsy and Jimmy Quill and their families suffered immense psychological strain from that evening – the questioning, the aggravation of trying to put back any kind of business the pub had before the murder. It had often been frequented by villains and thieves, who were no trouble to the Quills. In fact, the villains were often well known by either them or their staff. The pub's clientele was great before it became infamous because of the murder, but for a time at least that trade of villains could not possibly be seen using The Beggar, which was being watched, or even if it wasn't, appeared that way. In the aftermath of the murder, The Beggar may have got a few macabre sightseers or tourists, but as a former pub owner I can imagine just how they felt, more so Patsy Quill, for he was living there with his family.

These days, the three-storey, red-brick The Blind Beggar still stands proud and almost imposing in an area which is a hectic architectural mix. The sign, showing a medieval-looking man dressed in black being helped by a fair-haired maiden in red, sways slightly in the breeze as heavy traffic passes by. Nowadays, it attracts not only locals, but office workers, too, who pop in for typical pub fare. A sign says, 'Kids welcome in bar garden and conservatory only.'

A plantation fan circles a touch wearily. Mirrors and pictures hang everywhere, showing tranquil country scenes or waif-like children. A flashing fruit machine attracts no one. Nor does the jukebox. Although lunchtime, it is surprisingly quiet. The lighting is subdued, but the atmosphere cheerful enough. Pip, one of the pub's cats, is sitting on a Chesterfield sofa, his olive and black eyes sharp, missing nothing. One doubts whether any of the young, instantly attentive bar staff know of the pub's history.

Glancing at The Beggar's large, brick fireplaces, one

wonders just how many people have stood there over the years. What were their stories, lifestyles, triumphs and tragedies? For like all pubs, over the years The Beggar has been host both to celebrations and calamities.

Seen through the building's leaded glass windows, people continue to scurry by, some to market stalls, others to a branch of J. Sainsbury, which now lies behind The Beggar. The drone of traffic at the busy junction and slight smell of exhaust fumes fill the air.

Pip jumps off the sofa and, tail erect, walks majestically off in search of a different scene. Who knows: perhaps he will have nine lives? Unfortunately, George Cornell had only one. And, in a sense, Ronnie Kray lost his life that night, too, because one ordinary evening saw extraordinary events at The Blind Beggar . . .

the american way

'Hello, Laurie. It's Dru Harvey here.' Dru was an agent and manager of showbusiness artistes, married at that time to vocalist Jackie Trent. It was early 1967. Dru was calling with an idea that might interest me. Maybe we would be able to meet as soon as possible? He seemed anxious, but told me little apart from the fact that the music business would not be the topic of our meeting. My interest was aroused and we arranged to meet the very next day in Oxford Street, in an Italian coffee bar near to his office.

I arrived first and was sitting at a small table enjoying my coffee, watching the world go by, when I spotted Dru entering the café. He was a small man, casually dressed. Not for him the smart suit, collar and tie of music business agents of the day. Dru dressed to be comfortable.

Spotting me, he apologised for being a little late, adding as a cliff-hanging appetiser, 'Have I got something for us to talk about!' Getting him a coffee, I could not wait to hear the reason for his excitement.

'I've had a call from a firm of solicitors in New York,' he revealed. 'They wanted me to contact you with a tentative proposition to put to your mates, Reggie and Ronnie Kray . . .'

I could not think just what the proposition could be. I knew, along with hundreds of others in the East End, that Ronnie had murdered George Cornell and that the Krays had a reputation as gangsters, but that surely would not interest lawyers in America. How wrong of me!

'... Laurie, would the Krays be interested in writing a book, with the possibility of a film, about themselves?' asked Dru.

He began to explain that the New York solicitors were acting for clients in the matter, and wanted to contact me as they knew I had managed the Charles Kray Agency, with their elder brother, Charlie. I was to be approached at the outset to see if the Twins would be interested in the idea.

'Hold on a bit, Dru!' I exclaimed, having become suspicious about the proposition. Was the whole thing a plot so that when sufficient information had been recorded the British police would have enough evidence to arrest them? They had not managed to make anything stick in the past couple of years and, of course, wanted to nail them desperately.

'Why the interest in the Twins?' I asked.

'Well,' said Dru. 'They are considered to be the equivalent of the New York Mafia; they're seen as the guv'nors of organised crime in Britain, and they're very colourful, too.'

I was still a trifle suspicious, although not of Dru. I knew he would not dare to try anything untoward with the Krays, for their reputation as villains was awesome. I knew also that he had too much respect for me. We had known each other for quite a few years, and had, for example, concluded a few good deals in the rock business with the Moody Blues, Chuck Berry, Status Quo and other groups that I had sent to the continent for him. All in all, I knew that Dru was reliable.

We exchanged a few pleasantries, and I told him I would approach the Twins with the proposition and call him in a couple of days, after I had spoken to them.

Soon after, I arranged to meet Ronnie Kray at his mother's house, where we discussed the possibility of the project.

'A book about us!' Ronnie seemed surprised at the suggestion. 'How much are they offering, Lol?' he asked.

I said that I would not consider anything less than one hundred thousand dollars for the book, with the Krays retaining the film rights. His eyes immediately lit up with excitement.

'Do you really think they will pay that much, Lol?' he questioned.

'I can only ask, Ron. It depends what they are looking for – and how much you are prepared to tell them.'

Ronnie looked slightly puzzled by this, then quietly commented, 'We can't tell them everything can we, Lol?'

As I did not know what 'everything' was, I nodded in agreement with him, asking, 'Are you prepared to meet their representatives if they come to London?'

'Yes, Lol,' was Ronnie's immediate response. 'But only Reggie and me will be there, not Charlie. We'll split the money four ways if you can fix it for us.'

Things were going well in my chat with Ronnie, but before I got too carried away, I wanted to put right my position with him. 'I am working as an agent, Ron, your agent, for you and Reggie. I have another agent, Dru Harvey, who received the initial request. We will get ten per cent between us, then you and Reg will be able to give Charlie whatever you both decide.'

Suddenly, Ron became serious, '*No*, Lol,' he said. He did not shout. In fact, Ronnie was speaking quite softly, but he emphasised the word 'No' quite clearly. I knew when to argue with him – and the time was not right just now. I realised that Ronnie had always been fair with me, and now was treating me as a friend and not as an agent.

'Let's sound them out first, Ron,' I suggested. 'Then we can decide what it's all about.'

Ron was really excited about the book project. I think I had aroused his vanity. 'Make a meet when they come over and we will go to see them,' he decided on the spot. 'The Grosvenor House hotel will do as it's nice and private there.'

We agreed that I would be their agent, but Ronnie hastened to add, 'Don't tell anyone about our arrangement today. We don't want the Old Bill to think we are writing a book. They might try and stop it.'

As I was leaving, I knew Ronnie was immensely pleased with our talk. 'Marvellous!' he said. 'If you pull this off, Lol, we might even be able to retire!' He then broke into a loud, raucous laugh.

I went to my office and called Dru to arrange a meeting. He was delighted with the news. After a couple of days, Dru told me that the firm in the States would send two young junior lawyers over to London to meet the Twins as an initial contacting courtesy. He had also told them that the figure required for the project to proceed was not less than a hundred thousand dollars. They were not fazed by the figure, suggesting that the meeting should be arranged for the following week. These arrangements were relayed to Ronnie, who agreed to an evening meeting at the impressively high-class Grosvenor hotel in Park Lane, a five-star hotel in every possible way.

The junior lawyers appeared to be overawed by whatever their bosses had told them about who they were meeting. I met them at their hotel, the Selfridge in Oxford Street, and was shocked to find they were extremely nervous about the projected meeting. This was a bad sign, for why were they so on edge? I had expected a couple of assertive, over-the-top Yanks that I would have to curtail. This pair would hardly instil confidence in anybody, and were almost visibly jittery.

I ordered some coffee and calmed them down. It emerged that they had been talking to a doorman at the hotel and naturally asked him if he knew of the Krays. That was a wrong move as he told them the most horrific tales about the brothers.

'They are killers!' he warned, elaborating on things he had heard about them, and telling the two young men that they did not want to have anything to do with people like that.

I explained that the Krays were extremely hard gangsters: that was why their bosses had sent them to London for some initial contact. They would, I assured them, be safe with me, and should not get involved with talking about money. This was my job and I would discuss it with their company later.

We hired a taxi to the Grosvenor. The young lawyers, with their suits, shirts and ties almost matching, looked like two shop assistants. When we arrived at the front of the splendid Grosvenor House hotel, it was around 5 pm and still quite light, but the bulbs around the illuminated name sign shone brightly. The doorman, looking superb with his uniform and high top hat, opened our taxi door. Alighting on to the wide pavement, I saw Ron and Reg Kray standing nearby, a short distance away from the entrance to the hotel.

They portrayed an image of gangsters that was supreme – sleek, black hair greased with Brylcreem, smart, tailored suits, shoes shining bright, sober ties and immaculate white shirts. They greeted us warmly.

I introduced the lawyers, who were met with very firm handshakes. I think Ronnie was surprised by the fact that they were so young. He was not thinking about anything but the money, for he showed no sign of interest in either of them sexually.

'We can't use the hotel,' said Ron. 'There's a dance tonight, so we'll have to go somewhere else.'

Ron, who had been arranging things firstly with me and then Reggie, had taken on the leadership role. He wanted to change the venue, having seen entering the hotel an entourage of middle-aged ladies, done up to the nines with long dresses in the most atrocious colours. I could see his point, but did not want to tell him that the dance was in a part of the hotel hired for the purpose and not in the restaurant or coffee lounge which we would have used.

Ronnie suggested that we went to the nearby Mayfair Hotel. I did not think that was a good idea, especially as Ron had said he did not want anyone to know about the meeting.

'The security is much too heavy in the Mayfair, Ron,' I

said. 'We would be open to intrusion. It will be quieter for us at the Dolphin Square Restaurant in Pimlico.'

They did not know where it was, so I gave the Twins the address, agreeing to meet there as soon as possible. Off they went to get a taxi, with Ronnie saying that they had to phone someone.

We got a cab right away. Arriving at the restaurant entrance, we were directed to the bar area by a receptionist. A table was ordered for the Twins, who turned up soon afterwards. I decided I would not sit in, preferring to remain independent, as this was purely a meeting for introduction purposes only. I sat on a barstool with a white wine and soda for company.

Looking in to where they were sitting, I could see they were talking and hoped that the young lawyers were just listening and not getting too confident in their conversation. The Twins had a unique way of lulling opponents into a false sense of security by being polite. Then, when the adversaries thought they were listening to them, they would explode if things were not going their way: that was when you saw the wild side of the Krays.

I was silently thinking about that when the door to the bar opened and the quiet was broken by Alex Steene, a ticket agency operator, who was a very good friend of Reg and Ron. He never recognised me at all.

Alex was quite agitated. 'I'm late for a meeting with the Krays,' he blurted to the barman and, of course, to anyone else within earshot. So much for Ronnie's secrecy about the meeting!

'They are in there,' I said, pointing through the glass doors to their table.

Alex Steene hastily entered and caused chaos inside. I could see that as he was being introduced by Ronnie to the Americans. He proceeded to put two tables together, making more room, but drawing extra attention to themselves.

I knew then that I should have been in there with them, for the Americans would be totally overawed by the fast-talking Alex, who would tell them about his success as a negotiator in the fight game. I think Alex had a secret sense of insecurity, for he always wanted to prove himself and just loved mixing with villains. Everybody liked Alex, including me, but for this meeting it was not necessary to include him.

I was just hoping that the meeting would be alright when I glanced outside into the street to see the driver of a mini-van looking into the entrance of the restaurant. It was Albert Donaghue, a member of The Firm, and a criminal with form. What was he doing here, too? I left my stool and went out to him.

'Ronnie told us to come in case there is any trouble with the law,' Albert explained.

I looked into the small mini-van. It was windowless along the sides, apart from by the driver and passenger. It was then that I saw there were another three men from The Firm sitting in the back of the van!

'Ronnie thought the meeting might be a way of setting us up, so we've come armed.'

I could not believe what Albert was saying. They were prepared for a shoot-out in SW1! If they had been stopped by a patrol car, they would have been in the nick before their feet touched the ground.

'You'll get plenty of bird if you are pulled over around here,' I said. Albert stopped me in my tracks, saying,

'They're coming out now, Laurie.'

I turned to see Ron and the others coming into the street, oblivious of the mini-van and Albert. Ronnie called me over. He did not look too happy.

'Was everything all right?' I asked.

Ron replied with a serious tone to his voice. 'They tried to have us over, Lol. Asked us for two grand. We'll see you at Vallance Road. They're paying the bill. I think that's only right for messing us about.'

Immediately, I wondered what had gone wrong. Leaving Ronnie to give the orders to his men, I went into the bar area. The two young men were totally perplexed.

I explained that Ronnie had told me about the two thousand dollars. In the taxi back to the Selfridge Hotel, they said that initially all had been going to plan. Details were being finalised for them to take the Twins' orders back to the States to their bosses, when Ron asked, 'Well, we can expect a hundred thousand dollars, can we?'

Without thinking – and not knowing the deal that I had proposed – one of the lawyers said, 'Except the two thousand dollars for our expenses.'

Ronnie was used to similar negotiation in the villainy world: it was called nipping. He took the reply as meaning that they would want their expenses up front. Ron knew that was how con men worked: up-front money for expenses and never to be seen again. I think that only out of respect for our friendship he did not explode at the lawyers. Fortunately, Ron knew that I would not dare set something up against him and Reggie, so I was exonerated from blame.

Following the George Cornell murder, the law of suspicion

was very active. Although he never mentioned the fact to me, or that they were coming prepared for action with Albert Donaghue and an armed team in the van outside, Ron had been suspicious that he was being set up by the FBI and top detectives at Scotland Yard. I should have remembered my wrongly placed suspicion at that first meeting with Dru Harvey, and expected either Ron or Reg to have thought the same way as me. The Twins had more to lose than I did.

When I arrived at Vallance Road, Ron was waiting for me. Reg had gone out, but Ron listened intently to my explanation that the two junior lawyers should not have discussed money whatsoever. Ronnie was being very logical and then decided to tell me why he had arranged for the members of The Firm to be there. It was, he said, 'a safety measure'. Ron was justifiably paranoid that Scotland Yard were trying to nail them.

Further developments were discussed in the States, although the young lawyers sent to London had painted a very black picture of the Twins back home. They were scared about how the meeting had gone, with Ronnie walking out, having called them con men.

Discussions about the publishing venture went back and forth between Dru and myself. The interest in the States was still very much on, with publishers waiting for a possible synopsis. However, I could not pin Ronnie down about the book business.

He was too busy at the time, going off to America to meet some Mafia friends with Dickie Morgan, his old mate from the early days in the army. Ron liked Morgan, who had the same sense of humour as himself. This trip was orchestrated by Alan Cooper, an American who was at the time, unknown to any of The Firm, working for Scotland Yard as an *agent provocateur* against the Twins. He had won Ronnie's confidence and sealed it by arranging for Ronnie to travel. Despite the fact that both Ronnie and Morgan were ineligible due to their criminal activities, Cooper was able to get them American visas with the covert help of his associates at the Yard. Although Dickie and Ron had to travel to Paris to get their visas passed, this only appeared to give Cooper more power.

Ronnie enjoyed the fact that he was getting past the system to enter the United States and loved meeting his heroes, the American Mafia. In all, Alan Cooper made a big impression on Ronnie. This was to prove a disaster for Ron later, when Cooper helped to set him up with the Law.

unrest in the firm

It was some time after the meeting with the young lawyers sent from the USA that other negotiations were set up for the possibility of the Krays writing their life story.

It was late in 1967 and I had been dealing with Ronnie since that initial meeting at Dolphin Square and he was still as keen as ever to have their life story published. We had been discussing a writer to sort it out for them: the sum of $100,000, as promised, was still an achievable figure. But Ronnie had not been around for me to see for quite a while. It seemed he was staying away from his home in Vallance Road.

Then his mother told me that he wanted to see me urgently, so I went to Vallance Road one lunchtime. There had been strange things happening with The Firm, although I was never at their meetings. It was noticeable that something was not quite right. Whenever I bumped into any of them when visiting Mrs Kray, there seemed an air of secrecy about them.

When I knocked, Mrs Kray greeted me with, 'Come in, Lol!' Her usual friendly welcome was warmly appreciated. Going into the front room of the house, I was greeted by at least four members of The Firm. The atmosphere in that room was extremely sombre.

'Ronnie wants to talk to you about something, Lol,' said Billy Exley, the swarthy-looking, ex-fighter member of The Firm, who had been involved in the trouble outside Esmeralda's some years before.

'Where is he?' I asked, naturally expecting an address.

'We've got to take you to him, Lol,' Exley replied. 'He's in hiding.'

I felt distinctly uncomfortable. I had heard rumours of unrest among The Firm, and knowing Ronnie's bouts of depression, wondered if there was something more sinister in this request. Looking at Exley, I noticed he was carrying a shooter under his jacket.

'What's happening, Bill?' I continued. 'Why the gun?'

'We've got some business in Old Montague Street. We're getting out of the motor there.'

My suspicion was still acute. 'Who's driving?'

'It's a mini-cab,' Exley said.

Suddenly, Mrs Kray entered with a cup of tea for me, saying, 'Here you are, Lol. Can I see you a minute?'

Going into the passageway towards the kitchen, she motioned me to talk quietly. 'I don't know what's going on, Lol,' she said, 'but I think Ronnie needs you. He's only in Bow.'

That was reassuring. Mrs Kray was like a mother to me, and I relied on her judgement and felt confident that I would be safe. Going back into the room, I told Exley that we should go right away as I had a meeting with a solicitor later that afternoon. As we left to get into the car, I decided to sit in the front next to the driver, a pretty young blond boy.

'He's not coming to see Ronnie is he?' I asked. 'We'll never get back home!'

'No, Lol, he's a mini-cab driver, ain'tcha mate?' asked Exley, nodding in agreement.

I still had a feeling of uncertainty about getting into the car, but decided that if they didn't get out at Old Montague Street, then I would jump out of the vehicle at the first opportunity.

We left the Krays' house, going along Vallance Road, arriving at the top of Old Montague Street. The car stopped. Two of the men got out, leaving the driver, me, and one backseat passenger who wasn't familiar to me. 'See ya, Lol,' Exley said. There was no mention of any message for Ronnie.

Watching them leave the car, striding across Vallance Road to the beginning of Old Montague Street, I realised they were obviously up to no good, and was relieved that they had left the car.

Turning left into Whitechapel Road, the car went in the direction of Bow. The remaining man in the back seat knew where we were going and directed the driver, saying, 'Go over the fly-over, then take the first right.'

His directions brought us into Abbey Lane, off Bow Road, where he gave me the number of a block of flats, pointing them out to me. 'That tall block, Laurie,' he said, using my proper name and seemingly showing a friendly respect.

'Are you not coming, then?' I asked.

'No, Laurie, I'm going home with me brother,' he said, pointing to the blond driver. 'We live in Stratford.'

So he wasn't a member of The Firm at all; they were both local minicab drivers. How the mind plays tricks when there are guns around!

'How much is the fare?' I asked, to be told that they had been paid already.

I went into the block of council flats, looking for the floor and the number which had been given me. Getting the lift to the fifth floor, it was noticeable by the strong smell of urine and vomit that it had not been cleaned recently.

Once at the flat, I pushed the bell. The door opened, and I was face to face with a man I knew from a Whitechapel bookstall as Lennie Dunne. He did not recognise me. This was fortunate, for his reputation as a copper's nark went before him and I had noticed that he often spoke to the coppers on the beat at his stall. Lennie was a funny-looking, weedy man, not very tall, and a bit ferret-like.

'Who d'ya want?' he questioned me with a strange sense of superiority. I thought I had gone to the wrong flat.

'Is this the right flat for Ronnie?' I deliberately left out the surname, thinking that if it were not the right place, he would have crapped himself.

'Ronnie who?' he questioned. At that point, another man showed his face, saying, 'Hello, Lol!' It was the Twins' cousin, Ronnie Hart. 'Come in.'

As I entered, I could not help but notice that Ronnie Hart had that same look as Exley. It is what I can only describe as fear – kind of vacant, with no sparkle or fun, and too serious.

'Hello, Lol!' Ronnie Kray came into the lounge from another room. 'Thanks for coming, but it's urgent I speak with you about the book.'

I explained that I had been trying to contact him as well, as the publishers were very interested, but wanted a story from him and Reggie to match the Mafia in America. They would have to tell a few good stories of violence, and their rise to their position in the underworld.

I was shocked by Ronnie's appearance. He had left out a dental plate he wore with a couple of false front teeth, so had a gap right in the centre of his mouth. He hadn't shaved, was wearing a white singlet and had put on a bit of weight. His hair was a mess.

After a short while, he asked Ronnie Hart to get him something from a local chemist. When Hart left for the errand, I just had to tell Ronnie something. Going close to him, as I didn't want Lennie Dunne, who was in the kitchen, to hear me, I said, 'Ron, don't let anyone, including me, ever see you looking like this again. I'm selling your image to the Yanks. I don't want any of these, including Ronnie Hart, to take a photograph of you looking like this.'

'I've not been well, Lol,' croaked Ronnie. 'I've had the flu.'

Despite being so blunt, I did not feel at all frightened. On reflection, after seeing what Ronnie had done in the Le Monde to someone who called him fat, I must have looked and sounded sincere and confident. After all, I was right, and his image was really important.

Ron had that vacant look in his eyes, too. 'I know what you mean, Lol,' he admitted. 'I haven't been to work at all for a couple of weeks.'

Then I had the cheek to ask him, 'What work, Ron?' (another mistake really!).

'Collecting a few quid here and there,' he said, breaking into a grin.

I was relieved for the second time that day – once in the car when the men with the guns left, and now with Ronnie grinning and not getting angry. But his mood was soon to change as Ronnie Hart came in from his trip to the chemist. He gave Ron a bag.

As Ronnie Kray examined its contents, he roared 'You stupid bastard!' Hart looked in dazed amazement, wondering what on earth he had done. 'You've got me perfume instead of aftershave. Don't you think I've got enough trouble without wearing perfume, you bastard!'

At that very moment, I thought it would be best for me to leave. Ron's anger showed in his body language; he was raging mad, walking from one room to another.

'I'm going now, Ron,' I said, trying to defuse the situation.

'All right, Lol. Don't forget to let me know after you've seen the publishers.' Ronnie's personality changed as he spoke to me softly, but a tirade of abuse followed for Ronnie Hart. 'You can fuck off, too!' he told him.

As I left and was waiting for the lift, Hart appeared from the flat, and joined me in the lift when it arrived. I could not believe how he could stand that kind of abuse from Ron. It was violent. Obviously, he had upset him over something else. It could not just have been for making a mistake with the aftershave, but was a build-up of venom aimed at Hart.

'Why do you stand for that, Ron?' I asked Hart, as we travelled downwards in the lift together.

'I dunno, Lol – he's been miserable lately,' was his reply, nothing more.

'I couldn't stand that,' I added. 'I would sooner work driving or something. Anything would be better than that pressure.'

As we arrived at the ground floor level, Ronnie Hart and

I walked in the direction of Bow Road. 'Which way are you going, Lol?' Hart enquired of me.

'I'm going to have a slow stroll through to Mile End underground station, then catch a tube to Bethnal Green and home, Ron,' I replied quickly.

Ron said he was going round to see his brother, who had a business hiring lorries to contractors.

'I think I'll buy a lorry off him and start up on my own, Lol,' said Ron as he left. I could not help but notice how tired he looked.

That was the last time I was to see Ronnie Hart. Later, I was to find out why everyone I had seen that day – Exley, Hart and the others – all had a vacant look in their eyes.

what price glory?

Further to my meeting with Ron at the flat in Abbey Road, as promised, I had arranged for Ron to meet a director of a publishing firm in London. I knew the meeting took place, but Ron did not contact me afterwards. At the time, I imagined that all of my work with the introductions had been in vain and an opportunity had been lost for a deal that was both straight and quite lucrative. It was frustrating for me.

Unbeknown to me, it was in the end good fortune that I was not contacted by Ron after his meeting with the publisher. In fact, the net had been closing on the Twins after a series of events that, without my knowledge, had been going on even before that first meeting with the American publisher's young lawyers.

After the Twins' trial, the stories that emerged began to make sense of all the secrecy and suspicion surrounding The Firm at the end of 1967. Everyone in the East End knew of Ronnie's murder of Cornell; it was no secret. But since then, The Firm had been extraordinarily active.

At the end of 1966, the Twins had carried out their promise to free 'Mad Axe Man' Frank Mitchell from Dartmoor Prison. Ron had met Mitchell in Wandsworth

Prison ten years earlier and been impressed by his huge strength and loyalty, and when Reg did a short amount of time in the early sixties, also in Wandsworth, he, too, had befriended Mitchell. The Twins had helped the simple-minded Mitchell on several occasions when he had been in trouble in prison, and in return the Mad Axe Man idolised them, Ron in particular. Then, in the aftermath of the Cornell shooting, it was decided that it would be good for The Firm's prestige if they sprung Mitchell from prison.

Planning began in August and continued through the autumn months as various members of The Firm visited Mitchell in prison, and it was decided that he should escape from a working party on the moor. In fact, it was obvious that the escape would be the easy bit. In spite of his violent past, Mitchell was a trusted prisoner and was allowed a fair amount of freedom. The difficult part would be to hide this enormous and highly recognisable figure once he was out.

But soon everything was in place, and on 12 December, two of The Firm, Teddy Smith and Albert Donaghue, picked up Mitchell from the moor and sped to London. There, the fugitive was hidden by the Krays in a flat belonging to Lennie Dunne, whilst the Twins and Teddy Smith appealed to the Press and the new Home Secretary to get Mitchell's sentence reconsidered. If his punishment was reviewed, he promised he would hand himself in.

At this time, though, Ronnie, too, was in hiding, which is one of the reasons I saw him so infrequently. I found out later that he had been summoned to appear as a witness in a police corruption case, and although it would have helped bang up a bent copper, Ronnie refused to cooperate with the police on principle. He was also preoccupied with suspicions about members of The Firm. Les Payne, the so-called brain of The Firm had been rather quiet, and Ron suspected that he may have been talking to the police. Another of the Krays' associates had also become unreliable – Jack 'The Hat' McVitie, an East End hardman occasionally used by the Twins.

Meanwhile, members of The Firm – Donaghue, Billy Exley and others – tried to keep Frank Mitchell happy with huge amounts of food to fill his enormous frame and with endless games of cards. A girl was arranged for him, with whom he promptly fell in love. Reggie visited when it seemed safe, but Mitchell was getting frustrated. He wanted to see Ronnie. He had great dreams of Ronnie being the king of the underworld, with himself as his right-hand man. As the long days in the flat passed, some of the men minding him started to get worried, convinced he would break out of the flat on his own. They even got the girlfriend to try to persuade Mitchell to give himself up. Initially, he said he would do whatever the Twins wanted, but then he flew into a rage and demanded that Billy Exley give him his gun. Once armed, he calmed down, but still demanded that the Twins get him out of the flat straightaway. He was determined to spend Christmas with his family.

The Twins were not about to be ordered around by someone so in their debt. Mitchell had become a dangerous liability. According to Donaghue, who was to turn Queen's Evidence in the trial of the Krays, the Twins' friend Freddy Foreman laid on a van, supposedly to take Mitchell to Kent. Once inside, the Axe Man was shot several times, lastly in the head. It was Christmas Eve 1966.

For the moment, the police did not seem to have anything on the Krays to do with Mitchell and the hunt for the Cornell killer seemed to have petered out as well. Nevertheless, Ronnie had to remain in hiding for the first half of the next year until the corruption case against the police officer reached its time limit. He was unable to attend the funeral of Frances, Reggie's wife, who, suffering mental problems, tragically committed suicide on 7 June after several previous attempts. When Ronnie finally emerged from hiding in July, he found Reggie devastated by the loss, full of hatred and aggression. With Ronnie at large and Reggie in this sort of mood, punishment beatings and shootings became everyday work for the Twins.

Jack 'the Hat' was so called because he never took off the hat that covered his bald patch. As well as being a hard fighter, by all reports he was a drunkard and drug-taker and had a reputation for beating up women. He was not part of The Firm, but had been used by Ronnie on some small jobs. He made the mistake of cheating Ronnie and then ignoring warnings from both the Twins.

Perhaps to test his loyalty and put him in his place, in the autumn of 1967, Ronnie contracted McVitie to kill Les Payne, whom Ron was convinced was a police informer. Normally, Reg might have restrained his brother, but he was far too grief-stricken and angry about Frances' death. The killing was bungled or never attempted and McVitie showed no signs of returning the payment. Then he started threatening the Twins. Crisis point was about to be reached.

In early October it came. One night, a drunken McVitie turned up at the Regency Club in North London, brandishing a shotgun, saying he was going to kill 'the fucking

Krays'. The following night, Reggie went looking for him, accompanied by the Twins' cousin Ronnie Hart and the Lambrianou brothers, Tony and Chrissie, who were in the process of joining The Firm and were being checked out for loyalty and reliability. Not finding him in the Regency, the group made for a party in Evering Road, Stoke Newington. There, they met up with Ronnie and another member of The Firm, Ronnie Bender.

Ronnie was by now furious with McVitie and Reggie was drunk and aggressive, too. The party was cleared of non-Firm members and the Lambrianou brothers were despatched to lure McVitie to the party. Amazingly, he fell for the trap and arrived asking, 'Where're the birds and the booze?'

Straightaway, Reggie tried to shoot McVitie in the head, but his gun jammed. McVitie pleaded for his life, but Ronnie grabbed him and locked his arms behind his back. With a carving knife Reggie stabbed McVitie just below the eye. According to Ronnie Hart, who was to turn Queen's Evidence at the trial, Reggie then stabbed him in the body and then through the throat as McVitie collapsed on to the floor.

The Twins left straightaway for Harry Hopwood's flat in Bethnal Green where they washed and changed their clothes. Their soiled suits were burnt and Ron and Reg took a holiday in Cambridge. The Lambrianou brothers and the rest of The Firm cleared up the mess. Within a couple of days, the room in the flat had been completely redecorated and had new furniture. Even so, the murder of McVitie was to be the undoing of the Krays.

This crime was to bring tragedy, too, for Charlie Kray

and his good friend Freddie Foreman, who became involved in the anguish and stupidity of disposing of McVitie's body.

It was no wonder, then, that Ronnie and members of The Firm were on edge at the end of 1967 and the beginning of 1968. They had all been implicated in these murders, one way or another. It must have been frightening to have to rely on nobody cracking up. Suspicion within The Firm worsened when Teddy Smith went missing and it became clear that the American Alan Cooper had betrayed the Twins.

The paranoia I noticed on that last meeting I had with Ron in the flat in Bow now made sense. Moreover, at the time I assumed that the same flat was where they had harboured Frank Mitchell. But I was wrong in this respect. Many years later, I found out that Dunne's flat was actually on the ground floor of a house opposite the tall block I had visited.

It must have been at that time, too, that Ronnie Hart started protecting himself by meeting with Nipper Read, seeking immunity from a charge, even though he had been present and assisted in the murder of Jack the Hat. With hindsight, I looked back on that incident when Hart had mistakenly fetched the wrong aftershave from a chemist. I remember being surprised at Ron's attitude, calling him 'a stupid bastard'.

The chat I had with Hart in the lift going down is as clear now as then. I can still see the expression on Hart's face as I left him for the last time. His glazed eyes contained a look of total despair.

Any power Hart had acquired with his twin cousins had

vanished. He had enjoyed the ride of power and fame for just a few short years, but was already sealing his fate at the expense of others' freedom. What price his glory?

All my various introductions to publishers and agents finally came to fruition with the publication of *The Profession of Violence*, the Krays' biography, in 1972. The work I had started was finalised then, and although I had no further dealings with the book since the last meeting with Ron late in 1967, I have established the route taken.

The publishers in the USA contacted writer John Pearson, who was then staying in Italy, regarding the possibility of writing the life story of the most infamous gangsters in Britain.

Pearson, author of *The Life of Ian Fleming* and *The Life of James Bond*, was extremely interested. The publishers contacted Ronnie Kray, who was highly flattered that the writer of a James Bond book would want to undertake their life story with all the sinister action surrounding the Krays at that time. Ronnie's vanity still found the time to persuade his brothers to meet this man who had written a book on James Bond.

'He must be good,' he said, drawing himself up slightly and putting his shoulders back.

In attendance with close members of The Firm, Ron, Reg and Charlie arranged a meeting at the home of their good and trusted friend Geoff Allen. The venue was a lovely country mansion fit for a squire.

John Pearson discussed the details needed for a book to be written. I can only assume the mixture of fascination, fear, excitement and horror at the task ahead of him. For

John Pearson was going to be subjected to far more unbelievable stories than any Bond novel could produce. And these were fact, not fantasy.

A dingy flat was arranged for John Pearson in a Peabody Estate called Howard Dwellings near to St Anne's Roman Catholic Church off Vallance Road. The Twins called the flat 'the dungeon'.

According to Checker Berry, a good friend of mine who helped John Pearson with introductions to many East End folk, John Pearson began writing the book under considerable strain. Meetings were held in John Pearson's presence at The Old Horns pub in St Peter Avenue, Bethnal Green. The pub was owned by Checker's brother, Teddy.

John Pearson had the unenviable job of interviewing many people, which must have been difficult under normal circumstances, but even more so for him as the Twins became paranoid about him being a spy. This reminded me of the initial meeting with the young American lawyers at Dolphin Square and The Firm being in the van with shooters. Having the same paranoia as overcame him then, Ron was now aiming it at John Pearson.

When he was putting his experiences together, John Pearson wrote that if he were to put all the money he had expended together, there would be nothing left from any advance or future royalties. Thankfully, he has been well rewarded financially, for *The Profession of Violence* has been a continuing best-seller until this day.

But John Pearson never knew the real Ronnie Kray. At the time he met them, just before their arrest, the Twins were suffering the knowledge of at least three murders and

Ron in the early '60s (*Laurie O'Leary*)

Ron with Chunky Mor[...]
(*Laurie O'Leary*)

Ron, Chunky Morgan
(back), Reg and Jimm[...]
Williams (front), outs[...]
the Regal Billiard Clu[...]
(*Laurie O'Leary*)

to right: Peter Worley,
[...]sy Teapot, Ron and
[...]ky Morgan. Peter
[...]ey was the unwilling
[...]r in the so-called
[...]ese chase (*Laurie
[...]ary*)

[...]e Alford, Reg and me
[...]side the Regal Billiard
[...]lub (*Laurie O'Leary*)

Ronnie's favouri
photo. Left to rig
Eddie Pucci (Fra
Sinatra's
bodyguard), Ror
George Raft (mc
star and alleged
Mafia associate)
Reg, Rocky
Marciano (unbea
world heavywei;
boxing champio
and Charlie

The Krays' Wes
End club, which
managed in the

Reg's wedding to Frances Shea, April 1965. Their married life was to end in tragedy two years later, when Frances committed suicide (*Laurie O'Leary*)

The peer and the gangster scandal: Lord Boothby, Ron and Les Holt

The author (right) with Jimmy Murphy, trainer at the West Ham Boxing Club (*Laurie O'Leary*)

The marvellous painting of (left) and Reg by Jo Alleeso (*Laurie O'Leary*)

...rlie Kray and I bearing Ron's coffin, with Freddie Foreman behind me (*Dillon ...tinez*)

Scenes from Ron's funeral (*Laurie O'Leary*)

One of the last pictures to be taken of Ron Kray, in Broadmoor 1993

were rightly paranoid that the net of Scotland Yard was closing in on them.

As far as I was concerned, The Firm were acting more and more strangely. It was very peculiar. Something did not feel right.

My worries were confirmed when, very early in the morning on 9 May 1968, the Kray Twins were arrested, along with other key members of The Firm. In all, over twenty people were picked up simultaneously. Thanks to Cooper's evidence, the police were able to hold the Twins on remand in Brixton Prison while they went to work on the potential grasses. They wouldn't need long.

thirty years

When the Krays were arrested, I was promoting and managing the Speakeasy Club in Margaret Street in London's West End. This music business club was famous in the rock 'n' roll industry, although part of the club's policy on music had changed to psychedelic sounds with colours of a mind-blowing description being projected on to musicians playing on stage. Sometimes, oil-filled filters were experimented with to drag these mixed colours across an often light-coloured backdrop to create an illusionary effect with the music.

This was the time of free love and cannabis, which helped club members to relax to the sounds of groups with such fancy names as Pink Fairies, the lead singer of which was called 'Twink'. Other groups and singers had such names as Thin Lizzie, Osobisa, Vinegar Joe, Pacific Gas and Electric Flag. David Bowie, Marc Bolan, Eric Clapton, Keith Moon, Jimi Hendrix and Mick Jagger were all frequently seen at the Speakeasy, either playing on stage or being entertained socially in the restaurant, enjoying Luigi's superb food and intoxicated by the new sounds that always predominated at the Speak.

The scene here was far removed from our early days of

those old standard songs of Frank Sinatra, Dean Martin and other melodious singers, who generally had the backing of a full orchestra. The club's music would have made the Twins think I was insane, especially when one considers strobe lights and the introduction of LSD, the fashionable drug of those days, which caused trips, good and bad.

I am ignorant of drugs: three paracetamols and I would overdose! I only ever smoked cigarettes for about a week and that was when I was around twenty-five. I hated it. People would offer me a cigarette socially, so I decided to buy some of my own to offer back in case they thought I was a ponce. I disliked even carrying the bulky packet in my suit pocket, so gave them away as quick as I could. Stupid really.

Believe it or not, I have never tried any form of drug. I never had the need, for simply being around the Krays as kids was enough to get the adrenaline rushing through my veins, especially in the mid-1960s when they became the most infamous gangsters in London. Reg and Ron created a tremendous influence of fear across the country, which spread to gangsters in other areas of Great Britain. Photographs of the Krays were often shown in the national newspapers. They were always in the company of celebrities, who courted their infamy. Reg and Ron's vanity encouraged this to happen and it became something of a status symbol to be photographed with the Krays in the 1960s. Leading photographer David Bailey, himself an East Ender, took some of the finest and most popular photographs of the Krays. Since their arrest, they are the photographs of them most shown throughout the world.

To my mind, the sixties were fantastic times, although often worrying because of the tales I was hearing about the power of the Krays and how they were acquiring that power. Stories of brutal fights and of the strength of The Firm and their demand for power were circulating extremely fast.

Meanwhile, I was in a different world, the bright, brash, glitzy and sometimes glamorous world of the entertainment business, although it was hard graft. But I would still visit their parents' house regularly. The Twins' mother would keep me updated, but not about the violence; that was not how Mrs Kray expressed herself to me. She would just tell me, 'They're not in, Lol. Want a cup of tea? They've gone away somewhere.'

The purpose of my visits was natural. After all, I had been calling at the Twins' house for many years. It was almost like a second home. I knew they were violent and with Ronnie's illness still not under control, anything could happen – and it usually did. But Reg and Ron were still my mates, and had made the transition from healthy schoolboy boxers into heavy, mature gangsters quite naturally. It appeared to me the obvious transition. It was all about strength.

Unfortunately, the power of Ronnie Kray could not be harnessed.

On Tuesday, 8 March, 1969, the Clerk of the Court prepared himself to ask the jury for their verdict in the trial of Regina v The Krays. The court case, which had been running for thirty-eight days, was then the longest murder trial in the history of law.

The jury filed past the Clerk of Court and settled into their places in front of Judge Mr Aubrey Melford Stevenson, who had sent them to the jury room about six hours earlier, with a request to return with a verdict if possible.

'Would the foreman of the jury please stand?'

Proceedings began with the Clerk of the Court questioning the foreman.

'Would you please answer just "Yes" or "No" to the questions I ask you.'

'I will, sir.'

'Members of the jury, with regard to the defendant in the box, Ronald Kray, have you reached a verdict that is agreed by all?'

'Yes, sir,' the somewhat shaky voice of the foreman answered.

An eerie silence fell over the courtroom as the verdict on one of the most complex trials in legal history was about to be announced.

'Do you find the prisoner Ronald Kray "Guilty" or "Not Guilty"?'

'Guilty, sir.'

Ronnie Kray clenched his teeth, causing his jaw line to appear even more pronounced than normal. He was led down the steps to the cells below by a warder.

It had started badly for the Krays at their preliminary trial, at Old Street magistrates court on 6 July 1968, when Billy Exley appeared in the box for the prosecution. He proceeded to outline the harbouring of Frank Mitchell in his flat, and also gave details of the Krays' long firms. Then the barmaid of The Blind Beggar pub appeared and identified Ronnie as George Cornell's killer. It had looked hopeless for the Krays.

The main trial started in January 1969. In all, twenty-eight criminals were given immunity and protection in return for testifying against the Krays. Only the Lambrianous, Ronnie Bender, Ian Barrie and one other member of The Firm stayed loyal. Although the Krays were found not guilty of the murder of Frank Mitchell after Albert Donaghue's evidence against them was discarded, there was no way they could escape from the other charges.

The day after the verdict, the defendants – amongst them Ron, Reg and Charlie – were brought back to the Old Bailey for sentencing. The public gallery was packed, with the Press like vultures waiting for their piece of flesh. The jury had returned to hear the sentence. The Judge ordered the first person to be brought up from the cells below.

'Ronald Kray,' he said. 'I am not going to waste words on you. The sentence upon you is that you will go to life imprisonment. In my view, society has earned a rest from your activities. I recommend that you be detained for thirty years. Put him down.'

Like Ron, Reggie similarly received a recommended minimum of thirty years for the murder of Jack 'The Hat' McVitie. Charles Kray and Frederick Foreman were each given a ten-year term as accessories to the murder of McVitie.

But in the eyes of so many, three ordinary boys from London's East End had achieved extraordinary status, especially Ron and Reg. The legend of the Krays had begun . . .

valuable visitors

The Twins were only thirty-five years old when they were sent down. For the next quarter of a century, the brothers were imprisoned in various high-security prisons and secure mental institutions. Their entire lives – depressed or hopeful, healthy or sick – happened under guard.

Sometimes, the visits I made to Ron were full of sadness, at other times, circumstances managed to create some laughter. On one occasion, when Ron was at Broadmoor, he was operated on for a mastoid and did not want to be seen looking the worse for wear, banning all visitors. However, he was eventually persuaded to allow his father Charlie and myself to see him.

Arriving at the Broadmoor hospital, we were shown into a very sterile circular room with about four beds. It was lit with subdued down-facing lighting with large shades similar to those over snooker tables. The scene was like the film *One Flew Over the Cuckoo's Nest*, especially when Ronnie appeared with his head fully bandaged except for his eyes, nose and mouth. The sore ear, which had a large pad over it, was also covered by bandage. The overall look was quite comical. Naturally, we did not laugh, although it was difficult to keep a straight face and we then understood why

Ronnie did not want to see anyone.

Charlie tried to break the ice by saying that he looked quite well. This was a wrong move, although I knew just what he meant. We expected Ron to be in bed, so the fact that he was able to walk about the ward was a bonus.

'Fuck off, Dad, I look terrible, don't I, Lol?' said a slightly miserable-sounding Ron, looking at me.

'You look like the Invisible Man,' I replied, causing Ron to laugh with us about his condition.

During the visit, he told us that he was scheduled to travel to an outside hospital to have his wound dressed and see a specialist a few weeks later. The planned trip happened four weeks later and Ron was escorted by two warders he knew and trusted from Broadmoor.

After the specialist had been seen, the warders decided to have a walk around the shops in a local mall with Ron in tow. He told me that they offered to let him have a stroll by himself for half an hour while they had a coffee.

'No thanks,' he told them. 'It's best I stay with you both. I'll feel much safer.'

Describing the incident, Ron asked me, 'Did they think I was an idiot? If I had walked away as suggested, they could have reported that I had tried to escape, getting themselves a medal and plenty of coverage in the press. I'm mad, but not stupid. Anyway, where would I go if I escaped? We would never escape. There's nowhere to go, is there? We're too well known.'

On my visits to see him, we often talked about the days of our youth, the fun, the naivety.

'We were kids then, Lol,' Ron would say almost wistfully,

perhaps settling back in his chair just a little. 'It was all a long time ago . . .'

With his future taken away, Ron would console himself by reliving good times in the past. Ron and I loved discussing those memories. It was the best time – scraps in the street or on the war-time debris surrounding our homes; the junior amateur boxing matches at the York or Seymour Halls; the boxing booths at the fairgrounds; the characters we grew up with. We laughed as we remembered 'Prince' Monolulu, who was adorned with feathers. Then there were the boxers like 'Slasher' Warner and Stevie Osborne. We'd also reminisce about another character called 'Wagget', who was rather scruffy looking.

Gambling was then illegal, but Wagget produced a paper giving the results of the greyhound races. It was often just a sheet of cheap A4 paper with some badly typed results that he had the nous to get from the tracks by telephone. His paper gave the results of that night's dog racing from all the London tracks. Wagget sold it around the pubs for a penny or two to the many East Enders who loved gambling for coppers.

Because then there was no licensed betting, people used a street bookmaker. These characters were a law unto themselves. Trusted by the punters, who would often have a bet on tick, which meant paying later on, they were chased by a policeman when a look-out man warned of his approach. The bookies' runners would take bets in or around pubs. Punters often stood next to a Salvation Army soldier, bought a *War Cry* newspaper, then wrote out a betting slip without a moment of care. It was strange, too, to see people helping the bookie escape the arm of the law by opening their doors to let him hide when being pursued.

On Sunday mornings, Wagget would change into a street vendor, pushing a costermonger's barrow around the streets selling winkles, brown shrimps and celery, the food then savoured by working-class families of the East End. We would pick out the winkles from their small, black, shiny shells with a pin or needle, first removing the black, hard, thin round spot on the top of the body of the winkle, then gently easing the fleshy part out, twisting it as we went. You did not want to lose the thin tail as that was delicious. Putting them on a saucer – or in some cases in an egg cup – that had been prepared with some vinegar and pepper added to the flavour of this delicacy.

Like most others, families such as ours and the Krays only had a half pint of winkles and half pint of shrimps with the shells on to share between at least five of us. But a couple of slices of bread and margarine or butter would make a delicious sandwich with a few winkles or shrimps spread between them. If we missed the seafood man or had no money to buy anything, our delicacy turned to the dripping from the Sunday joint of beef. This was put into a pudding basin, the brown gravy settling at the bottom into a lovely, lightly salted jelly that in itself was superb. Sitting atop the jelly was solid, creamy, white dripping from the meat. Having cooled, it solidified into a soft spread suitable for making a dripping slice, finished off with a fine covering of the brown jelly that gave it a unique taste. A slice of dripping was a delicacy. My brother Alphi and his mate Dickie Miller would often go into a café in Bethnal Green and order two dripping sandwiches and a mug of tea for the price of a few coppers. It was a meal then.

Ron really enjoyed talking about those times, the reminiscences giving him a great sense of joy. 'I get sick of talking about violence and villainy, Lol,' he said one time. 'I dream about travelling the world if I ever get out of here. Your brother Alphi has travelled the world, hasn't he? He sends us cards from Japan, China and Australia. It must be marvellous.'

A wistful look crossed his face. Perhaps in his heart of hearts, Ron knew that yes, he would indeed leave Broadmoor one day, but rather than be whisked away in a black limousine, it would be a black vehicle of another description. In any event, that was what Fate had in store . . .

A poem Ron sent me that he had written called 'The Lifer' contains a plaintive point:

The years roll on by.
You can see winter turn
To summer by the sky.
Home seems far away
How much longer behind these walls must we stay?
I say a prayer for my fellow men behind bars
Who gaze up at freedom and the stars.
Let us waken from our sleep
And be as free as sheep.
Let our hearts soar high
As high as birds in the sky
As we think of being free
And at long last the end of the long road
We can see.

Over the years, Ron and Reg sent me literally thousands of

letters and poems. Some are written on scraps of paper, whilst others appear on official prison notepaper, which always begins with the prison's full address and the inmate's number and name. One I particularly treasure is written in black felt-tip ink on a torn-off piece of lined paper. Ron writes, 'Con man told me there is so much good in the worst of us and so much bad in the best of us it hardly becomes any of us to talk about the rest of us.' Perhaps he has a point . . .

Ron's writing and spelling are not the best in the world, but there is genuine depth of feeling behind the poems he wrote. Indeed, some are so poignant as to be almost painful. They show that within Ron was a caring, sensitive, thoughtful soul as opposed to the vicious villain, the mindless thug so often portrayed. Some poems are hand-written, others laboriously typed out on a now old-fashioned manual typewriter. Perhaps these verses were an emotional and physical outlet for the anguish he so often felt, a medium whereby he could openly express sensitive feelings even within the rigid regime of a sterile and secure institution.

It is noteworthy that when mentally ill, Ron's writing rapidly deteriorated. One scribbled note contains several lines crossed out. 'Mental trouble re complicated mind,' writes Ron, who adds, 'I want to make it quite clear that I don't profess to be like my poems, but these are my thoughts, dedications.'

Ron's poems cast a unique light on his complex and often troubled character. True, an expert on poetry might scoff at their metre, scanning and structure, but they reflect Ron's inner self. In fact, it seems he was able to express himself in verse more adequately than by any other method.

In September 1977, whilst still in Parkhurst, Ron wrote to me: 'I was really pleased that you may be able to make a song out of my poems. I am going to send you five poems that I have done. Laurie, I know I can trust you so could you get them copyrighted for me as I think that this is important.

'You know that it will make me happy if you can get them made into songs as then I will know that my life has not been all violence and that I have done something worthwhile . . . This has really given me something to think about.'

One of Ron's most poignant poems, sent to me in December 1989, is simply entitled 'Peace'.

Everything at peace in the valley
And on the hill
Everything so quiet and still.
Breathe in the country air and look at the beauty
All around
Only God can grant us this peace to be found.
See the fields of wheat
And hear the lambs bleat.
See the farmer with his pitchfork in the hay
And the farmer's son building a house of clay.
See the white dove in the sky
How free does it fly.
Walk down a country lane
Look at the old church
With its coloured windowpane.
Stop and look at the old church
Graveyard
Its old gravestones so old and hard.

Ron's letters and poems are a very real reminder of a friendship that lasted decades, but in 1994 he gave me another tangible sign. Ronnie bought three watches, giving one to me, the second to Reg and the third to Charlie. This was, he explained, because we were the three most important people in his life.

In his book *Profession of Violence*, John Pearson wrote that Ronnie did not have a sense of humour. I must contradict him. Ronnie had a terrific sense of humour. Sometimes it was rather sick, but other times very funny.

In the mid sixties Ron was amazed at a press story about a midget named Royston Smith, who was supposed to have been a contract killer for the Krays. Smith was a dwarf, and Ronnie had found great delight in humouring him to give him some form of status.

'I suppose we engaged him to do the knee-capping for us,' said Ron with a chuckle. 'Well, it would be all right for him as he's just about the right height!'

We had many laughs about the strange characters that Ron picked up along the way. One day, Ronnie noticed a very large black man sweeping the roads near to his mother's house in Vallance Road. He decided that the man would look like a minder from a James Bond movie if he were attired in evening dress with all the accessories, promptly sending Checker to hire everything for Cha-Cha, the name of Ronnie's new friend.

It was a difficult job due to Cha-Cha's enormous size. Eventually, they returned to Vallance Road, where Ron asked Cha-Cha to put the clothes on so he could see how he looked. Ron was pleased with how he looked and on impulse decided that Cha-Cha should join him at a meeting that very evening at the Victoria Sporting Club in the West End.

Cha-Cha was a very slow-talking, slow-moving individual, with little or no ability to converse. Ron explained that he would pay him to keep quiet and just sit down and await his orders.

Arriving at the club, the doorman was shocked at the size of this huge giant of a man, dwarfing Ronnie Kray as they entered the restaurant. This impressed Ron greatly, who introduced Cha-Cha to the American businessmen he was meeting.

They sat at a table to eat. Cha-Cha had never been into a restaurant before in his life and seemed rather nervous and apprehensive. The waiter asked Ron for his order.

'A prawn cocktail,' came his reply.

Turning to Cha-Cha the waiter asked, 'The same for you, sir?'

The response from Cha-Cha was an embarrassed, 'No thanks.'

Noticing this, Ron said to him, 'I'm having a steak. I'll get the same for you.'

Cha-Cha agreed with Ron, eating his meal ravenously. As the waiter went to pass the table, Cha-Cha tugged on his trouser leg. Turning around to see what it was, he saw a huge, shiny black face looking at him.

'I'll have that prawn cocktail now please,' said Cha-Cha. 'I'm thirsty.'

A dumbstruck Ronnie Kray cancelled the order and asked Checker, who had been waiting in an adjoining bar, to escort Cha-Cha from the table.

While in Broadmoor, Ron often sent money to people experiencing hard times. 'But how much harder than him being in Broadmoor?' I often thought. Sometimes, he sent off a donation to help someone's cause if he had read in a newspaper of some poor soul who was suffering. In essence, Ron could be the kindest person ever, but a real bastard on other occasions.

Even with his most trusted friends and family, Ron could get angry. Once, when I visited him at Broadmoor, Ron was persistent that I should get the address of the mother of Willy – the friend of mine he had fancied so many years before. He wanted to try and locate him.

I never obliged, much to Ron's anger. Subsequently, I received a letter from him telling me that he never wanted to see me again. At the time I was hurt and thought the letter totally unjustified.

In my frustration, I wrote and told Reggie about Ron's letter and that he did not want to see me again. Understanding Ron's moods, Reggie was not at all interested really, but understood that Ronnie was his own man, so would not interfere with his affairs.

But I had forgotten, when I had received the letter, that Ron was not well. At that point, he was in Broadmoor and had mood changes for which he was not responsible. It is important to bear in mind that the drugs and other treatment he was receiving also altered his mood.

Later, I did get a letter of apology from Ron, blaming the drugs, which was probably true. Soon after, he sent me a poem. Signed 'To my friend Laurie from Ron Kray' it is entitled 'I Care What He Thinks'. The typed original reads:

Does my friend think I am mad?
Does he think I am bad?
Does he think I am glad
When I should be sad?
Please God
Let him understand me
As clearly as he can see
The leaf of a tree.
And let him know that I love him like a son
As I would like him to be.
Like me he is in a cell
But if I could have a wish
From a wishing well
I would like to see him free
With his heart full of glee.

Over the course of his imprisonment, Ron also sent many letters to other close friends saying that he was fed up with seeing people and wanted them to leave him alone. They were nice people, having done nothing wrong to upset him. These letters were sent in complete frustration that he had to rely on others for his needs to be met. Others were similarly really hurt at the time, but like me they recognised the pattern and would act accordingly if they were able to. Soon, his letters no longer caused me anguish, for now I understood him and his moods much better.

While Ron was regularly visited by old friends, he was even able to make some new ones as well. Kate Kray met Ron in an unusual way. In fact, it sounds rather like a film script, but so often truth is stranger than fiction.

Kate was waiting for a train from Charing Cross Station to take her home to Kent. Having some time to spare, she browsed at the books on sale at the station and was drawn to one about the Krays. Purchasing it, Kate, 32, was riveted, skimming the pages, intrigued and fascinated by the Twins' life.

Her curiosity more than aroused, in 1987 Kate decided to write to Reg, who at that point was at Gartree Prison in Leicester. Having received her letter, Reg decided he wanted to meet Kate, so a visit was arranged.

Reg immediately enjoyed her bubbly personality, feeling comfortable enough after a while to ask if she would go and see Ron. Reg already had a number of female visitors and thought that Kate's lively character would appeal to Ron and undoubtedly make him laugh. In short, Reg was certain that Kate was just the tonic Ron needed, as his letters at the time were becoming rather morose.

Katie contacted Broadmoor Hospital and arranged a visit to Ron. As expected by Reg, they got on like a house on fire. Ron liked her attitude when he told her that he was bisexual. Rather than being appalled, Kate was amused by his refreshing honesty. In fact, Ron did not realise that Katie already knew, having read about it in the book.

Ron and Kate rapidly developed a close rapport, with Ron bombarding her with phone calls and beautiful bouquets of flowers. After about a year, Ron surprised Reg by proposing to Kate, surprising her even more. Eventually, she accepted.

Ron told Katie that although he was considered homosexual, he had been married before, whilst in Broadmoor. This was to Elaine Mildener, and it had only lasted a year or so. Ron rapidly divorced Elaine because she deserted him by not visiting him for the last five months of their marriage.

'I'm bisexual really,' he reassured Katie, 'and think it's only fair that I have an HIV test for AIDS.' Ron did and was clear.

Kate thought that the situation was quite bizarre as she knew the likelihood of any sex with Ron was extremely remote.

Nonetheless, in Kate Ron saw a very astute business-woman. After all, she had her own Rolls Royce chauffeur business and kissagram agency. He was enthralled by her enthusiasm and thought she would be an ideal manager of his affairs.

In turn, Kate could see the possibility of using Ron's reputation to enhance her standing. In a very short time, their friendship developed into a warm and very meaningful relationship, with genuine, deep-seated affection and a certain type of love on both sides.

We first met at their wedding reception in the Hilton Hotel at Bracknell, Berkshire, in 1989. My brother and I were invited. It was a really nice reception – and Kate looked fantastic dressed in a beautiful oyster-coloured designer dress. Naturally, lots of Ronnie's friends from London were there, so during the evening I was able to reminisce with a few old mates from Bethnal Green who had also been invited.

One funny thing happened when I went into the gents toilet. Standing next to a good friend Albert Smith – a member of the Smith family of wardrobe dealers from Bethnal Green – I said loudly for him to hear, 'You could always get a few quid with the Krays,' knowing that 'on the knocker' nobody gave anybody anything. The rule was no friends on the knocker. If you could have one or other over all the better, for it made you even more slippery, a feat to be admired in that fraternity.

Albert, who has been quite ill for some time, turned his head slightly to see who had said such a thing. 'Are you fucking sure, Laurie?' he asked quizzically. 'I've never earned a penny with them, not that I wanted to, of course.' It was typical East End banter.

Having met Kate, it was not difficult to understand Ron's feelings. She was indeed a warm, caring, sensitive person. Having been a good friend of hers for over a decade, I can vouch for the fact that she definitely did not marry Ron for his name or notoriety, and certainly not for his so-called wealth. I enjoyed talking about Ron to Kate. We would discuss Ron's wild temper and the fact that if you had never been called 'a slag' or 'a rat' by him, then you had never really been close. These were two of his expressions when he could not get his own way.

Whilst married to Ron, I know that even in their frustrating moments, Kate saw his deep sense of humour. Once, when visiting Ron in Broadmoor, Kate told him that she had left a tie for him at Reception, where all gifts for inmates had to be deposited.

'It's from Georgio Armani,' she said with a warm smile, hoping he would be really pleased with a designer item.

Ron's reply was made with a blank look. 'What's the matter with it?' he asked. 'Didn't he want it?'

It has to be said that their marriage was often volatile and ended in divorce because third parties deliberately tried to drive a wedge between them, spreading malicious stories. Certainly, Kate had some very heavy confrontations with Ron at visiting time in Broadmoor. I often tried to pacify her after such meetings had taken place. She would phone me in a state of anger.

'He's such a bastard, accusing me of marrying him for his money!' she said furiously. 'What fucking money? He's got none. And when he gets some, he can't wait to give it away!'

Then we would both burst into laughter. 'I had my own Rolls Royce and a thriving business when I married him, Lol,' Kate threw in for good measure.

Sadly, the end result was inevitable, and Ron issued divorce proceedings.

However, despite that, I have never to this day heard Kate speak badly about Ron. We often talk about their relationship and fondness for each other. Despite the divorce, Kate is still Kate Kray, even though the name conjures up an enduring infamy. Despite the unusual circumstances of their marriage, I know that Katie still considers it a very important and meaningful milestone in her life.

Kate is my mate and was very good for Ronnie. They had some great laughs together. When he asked me to write this book, I mentioned the fact that I would only be able to write nice things about Kate, and that as a friend I loved her. This prompted Ronnie to add, 'So do I, Laurie. So do I.' And he really meant it.

Ron was always delighted by visits from celebrities. On one occasion actor Ray Winstone went to see Ron in

Broadmoor with his friend actor Glen Murphy of TV's *London's Burning* fame. Ray is the son of one of my oldest friends from my teenage years, Ray 'Sugar' Winstone, who years before had changed my mind about working for Ron at Esmeralda's Barn, after first refusing the job. Ronnie told Glen Murphy that he knew his father Terry and that he was a good professional fighter.

'You were a good fighter too, weren't you?' Ron hastily added, obviously delighted that he could speak with some background knowledge. 'I read about you in a television book, and saw you playing the part of a fighter in *London's Burning*.'

Yet again, Ron was filled with pride that two East End stars had flattered him by making a visit.

'I'm going to hire a cruise ship when I come out, Glen,' Ron added. 'You can join me and my friends. It will be marvellous!'

Glen smiled in amusement. He could just imagine the faces of his wife and children when he told them.

'Ray's coming, aren't you?' added Ron. Then, with a teasing smile, he went on, 'I'll give you a really nice massage, won't I Ray?'

Ray replied rapidly, with a cheeky grin, 'You will, won't ya, Ron?' knowing that he was having him on.

It is no exaggeration to say that the Krays have fans throughout the world. However, these followers are not villains or potential gangsters, but ordinary people, fascinated by the Krays and the media hype.

The last fan to visit Ronnie, just days before his death, was Wayne Lear, a lad in his twenties, a hard-working steel worker from the West Midlands. Wayne recalls that the main thing he could remember about Ron was how smart he was. You could see your face in his shoes, he said. His shirt was crisp and white, and his black trousers were well pressed. He wore a tie and blue blazer.

Wayne showed Ron some photos of what the East End looks like now.

'Oh! It's changed a lot,' he said, going on to say that the youngsters today should not need to turn to crime with all the different sports they could do and youth centres and clubs to go to.

Ron told Wayne that he tried to keep himself busy by going into the garden if he could, and that he had a radio in his room. He added that his favourite record was *Madam Butterfly*. What kept him going most of all, he said, was what he wanted to do in the future when he was let out. Ron told Wayne he could be his chauffeur and take him for rides in the country.

There are thousands of fans like Wayne who love to collect photos, books and T-shirts. There is now an official Kray website and fan club. Some of the attention that the Twins have received, however, has been less welcome.

I was disgusted when, in a movie about the Krays, their mother was depicted as a foul-mouthed woman. That was entirely incorrect and unfair. Their mother Violet was, in my opinion, a very lovely lady. In the film she was portrayed as the dominant person in the family. But Mrs Kray was nothing like that at all. Neither were her sisters, Rosie and May. They were all characters in their own inimitable way. I loved them all, knowing them since I was a kid, and sharing many happy moments in their company.

In the commercial sense, the Twins were unable to bring happiness to their mother. A house they bought for their parents in Suffolk for a small sum of borrowed money was quickly sold again when they were arrested and sentenced. Mrs Kray had to borrow from close friends and family to visit her sons. At one time, they were in three separate prisons in England. She never complained, but it must have been strange for her to read about her sons' supposed wealth.

I remember when she received some money from the advance given for the film rights of their book. It was just over £1,000. Mrs Kray told me that she would be able to pay off a few debts to people who had loaned her money for visits. Such was the alleged wealth of the Krays.

The film also made out that Mrs Kray and her sisters were blamed for making the Twins into gangsters. This was also absolutely ridiculous. No one was able to control the Twins, least of all their mother and aunts, as has been suggested by many newspapers as well.

They became gangsters not because of any family influence, but because Ronnie liked the power. He made it happen because he would stop at nothing, even murder. This was to be their ultimate downfall. Ron liked the life that the power gave him, even if at times he would go into a huge depression, talking to nobody except his mother or aunts. But that did not make them responsible for his behaviour, for half the time they had no idea what the Twins had been up to until they read it in the newspapers.

Both Reg and Ron hated to worry their mother. I remember when we were only about sixteen years of age and standing outside a fried fish shop in Globe Road. A man who Ronnie had argued with a few weeks previously came out of a pub opposite with some of his friends. He was older than us by about six years and tried to treat us as kids.

'All right, son?' he called out mockingly, with a loud laugh.

That was like a red rag to Ronnie. As the man and his friends came across to the fish shop, Ronnie grabbed him around the neck. Both the man's eyes and Ronnie's eyes bulged – Ronnie's with incensed anger, the man's as he was being strangled. Then I heard Reggie shout loudly into Ronnie's ear, 'Think of Mummy!' Only then did Ronnie relax his grip. He threw the man to the ground. One of his friends, a huge, very nice man named 'Boy-Boy' Leaming, went to his aid. It was another example of Ronnie showing no fear, for it was just Ron who attacked the man while Reggie looked on, watching that he had nobody trying to jump on his back.

As we left that scene, it became obvious that Ron intended to leave his mark on anyone who tried to mug any of his family and friends. Of course, that story did the rounds of rumour, although a comeback occurred in the Mansford Club, with us having a fight with the man and his friends around a billiards table, broken cues and billiard balls being the weapons.

On hearing that I had been fighting with his landlord's neighbour, my older brother Arthur threatened never to speak to me again. Would you believe that his neighbour's son was training to be a copper and hit me with a truncheon issued to him as a cadet! Of course, I relieved him of it and hit him back with it. That's fair ain't it? There was no real damage done at all except a few bruises on most of us. It was not all one way, you know. We got hit, too. The East End was a tough place to live. Put simply, you had to fight to survive if you wanted respect.

voices from beyond

'Ladies and gentlemen. Would you please meet and greet Doris Stokes, the lady with voices in her ear.' From the side of the stage, I watched Tony Ortzen, then editor of *Psychic News*, introduce famous medium Doris Stokes, who I managed for four years.

Doris was clairaudient – and really did hear spirit voices in her ear. I know from personal experience how accurate her mediumship was, as she gave me some compelling evidence from my mum, including unusual details I am convinced she did not know by normal means.

Doris packed theatres, including the London Palladium on at least eight occasions. The first time, seats sold out within hours and people even queued overnight, the line stretching back around the block from the theatre. The sales of her seven books reached millions. A lovely mumsy figure who always wore flowing dresses on stage, much to her surprise she became the celebrity celebrities wanted to meet, becoming friendly with Pat Phoenix, Diana Dors, her husband Alan Lake, and many other household names.

Yet fame did not go to her head, for she never forgot her humble roots in Grantham, Lincs. Despite her later wealth, at that time she lived in a humble, two-bedroom, ex-servicemen's block in Fulham Road, south-west London, with her husband John and adopted son Terry. A high proportion of her earnings went to charity or individual worthy causes, for Doris neither needed nor wanted great riches. Doris may have been other-worldly, but truth to tell she was unworldly, almost naive, when it came to monetary matters. She was a medium with a message. To her all that mattered was that her sitters, whether famous or not, came to understand that physical death is not the end.

I watched Tony take his seat as Doris settled into hers. As usual, she told a few jokes to settle the expectant crowd at the packed-to-the-rafters Fairfield Halls in Croydon, Surrey, and allow herself a few minutes to tune in to her first spirit contact. Many of those who attended her public demonstrations were bereaved. All naturally hoped – and probably literally prayed – for a spirit message. Often I felt close to tears as details emerged of sons, daughters, mums, dads, lovers, friends and even pets dying in terrible and tragic circumstances. There were sometimes tears from those who received messages, too, yet Doris's demonstrations were also marked by humour as either she or a spirit contact made an amusing comment if an especially poignant story emerged. That lifted the atmosphere immediately, always causing laughter to race around a theatre.

Unknown to Doris, amongst the audience that night was Charlie Kray. Afterwards, Charlie went backstage with his girlfriend, Diana Buffini, to see Doris, who was very pleased to meet them. Just like the Twins, Doris always enjoyed meeting celebrities and well-known people.

Charlie explained that he thought the Violet Doris had mentioned towards the end of the evening was his mother, but had not known how to respond.

'Oh, that happens quite a lot, luvvie,' said Doris reassuringly. 'After a demonstration, people often come backstage telling me that a relative has come through, but they were too surprised or embarrassed in front of thousands of others to claim the contact. Then they want me to try and continue with the communication, but sadly I can't pick up the link to order when I have "closed down". Still, let's hope your mum will come back at a later date. I'm sure she will.'

Ronnie was thrilled when I told him I was managing Doris and asked if I could arrange a meeting. Doris was equally keen to meet him, too.

I picked her up at home. As usual, Doris was smart, but not overdressed for the occasion. Having looked after many top-quality stars in the past, I had arranged a black Daimler limousine to take us to Broadmoor, for Doris did not own a car. We started the long journey.

Doris, who was never, ever short of a word or two, became unusually quiet and pensive as we entered the grounds, looking to her left and right, taking in everything. The security checks over, the moment both she and Ronnie had been looking forward to arrived and I introduced them. Ronnie took her hand very gently, giving Doris a broad, warm, welcoming smile. Impeccably dressed as ever, Ron took Doris's overcoat, pulling out a chair for her. I could tell that Doris was impressed by his manners and overall courtesy.

'Here you are, Mrs Stokes,' he said gently.

'Oh, you can call me Doris,' came the instant reply.

Obviously feeling quite chuffed, Ronnie answered, 'Well then, you can call me Ron. Would you like a pork pie or smoked salmon sandwich?'

Momentarily, Doris looked a little surprised to be offered smoked salmon inside Broadmoor!

'No,' she said. 'I'll just have a cup of tea.'

Over the years, I saw Doris meet countless people, and it was obvious that on this occasion there was an instant rapport between her and Ron. She was immediately both captivated and charmed by him.

We settled ourselves around a somewhat tea-stained table. Suddenly, Doris turned to Ron, paused for just a split second and looked him straight in the eye. Shifting forward on her seat an inch or two to move just a little closer to him, she said quietly but confidently, 'I've got your mum here with me, Ron . . .'

Ronnie looked at her with a mixture of amazement and bafflement. Perhaps momentarily forgetting that she was a world-famous medium, he said, 'But Doris, my mum is dead.' Ron leant over and whispered in my ear, 'I think Doris should be in here, Laurie, and I should be out there!' With that, we both burst out laughing. Doris, too, was amused.

Doris talked about the visit and her meeting with Ron all the way back to London and many times afterwards. 'He was such a gentleman,' she kept on saying. 'I really can't get over it. Must be awful living there, Laurie.' A former nurse, she had compassion for everyone. They were so different in just about every way imaginable, but something sparked a feeling of instant friendship between them, as though they had known each other for years. Both felt incredibly at ease with each other. Ron mentioned Doris in letters to me more than once, asking me to pass on his love to her. In fact, on a few occasions, he wrote directly to Doris.

Doris was always thrilled he remembered her and counted her as a friend, even though they met just once. 'Give him my love, luvvie,' she would say to me. 'I know what he did was wicked and wouldn't want to justify it, but it's not right he's still inside after all these years. Surely, he's paid the price by now.'

For her part, Doris was, in a sense, a recluse in that she rarely ventured outside the front door of her home, generally only doing so to give a demonstration at a theatre or attend some other special event. In some ways, her behaviour almost bordered on the agoraphobic. The fact that she was both willing to visit Ron and wanted to do so was a terrific compliment to him, as she did not care for travel very much apart from for her work.

In short, Doris was a normal woman with a supernormal gift. Now she, too, is in the spirit world she did so much to promote, having died in a London hospital in 1987, after surgery to remove a brain tumour. I like to think that she and Ron have met in the life to come. If so, perhaps this time they are enjoying a smoked salmon sandwich! And doubtless Mrs Kray is there, too.

Having received hundreds of letters from the Twins, and as their handwriting had never been analysed, I asked leading graphologist Peter West if he would have a look at some of them. What he came up with tells much about the differences between the Kray brothers and about their lives in prison.

Peter has never read a book about the Krays, so had no previous in-depth knowledge of them. His only information was confined to general newspaper articles and reports on TV. I gave Peter several original letters written by Reggie and Ron, and one from Charlie. The sample of Charlie's handwriting was a note written to me with a black ink felt-tip pen on a sheet of Belmarsh Prison lined notepaper in the late 1990s, when Charlie was in his seventies. This is what Peter West made of it:

The writing strength is good. There is plenty of physical energy, shown not only by the varying pressures, but also by the force of what he has written. The script is basically upright with some left slanting. However, in a few words, the slant of the writing is in all three directions.

This suggests a fairly flexible personality who liked to keep the peace and did not like to be found or seem wanting. This script indicates a degree of amiability, tolerance and general goodwill, although there are signs of a temper.

At the time this was written, Charlie's script suggests a fair degree of adaptability. He had the ability to lead others, but it was not really his style. He seemed to be able to look after anyone if he thought they merited his help, but might have preferred to have seen a little effort being made by someone before he assisted them.

From his writing, it appears that Charlie liked everything to be just so, although he was not an intolerant man and it would have been rare for him to have been over-critical of others. While he was fairly perceptive in quite a few ways, somehow he just did not seem able to spot a fraud or someone ready to 'take' him – and that made him relatively easy to fool. The way he formed the letter 'w' indicates a self-defensive and self-protective inner approach. He liked the good life, the nice things. Not for nothing was he called 'Champagne Charlie'!

Almost all of his lower case 'i's are much smaller than the rest of the writing. Inwardly, he did not have a very high opinion of himself or his role in society. Nearly all his lower case 't's have a high cross bar, a sure sign of strong ambitions. The construction of the middle zone parts of the letters 'a', 'g' and 'o' shows he could keep his mouth shut when it became necessary to do so.

The way Charlie wrote his name as his signature shows surface confidence, but he could also bluff with the best of them. There was not a lot of attention to detail. It probably eluded him because of his inner nature, but he made up for it with quite a sense of humour. In some ways he was, curiously enough, a bit of a worrier, but not always for very long. Life was for living – and this he much preferred to do.

The first sample from Ronnie is dated August 1975, written a few years into his sentence and made on Parkhurst Prison notepaper when he was forty-two years old:

It is difficult to know where to start first. Ron has used a red ink Biro. Even without the benefit of a good magnifying glass, there are many obvious different speeds and pressures used.

Red ink suggests an impulsive nature, the excitable and active type who needs to be noticed, someone who must be at the forefront of everything. There is a love of being different, but the emotional nature of such a writer can be easily disturbed, for they are very much subject to their emotions. There is a strong need to experience everything at first hand.

Changeable pressure, especially if variable or misplaced, shows intense feelings with strong reactions. These pressure changes are both vertical and horizontal and are indicative of serious fluctuations in the writer's ability to express his feelings.

On almost every line, Ron used the occasional capital letters where they should be lower case. This is confirmation of a potentially violent nature with sudden or impulsive outbursts that are also over-reactive in their content. This, in conjunction with almost every line tailing off down the paper, shows fatigue, depression and disappointment. It can also be a sign of determination and obstinacy.

Inconsistent letter sizes reveal a nature emotionally off-balance for much of the time. Here, coupled with an inability to construct two consecutive letters like the double 'e' or 'l' in the same manner, are additional features implying poor emotional control.

The next two examples were written on the same paper by

both Ronnie and Reggie on March 9, 1979:

Ronnie's writing controls have deteriorated some-what, although this time he used a blue ink Biro and managed to keep to the writing line much better. The pressure is not as variable, but now the writing is more of a printing exercise rather than cursive script. People who write in this fashion tend to be open to the influence of the moment and can experience difficulty filtering out unwanted stimuli. As a rule, such a writer is emotionally excitable and often ego-centric, moody and inconsistent. He or she might well prefer to be on their own for what they term a sense of self-preservation.

On the same paper, Reggie penned a twenty-line note to Laurie. Reg's writing is firmer and has a heavier pressure than his brother's, but it, too, shows variations. It is written almost in an angular style in that the pen strokes seem to be made up of a series of straight lines rather than curves.

Angular handwriting implies a stronger sense of personal discipline, but such a writer finds it hard to adapt and often has difficulty in keeping personal relationships on an even keel. So here Reggie appears a lot more aggressive and suspicious than his brother. The formations of his letter 'k' show an exceptional stubborn streak.

Practically every middle zone vowel has a short line, sometimes two, in the centre of it. This indicates an inability either to face the truth or be as honest with himself as he ought to be. This, in turn, will stretch to some of his associations. Although Reg could seem far more controlled on the surface, he may not always have been reliable.

A strong sex drive blended with a very high level of intolerance is also present, clearly shown by the lower zone construction of the letters 'f', 'g' and 'y'. Reggie also slips in an occasional capital letter where it does not belong. Loops made in a script where they would not normally be seen show extreme sensitivity to any form of criticism, no matter how well meant it may be.

The next sample looked at was written a few months later, in June of the same year. By working through Ronnie's letters, Peter West was able to track his changing moods and spirits:

There is a noticeable change for the worse in that his writing has quite significantly deteriorated. Control has weakened, the spelling is poor and his construction of sentences is decidedly worse.

The letter has been written in short sessions over a period of time, for there is a stop and start mechanism that clearly shows up under a magnifying glass. Apart from using two pens, blue and black ink, it is obvious that Ronnie suffered mood swings between and during the completion of the letter.

There is far more evidence of his having 'touched up' words and written over what he thought were errors at the time. This is a clear sign of an inner worrying nature and shows inhibition and repression of his mental processes. He backs this by saying he has been in his cell for 'months' and hardly ever speaks to anyone.

We move ahead now to May 1990. Ronnie's state of mind has deteriorated badly. After the first sentence, he has barely managed to put more than two or three words to a line. In fact, most of them are unreadable, they are so badly formed. By now, prison life has taken its toll. Like Reggie, Ron was being watched not only for his health and safety, but they were both marked men, even though they were in jail.

The next sample of Ronnie's writing is dated March 30, 1994 and is on a sheet of A4 headed notepaper marked 'Ron Kray'. It is started reasonably well, but after four lines reverts back to two or three lines on the front while the entire reverse has only fourteen words, all of which are hardly decipherable. At the end he writes that he is well and asks Laurie to pass on his love to Doris. This was obviously a reference to the late Doris Stokes, who had died seven years previously. Ronnie had either forgotten or was confused.

From a graphology point of view, this letter marks the descent from normalcy to a paranoid schizophrenia, for which Ron was originally certified years before. Schizophrenia implies a split personality. This can come about through a disturbed or distorted emotional response or as an inherited problem that may miss a generation with some families. The drug treatment Ronnie received might have played a part as well.

Ronnie Kray died of a heart attack just under a year later on 17 March, 1995 in Wexham Park Hospital, Slough, Berks. He was sixty-one years old and a broken man, which is reflected in his writing.

Four days later, Roger A. Blackwood, a consultant physician/cardiologist at the hospital wrote to Reggie at Maidstone Prison to describe Ronnie's last hours. Although Ron suffered a couple of minor dizzy spells at Broadmoor, 'no abnormalities were found. The following day,' Mr Blackwood continued, 'it became apparent that he had had some bleeding from his stomach. At midnight on the night before he died, we performed an endoscopy, which is a procedure to look into the stomach and see what is going on.'

Writing on official hospital notepaper, Mr Blackwood said that 'small, insignificant tears were found at the top of the stomach, which can be associated with vomiting. However, these had healed and Ronnie was in good shape. He was receiving blood to replace that which he had lost and was comfortable overnight. Sadly, as you know, he had an unexpected massive heart attack from which he arrested and died at about 9 o'clock.'

The letter added 'Although Mr Kray was agitated by being in hospital, he seemed to cope with his illness as well as anyone can expect, and he did not complain to me of any symptoms at all. These episodes are sometimes a dreadful shock, but in a man who is a heavy smoker, it is a frequent occurrence to have large heart attacks and to die young.

'I think his smoking was of considerable comfort to him, and I know that he was on very little medication for his nerves when he came in. I think he was as brave as could be expected, but he sadly arrested, and I am sure he was thinking of his family at the time. I am sorry we could do no more to help him.'

the name was kray

Charlie Kray was released from prison in January 1975. This followed a ten-year sentence for being an accessory to the murder of Jack 'The Hat' McVitie. On his release, the publicity around him was exceptional. I had not seen Charlie at all during his sentence as he did not want to see anyone except his family. However, Mrs Kray kept me in touch with the news on our journeys to visit Ron and Reg. Charlie's attitude to visitors was understandable: he was no villain and wanted to keep away from any further possibility of going back to prison when he came out.

While serving his sentence, Charlie had set his goal firmly at enjoying family life with his wife Dolly and children Gary and Nancy. His contact with the Twins was very spasmodic, too. They had little in common during their time in different prisons, and it was common knowledge that the Twins did not care too much for Dolly.

An absolute bombshell was dropped on Charlie to shatter his dream of a quiet life when in 1973 Dolly elected to be a witness for and testify that she had slept with George Ince on the night he was supposed to have murdered Muriel Patience at Braintree in Essex. It became known as the Barn Restaurant murder case.

This was a very brave act for Dolly. Her husband was one of the infamous Krays, but she showed tremendous courage to support George Ince, a man she loved. There had been mention of an affair with George before Charlie went to prison, but it seemed to have fizzled out, for I never heard anything further. Not that George and I mixed socially, for we had a different set of friends.

The Ince family were well known to me from our working holidays to the hop fields of Kent, where we had some great times. George's sister, Betty, was often in our family's hut, being friends with my elder sister Kathy. My memories of those Kent hop fields are still very vivid, as are those of the Ince family. Mrs Ince was a truly warm character, and a lovely woman.

Dolly's decision absolutely knocked Charlie on his back, but his determination to survive kept him sane. Once again, his mother became his rock. Ronnie was furious about the allegations of Dolly's affair. His only consolation for Charlie was, 'I told you so years ago.'

Justice was done when the charge was dropped after two other men admitted the murder. George Ince was acquitted of the murder charge, and justifiably became a free man.

Charlie did find love with other women and was horror-struck when he was sentenced on Monday 23 June 1997 for his part in a £39 million cocaine smuggling scheme. Despite his age, he received a twelve-year sentence.

Who knows what the truth was? But I will say this. Firstly, the Krays *never* dabbled in drugs. Secondly, Charlie could never even have been a dealer. To quote someone at the trial, 'He could not deal a pack of cards.'

Unfortunately, fool to himself, Charlie liked to give the

impression that he had power and had equally powerful contacts. In reality, he had neither. Perhaps, in a strange kind of way, he felt inferior to the Twins and their reputation and believed that he, too, had to prove himself.

Charlie died in April 2000, following a series of heart attacks. He was seventy-three. Although the least well known of the brothers, his death and funeral still received extensive newspaper coverage.

As at Ronnie's funeral, the family asked me to be a pallbearer again, which is surely a true mark of deep friendship and even love, to use the word in the broadest sense of its meaning. To help carry someone to their final resting place is a very special privilege. I was honoured both to be asked and to accept.

Reporting the funeral on page five, *The Times* printed a large colour photograph showing some of the eighteen black stretch limousines and two hearses. Journalist Tim Reid said that Charlie was 'given the equivalent of a state funeral by London's East End. A vast crowd turned out to shower his last journey with immense amounts of respect, and to greet his handcuffed brother, Reggie, as though he were an emperor returned.'

The day of the funeral began outside English's Funeral Parlour in Bethnal Green Road where Charlie's body lay in an open coffin under twenty-four hour guard. Amongst those who sent floral tributes were Barbara Windsor and her husband Scott Mitchell, who chose lilies.

At 11.10 am, Reggie, on release from Wayland Prison, Norfolk, just for the funeral, stepped from a people carrier. Wearing a smart grey pin-stripe suit, he was, as a second colour photo in *The Times* showed, handcuffed to a plainclothes woman prison officer. Immediately, and quite spontaneously, the crowd displayed its enduring affection and admiration for him, with people shouting, 'We love ya, Reggie!' at the tops of their voices.

The cortege made its slow and sombre way through the packed streets, pausing at the bottom of Vallance Road. Some bowed their heads in respect, donning their caps and hats. People hung out of windows and looked from shop doorways as trade temporarily ceased.

Charlie's hearse boasted two huge red and white floral boxing gloves from friends at Parkhurst Prison, a massive carnation teddy bear to 'Grandad' and a display comprising white roses which spelled out 'Gentleman'. And he was certainly that.

In his account, Tim Reid said that once at the church, the congregation was kept out until Reggie arrived. Inside, friends 'lined up to kiss him, Mafia style'. Three hymns were sung at the service – 'Morning Has Broken', 'Fight the Good Fight' and 'Abide with Me'. Also played was a recording of 'As Long as He Needs Me', by Shirley Bassey, one of Charlie's favourite songs.

The service over, thousands lined the route to Chingford Mount Cemetery . . . and all because the name was Kray. After the ceremony, amongst those who led three cheers for Charlie and one demanding Reggie's release was 'Mad' Frankie Fraser. Charlie was buried in the same grave as Ron.

reggie's last round

Sunday 1 October 2000 was a day of mixed feelings for me. My brother Alphi called to give the good news that Audley Harrison had won a gold for Britain at heavyweight boxing in the Sydney Olympics.

Alphi added that he had thanked the Repton Club and Tony Burns for helping him to achieve this feat. We discussed the fact that even with the euphoria of the day, coupled with the jubilation of winning, Audley Harrison never forgot those responsible for his support, letting millions of people around the world know it. It was a triumph for us all. How proud I felt that he had achieved his goal.

However, less than two hours after the delight of Audley's success in Sydney, I was shocked by a call from actor Billy Murray, a friend of many years, who gave me the sad, if expected, news that our friend Reg Kray had passed away only minutes before. Home Secretary Jack Straw had only agreed to Reg's release from prison after it was discovered he was suffering from inoperable bladder cancer.

Many thoughts flashed through my mind. Projected clearly was the similarity of those two East End families I had grown up with. The Krays and the Burns were both from poor tough breeding. Both had an upbringing in the boxing world.

It would have been easy for the Burns brothers to have entered the world of villainy. They were tough. There were quite a few brothers and cousins. But it was not for them. They chose to be guided by their fathers into the world of business. There was some wheeling and dealing, within the law of course, which gave them the experience to become the shrewd businessmen they are today.

Tony Burns is the backbone behind the Repton club, teaching and training up-and-coming amateur boxers, many of them champions like Audley Harrison. But most of all, the club keeps young kids off the streets, giving them the opportunity and incentive to be champions, and to be able to look after themselves in the outside world. Tony was greatly admired by Reggie Kray, who kept in touch by telephone and through visits until his dying day.

Through their brother Charlie, the Kray twins learned how to box at an early age after Reggie was bullied at school as a kid. The rest is history. Reg and Ron chose a life of crime, becoming infamous as 'those powerful Kray Twins'. Boxing was their first love, too, but with Ronnie power became his god.

His idol was Al Capone and Ron set out to emulate him. In killing rival gangster George Cornell, he felt he had achieved the same status. Ronnie Kray loved the challenge of gang warfare, paying the penalty with the sentence of thirty years minimum along with brother Reg.

When Reginald Kray died in his sleep on 1 October 2000, it made headline news on national TV and radio stations. The controversy over the arrangements for his funeral caused about as much press coverage as the ceremony itself.

The morning after he died, newspapers showed pictures of Freddie Foreman, Johnny Nash and Joey Pyle, friends of Reggie since the fifties. It was fitting that they were with him when he finally passed over at the Town House Hotel at Thorpe St Andrew near Norwich.

'I only want you to be the pallbearers,' Reg was quoted as saying to his close mates at his bedside. This was later disputed by his second wife Roberta, who gave a totally different version of his request. She was quoted as saying, 'He doesn't want any gangster friends as pallbearers.'

Nobody would deny that Reg was a gangster. He wrote books to this effect; his loyal and best friends were gangsters and would not deny it. They could not understand the snub by those organising the funeral to exclude friends who were closest to him during his years of power.

Many true friends were unable to attend the church service after being turned away at the door. Others, such as Freddie Foreman and Tony Lambrianou, chose not to attend at all. I know how Ronnie Kray would have reacted to the behaviour of those responsible for the disrespect shown towards his valued friends. He would have been so furious that the air would have turned a bright and unforgettable shade of blue. With colourful characters like The Who's Roger Daltrey, manager Bill Curbishley and others deciding not to attend in protest at the arrangements, a host of the Krays' friends had called me asking if they could get into the church. All were bitterly disappointed when I told them that it was invitation only and that sadly I had no influence at all.

The congregation in the church was rather mixed, split into sides, with place names on the seats. Actor Billy Murray and I sat beside Johnny and Ronnie Nash, alongside Mr and Mrs Joe Lee, Rita Smith and her daughter Kim. Being the closest relatives, they were front row.

Pitiful was the fact that two rows of at least twelve seats remained empty throughout the service when so many of the Krays' other true friends were unable to get into the church. A long, boring address by Dr Ken Stallard, an Evangelical Free Church minister, was mildly interrupted by the sound of a mobile telephone owned by a guest of actor Steven Berkoff, who appeared in the film about the Krays. Rather than being irritating, it was light relief from the awful attempt by Dr Stallard to emulate a Cockney voice, suggesting that was how Reg talked. He obviously did not really know him at all. A short, sharp address was all that had been necessary. At least ninety per cent of the congregation hadn't a clue who he was.

Noticeable, though, was the genuine grief shown by Joey Pyle, one of the Twins' oldest and most faithful friends. Joey stood next to me, away from the graveside. Like me, he did not wish to get among people that he did not know as they packed the graveside. When I asked him if he was all right, Joey was so emotional he could hardly talk to me.

In my opinion, Reg's funeral was expected to be a final chapter in the life of the Krays. Sadly, it was an anti-climax, even though the glass-sided Victorian hearse was drawn by six horses wearing black plumes and draped in black and purple coats. Sad and sombre though the occasion was, it still made a magnificent spectacle and sound as the groomed-to-perfection horses clip-clopped their way through the normally busy east London streets. The horses were preceded by the head undertaker wearing a silk top hat, his colleagues walking either side of the horses and hearse. The pavement outside the undertakers was covered in floral tributes. Some of the papers made much of the fact that one hundred and fifty security guards wore ankle-length overcoats, 'RKF' (Reg Kray Funeral) badges and bright red armbands.

An eighteen-car cortege went down Vallance Road and on to St Matthew's Church, but only at strategic crossroads was there any weight of crowd. Between these points, the expectancy of onlookers along the route diminished. The strength of the crowd only showed itself at the run-up to Chingford Mount Cemetery, where the dense throng clapped as we passed in the third car.

I understood them applauding Reg at both Ron and Charlie's funerals. However, from my point of view, the Reg Kray I knew had died too when his brother Ron died in 1995.

Reg was buried alongside his parents, brothers and first wife Frances. He was very strong, and attracted public sympathy by his length of prison sentence and continual publicity. But it is undeniable that the gay, mad killer Ronnie Kray was most definitely the Power of the Krays . . .

the kray letters

During the thirty years of regularly visiting Ron and Reg in various prisons – and in Ron's case, Broadmoor – it became noticeable from their letters that they were suffering mentally.

In 1970, Ron would write across the page edge to edge, without a margin, completely covering it with legible hand-writing. However, in the last few years of his life his letters became almost illegible with very few words on a single page, revealing his great emotional turmoil.

Reg, too, showed in his 1970 letters a kind and caring nature with readable handwriting and reasonable requests. This deteriorated during his last period of imprisonment when the letters became demanding and almost unreadable, possibly due to his frustration at his long incarceration.

The following are a selection from the many hundreds of letters I received from Ron and Reg over the years.

A joint letter from the Kray twins, written from Parkhurst in the 1970s.

> DEAR LOURY.
> ME AND Reg WANT to
> THANK YOU FOR all
> YOU HAVE DONE. THANKS
> FOR the BOOKS. AND FOR
> TAKEING my mother
> OUT. IT IS VERRY NICE
> OF YOU. DO YOU KNOW
> LOURY YOU are
> OUR OLDEST FREIND.
> THANKS FOR BEING SO
> LOYAL to us.
> YOUR Pals.
> RON AND Reg

Letter from Reg, dated 5 April 1974, giving an interesting insight into his tastes in food: frogs' legs and octopus. Surely not prison fare?

6/4

In replying to this letter, please write on the envelope:—

Number 058111   Name V. KRAY

H.M. PRISON,
PARKHURST,
NR. NEWPORT,
ISLE OF WIGHT

Dear Mania,
                          Saturday 6th April.
        Thanks you coming along today. We enjoyed the visit a lot.
        It was good to see you looking so well.

        We watched the film for awhile, but then came upstairs as the sound was useless so we couldn't hear a thing after looking forward to it all the week.

        Say Hello to Eileen, your Dad and Alfie for us.

        We hope Alfie has a speedy recovery.

No. 243 30141 8-2-68

2

Hope you had a good trip home.

Thanks for the money, well get some food with it.

Have you tied your legs? they are good.

~~Octopus~~ Octopuss is good too.

Well look forward to seeing Mum next Saturday.

Thats all for now.

God Bless you all.

your son Reg.

May 1977: Ron claims here he doesn't smoke, drink tea or take sugar any more. Plus he's become a vegetarian!

In replying to this letter, please write on the envelope:—

Number 058110   Name KRAY

H.M. PRISON,
PARKHURST,
NR. NEWPORT,
ISLE OF WIGHT

2ND
MAY.

DEAR LAURIE
I am enclosing
two of my POEMS.

MAY BE you can GET
THEM MADE in to
SONGS.

I HOPE you LIKE
THEM.

WRITE Soon
LAURIE.
your pal
RON.
P.T.

No. 7-5 30141 6-267.

g DON'T DRINK
TEA ANY MORE
AND g DON'T
TAKE SUGAR,
AND DON'T
SMOKE.
AND AM NOW
A VEGATARIAN

———————

October 1977: This letter from Reg reveals his frustration at Ron's behaviour.

6

C58111   Kray R.

H.M. PRISON,
PARKHURST,
NR. NEWPORT,
ISLE OF WIGHT

Dear mummy, I am just writing to do visit with you at Mums, all I no really I pleased to see you today, I havent seen Ron for 3 days) I do live in over the Hospital.
The other night we Smashed up the cell of Assault the officer the following morning. He goes up for Punishment on monday.
will you write Him a letter direct to the Hospital I try to tell Him what a fool he is being. Tell Him to try and settle down. Dont Pull any Punches in your letter, be firm with Him. It's about time He thought of any Matter more as She worries. I'll write more after the visit, I'm going to get ready now.
well I hope we had a good visit with Mum and Uncle Albert. Mum told me about the mix up with Phoning you, but we hope to see you in 2 with weeks good time.
we will be seeing each next

When you write to Ron you can tell
Him   about the   Poetry Book too.
Ron   Seemed a lot   better   today on
the   visit. We get a Pay Rise
next week?   which   pleases me.
As the wages have been diabolical.
I have   not   been training
lately as I have had too
Much   to   worry about.
Ali   fights again   in February
yul   Spureed   wins Easily
Enough.
Say   Hello to all the   family for us.

theres not a lot more   to   write
about, So will   come to A close.
God bless you all.

your friend Reg.

PS, I hope you liked the
Painting   Mum has
Please give this letter   got for you.
letter to   Mum to read.

The poignant ending to this letter ('Starting in October we have only got to do 7 months and we start our 11th year') gives a sense of how time drags in prison.

In replying to this letter, please write on the envelope:—

Number. 058110 Name. KRAY (RON)

H.M. PRISON,
PARKHURST,
NEWPORT,
ISLE-OF-WIGHT. PO30 5NX

LAURIE

I HOPE YOU

LIKE THIS

POEM

GOD BLESS

FROM RON

LOARIE WOULD YOU

THANK the GROUP

CHICITS FOR the

RECORD IT WAS

LERRY NICE, DTO

No. 243 30563 7-10-68

OF them to Give
IT to US -

LAURIE PLEASE
LET me Know
IF you LIKE
my LATEST POEM.

LAURIE STARTING
IN OCTOBER. we
HAVE only GOT
to DO 5 MONTHS

AND WE START
OUR 17TH YEAR.

From Ron, 1977: one of a whole series of letters concerning the publication of his poems, which he had asked me to organise . . .

16 MAY 1977

In replying to this letter, please write on the envelope:—

Number 058110 Name KRAY

Security
15 TH
May,

H.M. Prison,
PARKHURST,
Nr. Newport,
Isle of Wight

DEAR LAURIE. THANK YOU
FOR YOUR LETTER, I AM
PLEASED THAT YOU LIKE the
POEMS. LAURIE IF YOU DO
GET A SONG WROTE. ON the
POEMS - I WANT IT TO
BE DONE IN MY NAME.
AND IF YOU DO IT SHOULD
MAKE YOU AND US A BIT
OF MONEY. WHAT IS YOUR
OPINION. ON THIS. DO YOU
THINK GLEN CAMPBELL.
WOULD LIKE THEM. ? I HOPE
YOU DOIT THINK I AM
GETTING BIG HEADED. BUT
I WOULD LIKE THEM IN
MY NAME. LAURIE OR
THURSDAY. WE START. PTO

No. 243 33141 8-2-65

our 10th year,
they sends you his
best wishes.

Laurie if you do
get it done in
the States - it will.
Be in my name
want it.?
I am just sitting
in my cell. we get
unlocked at 6 o'clock.
the sun is shining
on the windows.

Laurie

I am enclosing
another one
of my poems.

I think this
is the best
one.

God bless
you all

Ron

P.S. Please
write soon.

... But a year later, 1978, he has changed his mind again.

In replying to this letter, please write on the envelope:—

Number OS8110 Name KRAY. R

12th January

H.M. PRISON,
PARKHURST,
NEWPORT,
ISLE-OF-WIGHT. PO30 5NX

MY DEAR FRIEND LAURIE. I HOPE
YOU AND ALL THE FAMILY
ARE WELL. LAURIE I ASK MY
MOTHER TO TELL YOU THAT I
DONT WANT MY POEMS
PUBLISHED YET. I WANT TO
WAIT TILL I HAVE DONE
MORE AND WHEN I HAVE GET
MORE WISDOM IN MY MIND.
I AM VERY SORRY TO MESS
YOU ABOUT. I HOPE YOU
UNDERSTAND. COULD YOU KEEP
ALL THE POEMS. AND WRITING
NEW PROJECTS. APART MINING
TO THE BOOK. FOR ME. AND
LOOK AFTER THEM. I HAVE DONE
A POEM LAST NIGHT. WHEN
THE GALES WERE BLOWING.
I WILL SEND IT ON TO YOU.
COULD YOU SEND ME 3. COPPIES.
OF THE ONE CALLED (AND SO
WILL YOU.)

No. 243 30563 7-10-68

PTC

279

THAT you HAVE GOT. LAURIE
DO you THINK you
could come to see us
NEXT week. ANY DAY AFTER
~~FRIDAY~~ TUESDAY. AS BILLIE
BOULTER IS coming to see
us THEN. we DONT LIKE
seeing two people AT
ONCE. AS you CANT THINK
PROPERLY. SO could you
come on your own. ANY
DAY OTHER. THAN
SATURDAY. OR SUNDAY.
would you DROP
us A LINE.
AND LET US
know IF THIS
will BE POSIBLE.

I think I will
start doing
some poems.

Ready for the
day. I do have
them perccusion

Hea many times
you get
them Laurie?

Would you
Let me
know...
write soon
your pal.
Ron.

February 1981: Ron's 'Dear John' letter to me, saying he didn't want to see me any more.

A Song to Give to
ERIC CLAPTON.
AND I HAVE
HEARD   nothing
from him . y

I DON'T THINK
you want
me to meet
him .   you
DON'T SEEM
to think my

3

IS GOOD ENOUGH to
meet CERTAIN
people.

AS I SAID I
no longer
wish to see
you.

Ron Kray,

Less than a week later, he has repented, claiming that 'being in these places distorts the mind at times'.

3D MARCH, TUESDAY NIGHT

O my dear friend
Carrie - I am sorry
for sending a
note to you like
I did. I am very
sorry if I hurt
your feelings and
I know I must
have done so.
It was not very
nice of me, as
you have been
a good friend
to me and Reg.
If you still feel
you could P.

like to tell me. I
now like you
to come to tell
me WHEN you
ARE NOT BUSY.
Being in these PLACES
DISTORTS the mind
AT TIMES. I AM
very sorry LAURIE

GOD BLESS

your pal
Ron Kray

July 1981: Ron always had a fascination with the world of showbusiness, as this request to Eric Clapton shows.

Another Reg demand, written some time in the mid 80s.
The haggling over £2 demonstrates only too clearly that it
was a myth that the Krays made millions.

```
                                              24th JULY
Laurie,
        Thanks for letter.
        Irene work would have been minnimal so i am adamant that
        the two pound you say should go to your administration is to
        be split by Ron and I my share going to OPauls name.
        With due respect i feel that the six pound is enough for you
        for the work you are doing.
        I hope that you agree so that we can start earning some money.
                GOD BLESS
                FRIEND REG
```

A typical letter from Ron, written just before his birthday, asking for £50.

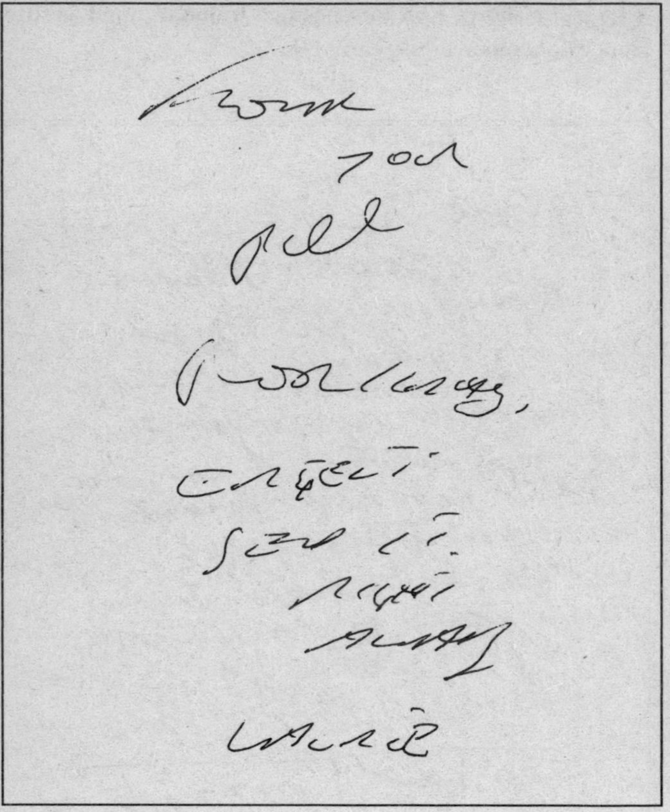

This letter shows Ron in a positive frame of mind, written from Broadmoor in the early 80s . . .

WOULD YOU PUT THAT. I DONT LIKE FLASH PEOPLE. I BELICE IN THE SAYEING THAT, THEIR IS STRENGTH IN HUMILITY, OUT OF THE BIBLE. WOULD YOU ALLSO PUT THAT THESE ARE MY THOUGHTS ON LIFE. I BELICE THAT I HAVE BEEN BROUGHT IN TO THIS WORLD FOR A PURPOSE. I DONT YET KNOW WHAT IT IS.

AND THAT I AM HOMOSEKSULL. AND AM PROUD OF IT,

AND THAT I LOVE LIFE BUT AM NOT AFRAID TO DIE.

P.T.O

AND THAT I BELIVE LIFE
SHOULD BE LIVED to the
FULL. (WHAT I WOULD)
(ALL the SCHOOL
OF LIFE.

AND THAT I DO, NOT Regret
ANY OF my PAST LIFE.

I BELIVE IN AFTER LIFE
AND GOD, AND FATE, I
BELIVE IN the SAYING,
WHAT IS MEANT FOR you
WONT GO BY YOU.

You HAVE now ALL MY
THOUGHTS DEDICATIONS. AND
POEMS.

. . . However, only a few years later, in September 1986, this one gives a disturbing insight into Ron's increasingly troubled thoughts.

> 4th Sep
>
> ① Dear Laurie
> would let
> everyone
> know that it
> was all all
> all lies
> lies in ...
>
> I ...
> would get
> out now
>
> God Bless ...

In this letter, written around 1989, Ron is saying that Reg and he both want to include me in their book (*Our Story*) as a close friend. When I first read it, I thought it said 'we *don't* want you in it'!

THANK you for
your kind letter. it
was very

nice of you
to write such a
nice letter.
Hope to see you
soon
God Bless
from
your pal
Ron
Kray.

1981.

Two letters written just before Ronnie's death, one from January 1993 and the other from March 1994. In each, Ronnie describes me as his oldest friend. Note the deteriorating handwriting by this stage in his life.

2

FRIENDS

NOW

AND

STILL HAVE

— LEFT

TOOK — A

TRYING TO HELP

PETER

SAMMS

HE IS A VERY

GOOD ENTERTAINER

R x

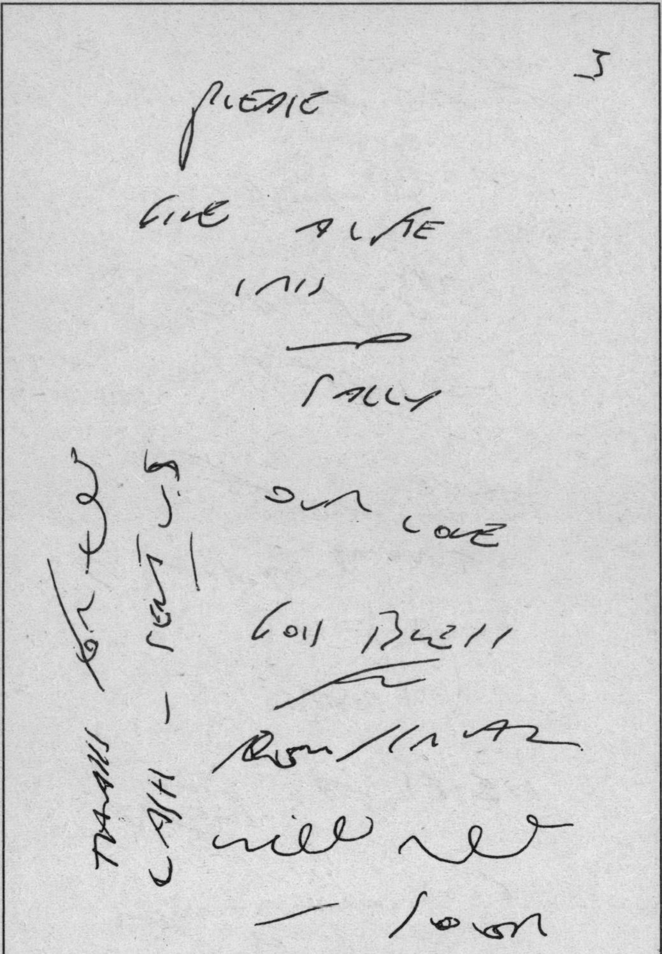

30 MARCH. 1994

Ron Kray

RK

MY DEAR FRIENDS LAURIE

ULN. THAT MAKE

HAPPY. MADE ME

PLEASE GIVE

INSI ALF OUR

BEST WISHES

YOU ARE ONE

OF OUR OLDEST

FRIENDS

IN FACT OUR

OLDEST FRIENDS

MAY

God Bess

-

? Ra

Mistar

Y am well

Please give

my love
to Doris XX

One of Ron's poems, 'Do I Speak in Vain?'.

index

Now you can buy any of these other bestselling non-fiction titles from your bookshop or *direct from the publisher*.